SO-AZI-574

HOLY SPIRIT LIBRARY

CABRINI COLLEGE, RADNOR, PA.

Mind-Body Identity Theories

The Problems of Philosophy:
Their Past and Present

General Editor: Ted Honderich
Grote Professor of Philosophy
University College
London

Each book in this series deals with a great or significant problem of philosophy. The series is intended to be easily accessible to undergraduates in philosophy, as well as to other readers at a more advanced level.

The first part of each book presents an introduction to and history of the problem in question. The second part, of a contemporary and analytical kind, defends and elaborates the author's preferred solution.

Already Published

RELIGIOUS BELIEF AND THE WILL
Louis P. Pojman

PRIVATE OWNERSHIP
James O. Grunebaum

THE RATIONAL FOUNDATIONS OF ETHICS
T. L. S. Sprigge

MORAL KNOWLEDGE
Alan H. Goldman

RATIONALITY
Harold I. Brown

PRACTICAL REASONING
Robert Audi

PERSONAL IDENTITY
Harold Noonan

IF P THEN Q
David Sanford

Forthcoming

THOUGHT AND LANGUAGE
Julius Moravcsik

Mind-Body
Identity Theories

Cynthia Macdonald

Routledge
London and New York

#16988911

First published 1989
by Routledge
11 New Fetter Lane, London EC4P 4EE
29 West 35th Street, New York, NY 10001

©1989 Cynthia Macdonald
Typeset in 10/12 Times by Columns of Reading
Printed in Great Britain by TJ Press (Padstow) Ltd,
Padstow, Cornwall.

All rights reserved. No part of this book may be reprinted or
reproduced or utilized in any form or by any electronic, mechanical,
or other means, now known or hereafter invented, including
photocopying and recording, or in any information storage or
retrieval system, without permission in writing from the publishers.

British Library Cataloguing in Publication Data

Macdonald, Cynthia
Mind-body identity theories – (The problems of philosophy:
Their past and present).
1. Mind, philosophical perspectives
I. Title
128'.2

ISBN 0–415–03347–0

Library of Congress Cataloging in Publication Data

Macdonald, Cynthia, 1951–
Mind-body identity theories.
(The problems of philosophy. Their past and present)
Bibliography: p.
Includes index.
1. Mind and body. 2. Identity.   I. Title.
II. Series: Problems of philosophy (Routledge (Firm))
BF161.M35   1989   128'.2   88–32543

128.2
mac
1989

Contents

HOLY SPIRIT LIBRARY

90 6709

CABRINI COLLEGE, RADNOR, PA.

PART II

Preface and Acknowledgements

One of the most central and familiar problems in the philosophy of mind is that of explaining the relation between mind and body. It is commonly thought that a person, in contrast to a mere animal, has both physical and psychological characteristics: like many other physical organisms, he can sleep, eat, and move his limbs, but unlike many of them, he is capable of having beliefs, desires, and thoughts. The mind-body problem, as we may term it, has its source in the view that these two sets of characteristics are unified under one concept, the concept of a person. It is further complicated by the belief that there are causal relations between the phenomena of which these two sets of characteristics are typical. This appearance of causal interaction is evidenced in countless ways in everyday experience: surgeons perform operations on brains to change mental states, for instance; and experiences of extreme pain often issue in tears. It seems that whatever mind is, it is inextricably bound up with the body of a person. What exactly is the relation between mind and body?

Many contemporary discussions of this question centre on the thesis that the mind is identical with the body. This thesis has taken a variety of forms; but the most forceful and persuasive of these are what may be termed 'event-identity theses' of the mental and the physical. Under this heading fall the strong, type-type identity theories of J.J.C. Smart and U.T. Place, the causal-role identity theories of D.M. Armstrong and David Lewis, and the so-called token identity theories of Jaegwon Kim and Donald Davidson.[1] It is part of the aim of this book to survey and evaluate such theories.

What is the problem of mind-body identity? Roughly speaking, it is that of explaining how it is that mental phenomena and/or types of phenomena can be such as to be identical with phenomena or types of phenomena whose natures are physical. All mind-body identity theories are physicalist at least to the extent that they are committed to the view that every phenomenon that has a mental description (i.e., a description in everyday folk-psychological terms, as do pains, itches, hopes, desires, beliefs, and the like) has a physical description (i.e., a description in the vocabulary of physics), which is to say that it is a physical phenomenon. (None of the theories that will be considered in the present study is committed to the stronger physicalist thesis that mentalistic terms and concepts are reducible to physical ones.) Commitment to this thesis poses a number of problems for any mind-body identity theorist. Two in particular seem to present insuperable difficulties for some, if not all, such theorists.

The first has its source in what is often referred to as the possibility of variable realization: the possibility that one and the same mental type of state – say, pain – should be realized internally in different creatures (or by the same creature at different times) by diverse physical types of state. Our instincts are to say that creatures whose internal physical make-up differed from ours would not thereby be prohibited from possessing the same mental properties as we possess provided that those creatures satisfied the commonsensical introspective and behavioural criteria which serve as our basis for attributing mental properties to persons. But this intuition is incompatible with the view that each mental type of phenomenon has a single physical type of nature. The possibility of variable realization is therefore incompatible with the strong type-type event-identity theories of the sort advanced by Smart, i.e., ones which assert the identity of mental and physical properties (though it does not similarly pose problems for causal-role and token event-identity theories).

The second and more serious problem has its source in the belief that mental phenomena and/or types of phenomena have properties that no physical phenomenon or type of phenomenon has. This, given the evident truth of Leibniz's Principle of the Indiscernibility of Identicals (according to which, if, for any objects x and y, x is identical with y, then x and y share all properties), shows that no mental phenomenon or type can be identical with a physical one. In the form in which this problem is most frequently voiced, it is known as the objection from phenomenal properties and applies specifically to sensations. These, it is argued, are essentially felt in a characteristic way: the quale or felt quality of a sensation not only serves as the means by which its subject typically identifies it, but gives the very essence of the sensation itself. Qualia – the throbbing of a pain, the burning of an itch, the colour of an after-image, etc. – are essential features of sensations in the sense that they cannot occur without being felt. Since no physical phenomenon or type is essentially felt, no sensation can be a physical phenomenon or type.

This objection has an analogue for the so-called propositional attitudes; beliefs, hopes, desires, and the like, which consist in a person's standing in a psychological relation to a propositional content, usually specified by a 'that' clause in sentences imbedding a verb of propositional attitude, as in 'Albert hopes that the examination will be easy'. These, it is argued, have their contents essentially. It is of the essence of the belief that Ben Franklin invented bi-focals, for instance, that it have the content it does (that Ben Franklin invented bi-focals). Propositional attitudes characteristically bear logical, and not merely causal, relations to one another and to the actions that they typically cause in virtue of having the contents they do. Thus, my belief that there is a red house on the corner of Lapwing Lane, bears logical relations to my belief that there is a house on the corner of Lapwing Lane, in that the sentence specifying the content of the former belief entails the sentence specifying the content of the latter. Because of these logical relations, the ascription of propositional attitudes is answerable to constraints of rational consistency and coherence as a whole (e.g., absence of contradiction, the use of principles of inductive rationality, transitivity of preference, etc.) in a way in which the ascription of sensations is not.[2] Hence, propositional attitudes are said to be essentially rational (or irrational) in virtue of the logical relations their contents bear to one another and to the actions they typically cause. Such constraints, being normative – they license judgements about how an agent ought to behave or to think given other of her attitudes – have no place in physical theory. Since it is not part of the essence of any physical phenomenon (type or token) that it be rational, no propositional attitude or type can be identical with any physical phenomenon or type.

This second problem presents the most formidable of objections to any mind-body identity theory for two reasons. First, versions of it can be seen to apply to propositional attitudes and sensations alike; and second, they apply to both the strong, type-type identity theories and to the token-token ones. For this reason, it serves as a focal point for discussion throughout the present study.

This book is divided into two parts. The first surveys three types of position that have been held in the relatively recent history of literature on mind-body identity and go under the name of event-identity theories of the mental and the physical. Chapter One examines the straightforward type-type identity theories of the sort advanced by Central State Materialists J.J.C. Smart and U.T. Place. Chapters Two and Three survey, respectively, the causal-role identity theories of D.M. Armstrong and David Lewis and the token event-identity theories of the sort advanced by Donald Davidson and Jaegwon Kim. All three types of position are evaluated in the light of the two problems mentioned above; notably, in the case of the second problem, in the light of the objection from phenomenal properties. Part Two constitutes an extended discussion and defence of one of the token event-identity theories surveyed in Chapter Three, viz. non-reductive monism, in the light of this second, and other, problems.

Event-identity theories of the mental and the physical have been thought by many to be the most plausible of identity theories because they avoid the objection from phenomenal properties in its original form. However, that objection can easily be reformulated so as to apply to events (types and tokens); and in this form it is decisive against both the straightforward type-type and the causal-role identity theories. Whether it is decisive against token identity theories as well depends crucially on the kind of metaphysical view of events that underlies them. As Chapter Three makes clear, one's conception of events will determine in an important way both the kind of token identity position that can be held and the means, if any, by which it is able to avoid objections from phenomenal properties.

Part Two therefore begins with a chapter devoted exclusively to an examination of some well-known conceptions of events. This chapter is crucial for two reasons. First, token event-identity theories are ontologically committed to events construed as non-repeatable, dated particulars: in the absence of other mental objects, events must serve as the relata of the identity relation. Thus the question of which, if any, conception of events is intrinsically more adequate than others *vis-à-vis* justifying the claim that events comprise an irreducible category of particulars must be addressed. But second, when one has addressed this, there is a further question to be considered as to whether any such adequate conception of events can be consistently combined with a token identity theory of the mental and the physical in such a way as to avoid objections from phenomenal properties. Part Two is therefore concerned with not one but two issues: whether an adequate conception of events, mental or physical, is forthcoming; and whether, if one is, it is capable of consistent combination with an argument for psychophysical token identity in a way that skirts objections from phenomenal properties. The argument in Chapter Four is that a certain version of the property-exemplification account of events, developed by Lawrence Lombard, is intrinsically more adequate than others and capable of consistent combination with non-reductive monism in such a way as to avoid objections from phenomenal properties.[3] Chapters Five and Six take up the most notable of objections to non-reductive monism thus construed.

The book is incomplete in two ways. First, mental phenomena as a whole – sensations as well as propositional attitudes – do not figure extensively in much of the discussion of various positions and their attendant difficulties. Certain difficulties, e.g., the qualia of sensations, that arise with regard to mental phenomena of one type do not arise with respect to phenomena of the other; and certain theories are better equipped to deal with one or the other, but not both, of these types of phenomena (e.g., causal-role identity theories seem better able to deal with the propositional attitudes than with the sensations). This sometimes makes for uneven discussion of the entire range of mental phenomena. Also, certain types of mental phenomena, particularly the emotions, do not easily fit into either of these two main categories. Such phenomena seem to share features with both the sensations and the propositional attitudes; and a promising way of handling them might be to construe them as consisting of two distinct components. As they present special problems of their own, however, attention has been restricted to phenomena that fall squarely within either the category of sensations or the category of propositional attitudes. Wherever possible, the sensations and the propositional attitudes have been discussed jointly; and this has occurred more in the second half of the book than in the first. In general, the propositional attitudes have played less of a prominent role than is ideal simply because of the role played by objections from phenomenal properties throughout the book. That fact notwithstanding, many of the arguments in its second half (e.g., for the claim that mental properties are not essences of the events that have them) are quite general and apply equally to the sensations and to the propositional attitudes.

Second, the discussion of theories of events is incomplete in a way that is apt to invite objections. Specifically, the version of the property-exemplification account endorsed in Chapter Four construes events as changes as *distinct* from standing conditions or states; and it is unclear how this theory is to apply to the propositional attitudes. Unlike sensations, many of the propositional attitudes (e.g., beliefs) do not seem to last for a specific amount of time during which their subjects are consciously aware of them.

While this issue has not been explicitly addressed, the question of whether events in general are best construed as states, where these are understood as standing conditions, is discussed at length in Chapter Four in the context of Kim's version of the property-exemplification account. It is argued that this construal obscures the distinction between events and other particulars (notably physical objects), thus undermining the claim that events constitute an irreducible category of particulars. In the light of this, the most obvious move is to attempt to supplement Lombard's version of the property-exemplification account in such a way as to accommodate phenomena like the propositional attitudes. These might be treated within the theory as concatenations of events, perhaps; or as events only when manifested, in something like the way that the solubility of a substance might be treated as an event only when it manifests itself by dissolving in a medium. As this analogy suggests, the problem is not peculiar to mental phenomena like the propositional attitudes alone. The claim here is that, however standing conditions or states are to be treated, they ought to be seen as dependent on a more fundamental conception of events as changes.

I wish to thank a number of people for their advice and comments during the various stages of thinking about and writing this book. Discussions with Barry Taylor have influenced my thinking about events over the past ten years, though not, I am sure, in ways that he would entirely approve. Graham Bird, Roger Fellows, Martin Davies, John Campbell, Michael Morris, Andrew Clark, Harry Lewis, and Ted Honderich have all helped to improve my thoughts about various issues in the book, particularly in its second half; and Eve Garrard and Steven Edwards have helped to make the first half clearer and more readable than it otherwise would have been. Lawrence Lombard has been an unfailing source of advice over many years on many philosophical issues, particularly on ones relating to events. Virtually every chapter in the book has been greatly improved as a result of his comments. My greatest debt is to Graham Macdonald, whose exacting critical standards have served as an ideal toward which I continue to strive. Discussions with him over the past thirteen years have influenced my thinking in countless ways; and every part of this book has benefited from his careful comments. I wish to thank the publishers of *Philosophia* for permission to reprint material from my paper, 'Constitutive Properties, Essences, and Events' (vol. 16, no. 1 (April 1986), pp. 29-43); the publishers of *Philosophical Studies* for permission to reprint material from 'Mind-Body Identity and the Subjects of Events' (vol. 48 (1985), pp. 73-81); and the publishers of *The Philosophical Quarterly* for permission to reprint material from my paper, written jointly with Graham Macdonald, 'Mental Causes and Explanation of Action'(vol. 36, no. 143 (April 1986), pp. 145-58). Finally, and most importantly, I wish to thank my parents, Vilma and Eugene, for instilling in me a love and respect for ideas, and for sacrificing so many things over the years in order to foster that love and respect. This book is dedicated to them.

C.A.M.

PART ONE

Chapter One

The most plausible arguments for the identity of mind and body that have been advanced in this century have been for the identity of mental events or states of persons and physical events or states of their bodies. Instead of construing the relation between mind and body as one holding between substances (the mind and the body) or between mental objects (such as pains, itches, beliefs, or desires) and physical phenomena (such as brain processes), these arguments have construed it as a relation between mental phenomena, such as the havings of pains, or types of phenomena, such as the type or property of having pain, and physical phenomena or types of phenomena. The move from a substance or object conception of the mental to an event or state one was precipitated by the most formidable of objections to mind-body identity theories, viz. the objection from phenomenal properties.[1] We may call the group of theories that resulted from this conceptual shift 'event-identity theories of the mental and the physical'. Under this heading fall the straightforward type-type identity theories, such as those put forward by Central State Materialists J.J.C. Smart and U.T. Place, the causal-role identity theories, such as those advanced by D.M. Armstrong and David Lewis, and the straightforward token-token identity theories, such as that advanced by Donald Davidson. Our survey begins with attempts to counter the objection from phenomenal properties by Smart, considered against the background of objections voiced by Saul Kripke, Thomas Nagel, and Frank Jackson.[2] It then turns to a second problem that faces type-type identity theories, viz. the problem of the variable realizability of any given mental type or property. Before proceeding, however, a preliminary issue needs to be addressed. How are events or properties to be taxonomized as mental or as physical?

1. Criteria of the Mental and the Physical

Any theorist whose aim is to show that what is mental is physical must have some conception of what is characteristically mental and what is characteristically physical. Coming by a workable conception of either, however, has proved to be notoriously difficult. One problem is that certain conceptions of the mental and the physical can actually preclude the truth of any form of the identity theory, while others can ensure their truth, thereby trivializing them. Suppose, for example, that we define the mental as that which is infallibly knowable or as that which lacks spatial dimension. Then, by defining the physical as whatever is fallibly knowable only or as whatever has spatial dimension, we can foreclose the possible truth of any identity theory of the mental and the physical. Suppose, on the other hand, that we define the mental as that which is describable by any expression (definite description or open sentence) which contains a mental verb or term (e.g., 'believes', 'desire') non-eliminably (as in, for instance, 'John's realization that the earth is round'). Then, on the assumption that there is some mental event spatiotemporally related to every event, it can be shown that *any* event counts as mental by this criterion.[3] Suppose that there is a purely physical predicate '*Sx*' true of the (one and only) sinking of the *Titanic* and that John only comes to realize that the earth is round once in his life. Then, given that the sinking of the *Titanic* bears spatiotemporal relation *R* to John's realization, the following will count as a mental description of the event which is the sinking of the *Titanic* since it contains a mental term non-eliminably: (ιx)(Sx & x bears spatiotemporal relation *R* to John's realization that the earth is round). The result would seem to be that every event for which there is a purely physical predicate will be one for which there is a mental description.

Suppose now that we proceed in a similar way to define as physical that which is describable in terms which contain no non-eliminable mental verbs or terms. Then, assuming only that there is some physical event spatiotemporally related to every event, it can be shown that *any* event counts as physical. Suppose that all events are spatiotemporally connected, no matter how distantly, to the one and only sinking of the *Titanic* (*Sx*). Then, given that John comes to realize that the earth is round only once in his life, the following counts as a physical description of the event (ιy) which is John's realization that the earth is round: $(\iota y)(y$ stands in spatiotemporal relation R_* to $(\iota x)(Sx))$. Minimal assumptions about spatiotemporal connectedness between mental and physical events suffice to show that this second way of defining the mental and the physical entails the trivial truth of any mind-body identity theory (a point to which we return below).

Both definitions suffer from the fact that they define the mental and the physical in terms that are logically interdependent. Evidently, it is only by working with conceptions of the mental and the physical that are logically independent of one another that the non-trivial truth of some form of the identity theory will remain a viable possibility.

A second problem that dogs attempts to provide a taxonomy of mental and physical phenomena or properties concerns the apparent heterogeneity of the mental domain itself. Many philosophers have noted that mental phenomena seem to comprise at least two very diverse categories. The first of these is often loosely termed 'sensations', and the second, 'propositional attitudes'. Within the first category are included not only those experiences with qualitative 'felt' content, such as pains, tingles, and itches, as well as auditory, tactile, gustatory, and olfactory experiences, but also perceptual experiences or sensings with qualitative but unfelt content, such as seemings to see something red. (There are differences between sensations and perceptual experiences – notably that we are inclined to ground the qualia of the latter but not the former in objects that exist beyond the confines of subjects' bodies – but they will not play a prominent role here.) Within the second fall those mental phenomena that consist in a person's standing in a psychological relation to a propositional content, typically specified by a 'that' clause in sentences containing a verb of propositional attitude, as in 'John believes that the earth is round'. Such phenomena are taxonomized partly by the attitude types into which they fall, e.g., belief, desire, hope, etc., and partly by the propositional types toward which the attitudes are directed, e.g., the proposition that the earth is round.

Phenomena falling within these two categories seem to be of radically diverse types, suggesting that there is no single conception of the mental forthcoming. Sensations, it is said, are essentially consciously felt or undergone; beliefs and other propositional attitudes are not. Sensations are directly apprehended from the first person perspective (subjectively) only, whereas propositional attitudes seem to be equally amenable to first- and third-person perspectives. Sensations have a felt, or phenomenal content, whereas propositional attitudes have no particular feel associated with them at all. If they do have content, it is propositional content, analogous to the semantic content of expressions embedded in clauses following the verbs of propositional attitude used to ascribe them. Such connections as may exist between propositional attitudes themselves are thought for this reason to be not merely causal but logical. Thus, Susan's belief that barns are both three-dimensional and red is logically related to her belief that barns are red in virtue of the logical relations that hold between the content clauses that truly describe her beliefs. No analogous conception of content is applicable to sensations. Nor, for this reason, are sensation ascriptions constrained by what has been termed the 'ideal of rationality' – the constraint on propositional-attitude ascriptions that they be rationally consistent (by the ascriber's lights) with other attitudes of the agent to whom they are attributed and with his or her behaviour.[4] Propositional attitudes, it is said, are rationally or irrationally held; sensations are not.

This second difficulty has led contemporary philosophers to opt for one or the other of two quite different types of criteria of the mental. The first is broadly epistemic in character and is intuitively geared toward the sensations, concentrating on the 'direct' or privileged accessibility of such experiences to their subjects. The second is concerned with the intentional nature of certain types of mental phenomena, and is intuitively geared toward the propositional attitudes. Both types of criteria are amenable to *linguistic* formulation or *metaphysical* formulation.[5]

Intentionality as a defining characteristic of the mental is a view widely known to have been held by Franz Brentano, who claimed that mental phenomena are exclusively characterized by the property of 'intentional inexistence' or of 'including an object intentionally within themselves'.[6] Contemporary proponents of the intentionality criterion prefer a linguistic formulation of this criterion. As is well known, the semantic behaviour of expressions typically used to describe phenomena intentional in

Brentano's sense differs markedly from that of expressions normally used to describe physical phenomena. In particular, certain sentences, usually containing a subject term and an active verb, e.g., 'thinks', 'perceived', etc., followed by a sentential clause, usually (though optionally) introduced by the word 'that', differ in semantic behaviour from sentences used to describe physical phenomena in at least two respects. First, they create contexts in which substitutions of co-referring expressions in the sentential clause following the verb appear to fail; and second, existential generalization on the terms in the sentential clause appears to fail. These two characteristics demarcate a large class of sentences containing peculiarly 'mental' verbs. Thus, Chisholm characterizes intentionality as a semantic property of linguistic expressions (sentences, in the first instance); specifically, ones in which the usual rules of substitution and existential generalization fail.[7] And Davidson defines an event, m, as mental just in case m is describable by an expression or sentence which contains some 'mental' verb non-eliminably. It turns out that 'mental' verbs are ones that occur in contexts in which the usual rules of substitution and existential generalization fail, i.e., are verbs of propositional attitude.[8]

Both of these versions of the intentionality criterion have been sharply criticized. It has been claimed that the intentionality criterion itself is too narrow since it fails to cover most if not all of the phenomena that fall within the category of sensations.[9] But in fact both versions are too wide rather than too narrow: any event intuitively deemed mental would count as mental by them provided that there is some mental event spatiotemporally related to every event, since any event can be shown to be mental on that assumption by the argument cited earlier (p.4). Nor is the required assumption an implausible one. One needs only to suppose that there is at least one physical event to which all physical events are spatiotemporally related and that that event bears spatiotemporal relations to some mental event to which all other mental events are spatiotemporally related. The second conjunct of this supposition may strike some as contentious; but, given the frank rejection of any substance conception of the mental by all event-identity theories of the mental and the physical and the independently plausible thesis that mental events are ones whose subjects (persons) have bodies and so are to be located where their subjects' bodies are, it is reasonable to maintain that mental events bear spatiotemporal relations both to one another and to physical events in virtue of being in or occurring to their subjects at (or during intervals of) specific times. In any case, essentially the same conclusion can be reached assuming only that mental events bear temporal relations to other mental and physical events – an assumption even Cartesian dualists would find acceptable.

The generous construal of the mental by linguistic formulations of the intentionality criterion should not (as an overly restrictive conception should) present a serious worry for those whose aim is to show that every mental event is a physical event. Thus Davidson, noting the above consequence, goes on to exploit it. Counterintuitiveness notwithstanding, both versions of the intentionality criterion accomplish what they must to be adequate, viz. circumscribe all that is mental. That they do not circumscribe only what is mental is irrelevant to the purposes of the identity theorist.

The real worry for proponents of linguistic formulations of the intentionality criterion is that they entail the truth of some version of the identity theory, thereby trivializing it. As was noted earlier, any method by which it can be shown that every event counts as mental by the criterion can similarly be used to establish that every event counts as physical, if, by 'physical', is meant 'any phenomenon describable by expressions which contain no non-eliminable mental verb or term'. The problem here is not with the criterion of the mental; it is with the criterion of the physical. Specifically, it is with the fact that the criterion of the physical typically used in conjunction with the intentionality criterion is formulated in terms that are not logically independent of that criterion. What is needed is a stronger conception of the physical.

One suggestion is that what is physical has spatial location or spatial extent. Formulated linguistically, the suggestion is that a predicate or expression P is physical just in case, for any object x, 'x has P' entails 'x has extension', or 'x has spatial location'.[10] This would seem to have the desired effect of covering all and only physical expressions, since it is plausible to suppose that no mental expression M is such that 'x has M' entails 'x has extension' or 'x has spatial location', even if it happens to be true that all events have spatiotemporal location. However, it quickly leads to problems.

Consider such predicates as 'x is to the left of y' or 'x is taller than y'; or 'x is 3 inches long' or 'x weighs 50 g'. These do not logically entail 'x has extension' in the straightforward way that 'x is a red barn' entails 'x is red'. Rather, one might wish to argue, it is only in virtue of the existence of certain 'constitutive principles' or 'meaning postulates' which govern our use of such predicates that they entail 'x has spatial location' (this is perhaps clearer for predicates like 'x is warm', 'x is furry', or 'x is red'). The trouble is that this can seem to be equally true for many mental predicates; for instance, 'x is a perceptual experience', 'x is a throbbing pain', or 'x is a feeling of fear', where x is taken to range over events. How, one might ask, can perceivings occur, but not where the perceiver's eyes are? Or pain occur which isn't somewhere in a sentient creature's body? Indeed, how can experiences or feelings occur without occurring in a body? It does not seem possible that any conception of entailment which is wide enough to cover all that is physical will not also cover much of what is mental. But if this is so, then the trivial truth of some version of the identity theory follows.

It may be tempting to respond to this by saying that although any conception of 'entails' adequate to cover all of what is physical will cover some of what is mental, not all mental predicates will count as physical by the criterion. Specifically, predicates like 'x is a thought' or 'x is a desire' do not entail 'x has spatial location' on any conception of 'entails', however loose. But once one gives up the idea of mental substances existing in addition to physical ones, it is plain that this response will not do. For the conclusion that mental phenomena have spatial location in virtue of occurring in or happening to their subjects, persons, who have bodies even if they are not identical with them, is then virtually unavoidable. The idea that mental events have spatial location is as intuitive as the idea that persons themselves do. The reason is that mental phenomena are ones whose subjects are persons, and persons have bodies.

Evidently, the problem with the spatiality criterion is not that it takes spatial location to be a necessary condition for any phenomenon's being physical, but rather, that it takes that condition to be sufficient. It is hardly credible that mental events do not have spatial location in the minimal sense just specified. But if spatiality is taken to be sufficient for any phenomenon's being physical, it follows from the conception of the physical alone that mental phenomena are physical. Construed in this way, the spatiality criterion is clearly too weak a conception of the physical.

A second suggestion is that those events are physical that have descriptions which instantiate a physical law.[11] This criterion does not have the consequence that events possessed of descriptions which instantiate physical laws have no further descriptions (specifically, mental ones) by which they fail to be so subsumed. It therefore leaves open the possibility that events deemed mental by linguistic versions of the intentionality criterion may be physical in virtue of being possessed of descriptions which instantiate physical laws. Nevertheless, it too suffers from a problem, viz. how to characterize what it is to be a physical law. If the best that we can do is to say that a physical law is a true, lawlike generalization which either is expressed by or contains physical terminology, then it isn't clear that the appeal to physical laws gets us any further in the attempt to provide an adequate criterion of the physical than the original, unsatisfactory suggestion that an expression is physical just in case it contains no non-eliminable mental terminology.

The threat here, of course, is one of circularity; and it may be that no non-circular criterion of the physical is forthcoming. Nevertheless, the appeal to physical laws does to some extent further the attempt to characterize the physical. By whatever intuitive conception of a physical predicate with which we may work, not every such predicate will figure in the antecedent or consequent of a physical law. So the appeal to lawlike subsumption represents a further culling of the set of events as physical. Specifically, events described in such terms as '(ιy) (y bears spatiotemporal relation $R*$ to $(\iota x)(Sx)$)' no longer qualify as physical simply by virtue of being describable in terms that contain no non-eliminable mental terminology. Such events must be possessed of predicates that figure in the antecedent or consequent of some physical law.

However, this in itself is the source of another worry, and that is that not all *physical* events may be such that they are possessed of descriptions which instantiate laws. Think of events like earthquakes and avalanches. There are no laws in physical theory governing events under these descriptions, even if there are ones covering events of which these are composed. If the composition relation is not one of identity, however, then being describable in terms which instantiate physical laws is too strong a constraint to place on the physical: the criterion may be sufficient for a phenomenon's being physical, but it does not appear to be necessary.

A number of responses can be made to this challenge. One is to argue that events like avalanches and earthquakes are in fact possessed of descriptions by which they instantiate physical laws. This is further explored in Chapter Five. Another is to argue that the criterion can be extended to cover events like avalanches and earthquakes by containing a clause to the effect that such events, if not themselves possessed of descriptions which instantiate physical laws, must be composed of events, all of which possess descriptions that instantiate such laws. Yet another strategy is to argue that it does not matter for the purposes of showing that every mental event is a physical event that the criterion of the physical does not cover all physical events. What matters is that all mental events can be shown to be physical in some sense of 'physical'; and for this it is enough to show that they are physical in a sense specified by a criterion whose conditions are sufficient but not necessary for every event to be physical. This is not necessarily to say that the criterion fails to specify conditions necessary for *any* event to be physical. It is rather to acknowledge that there may be, after all, more than one sense of 'physical'.

None of these responses is without problems; but all have a degree of initial plausibility. How they fare in the end must remain for the reader to consider. Whatever the result, it is clear that a workable conception of the physical is at least as, if not more, difficult to come by as is an adequate conception of the mental. Indeed, problems often attributed to linguistic formulations of the intentionality criterion have more to do with the criteria of the physical with which they are associated – specifically, with the fact that these are typically formulated in terms that are not logically independent of those used in the formulation of the intentionality criterion – than they have to do with inadequacies inherent in intentionality conceived of as the earmark of the mental.

That fact notwithstanding, many philosophers prefer criteria of the mental that are broadly epistemic in character, which attempt to circumscribe phenomena as mental by reference to their 'direct' or 'privileged' accessibility to a subject. Unlike intentionality criteria, epistemic ones tend to be formulated in metaphysical rather than in linguistic terms. Kim, for instance, characterizes an event as mental just in case it is an exemplification or instantiation of a phenomenal property at a time in an object (where this is identified in terms of the epistemic characteristic of direct awareness), events in general being conceived of by him as exemplifications of properties at times in objects (a view discussed in detail in Chapter Four).[12] Similarly, Levison defines an event, S's ϕing at t, as mental just in case it is logically possible for a subject S to be *de re* directly aware of herself ϕing (then or now).[13] Both begin with a certain conception of an event, and then attempt to characterize a subclass of events as mental by reference to the epistemic property of direct awareness.

Epistemic criteria of the mental also suffer from well-known difficulties. A crucial one concerns the fact that contexts in which epistemic terms occur do not sustain substitution either of co-referential expressions or of logically equivalent ones (i.e., are non-extensional). It may be true, for instance, that I am directly aware that this pen is red, true that this pen is the instrument that caused Jones's death, but false that I am directly aware that the instrument that caused Jones' death is red. Or it may be true that I am directly aware of myself being in this room, true that I am the next person in line for promotion, but false that I am directly aware of the next person in line for promotion's being in this room. Similarly, I may be directly aware of this shape's being four-sided but fail to be directly aware of this shape's being square, despite the logical equivalence of 'square' and 'four-sided'. This presents difficulties for epistemic criteria because failure of substitutivity shows that the class of mental events circumscribed by them is not well defined.

Kim attempts to circumvent this difficulty by amending his characterization of a phenomenal property as a property (F) such that, if any person S exemplifies F, S is the only person directly aware that S exemplifies F to this:

Property *F* is a phenomenal property if and only if for any *S*, if *S* exemplifies *F*, there exists *S'* and *F'* such that *S* = *S'*, *F* = *F'* and *S* is the only person who is directly aware that *S'* exemplifies *F'*.[14]

The amended version is intended to block objections to the original based on the fact that the definiens might be satisfied when terms like 'pain' replace '*F*' but fail to be satisfied when terms like 'C-fibre stimulation' do, despite the (supposed) truth of 'Pain = C-fibre stimulation'.

However, there are also problems with this version. Suppose that Sue (*S*) is alone in a room facing a mirror and seeing a reflection of herself for the first time. She does not realize that she (*S*) is the person reflected in the mirror (*S'*). Looking into the mirror, she has a certain visual experience (say, she exemplifies the property of seeing a person) of which it is plausible to say she is directly aware. Is she directly aware that the person in the mirror is having a certain visual experience? One's instincts here are to say 'no', since Sue is unaware of the fact that she is the person reflected in the mirror. But to do so is to acknowledge that 'directly aware' is functioning non-extensionally even in the amended definition of 'phenomenal property'. If it were not, the definiens would tolerate the substitution of *S'* for *S*. A similar complaint can therefore be voiced against the amended version: while the final conjunct to the definiens is satisfied when 'Sue' replaces both *S* and *S'*, it is not satisfied when 'Sue' replaces *S* and 'the person reflected in the mirror' replaces *S'*, despite the fact that Sue is the person reflected in the mirror.

Levison's formulation appears to avoid this problem by requiring that a subject *S* be *de re* directly aware of herself φing, though this requirement stems more from a concern to the conclusion that all direct awareness is propositional or *de dicto* in form than from one about the non-extensionality of epistemic constructions. As he sees it, there are experiences, mental events, of which subjects are directly aware no matter how described; the awareness is *de re*. An adequate characterization of the mental in terms of direct awareness ought therefore to sustain substitution of co-referential expressions: if *S* is directly aware of being in pain, and being in pain is being in neurophysiological state α, then it should follow that *S* is directly aware of being in neurophysiological state α irrespective of whether *S* knows or believes this. The criterion is formulated in such a way as to meet this condition:

> *S's* φing at *t* is a mental event = *df*. It is logically possible that *S* at *t* has *de re* direct awareness of the occurrence of (either) himself then φing (or φing now).[15]

Both versions of the epistemic criterion construe 'direct awareness' as meaning something like 'privileged epistemic access' or 'immediate experience', where these latter are taken as primitive. On the face of it, this makes them too narrow (strong), since many of the phenomena that fall within the category of propositional attitudes are dispositional rather than occurrent, and so are not consciously experienced at all, let alone directly or immediately experienced. One might suppose that the inclusion of 'logically possible' in Levison's version can meet this complaint, it being intended to cover unconscious mental events. However, in the form in which it occurs above, it can only cover unconscious sensations. Propositional attitudes, being attitudes toward propositions, are not the sort of mental phenomena of which one can have non-propositional (*de re*) direct awareness. If they are to qualify as mental by dint of possessing the epistemic property of direct awareness, then some other formulation of the criterion is needed.

Levison suggests that a person *S* is *de dicto* directly aware of something only if *S* has the concept of that thing and is able to form beliefs about it, and formulates a criterion for *de dicto* direct awareness of an event thus:

> *S* has direct *de dicto* knowledge that he himself φs (where φing is an event of which *S* is the only subject) iff (a) *S* has *de re* awareness of himself φing; (b) *S* has the concept of φing and understands what it is to φ; (c) *S* truly judges that he himself φs; and (d) *S*'s justifying reason for so judging is either (i) his *de re* direct awareness of himself then φing, or (ii) his disposition to report that he himself is φing.[16]

As (a) makes clear, direct *de dicto* or propositional awareness of an event qualifies it as mental only if its subject has *de re* direct awareness of the event that the corresponding proposition is 'about'. Thus, for example, S is *de dicto* directly aware that he himself is in pain only if S is *de re* directly aware of himself being in pain.

This criterion effectively covers, not propositional attitudes, but propositional awareness of sensations. Suppose, for example, that we wish to know whether S's belief that $2 + 2 = 4$ counts as mental. It doesn't qualify as mental by the *de re* direct-awareness criterion, since S's belief is propositional; whether S can be said to have that belief does depend on how it is described. If it is to count as mental, then, it must do so by the criterion of *de dicto* direct awareness. Does S have direct *de dicto* knowledge that she herself believes that $2 + 2 = 4$? Only, it would seem, if S has direct *de re* awareness of herself believing that $2 + 2 = 4$. But it is not plausible to suppose that S has direct *de re* awareness of her beliefs. This is not because propositional attitudes, and beliefs in particular, are largely unconscious: the criterion for *de re* direct awareness covers these as well as unconscious sensations by dint of the phrase 'logically possible'. It is because 'direct *de re* awareness' is fleshed out either in terms of the notion of immediate experience, where any phenomenon that is immediately experienced is something that necessarily is as it appears to be, or in terms of privileged epistemic access. The trouble is that one's knowledge of one's own attitudes is characteristically defeasible by behavioural evidence. This is particularly true in the case of beliefs. Sue's claim to have no preference either for a boy or for a girl can be shown to be false by her disappointment at discovering that the baby she has produced is a girl. Similarly, I can be surprised to find that my belief that I prefer apples to oranges is mistaken, my behaviour consistently showing me to prefer oranges to apples. Even supposing that all attitudes are at some time or another consciously undergone by their subjects and so appear to their subjects in one way or another, still they are not necessarily as they appear to be to their subjects. Nor are they phenomena towards which their subjects have privileged epistemic access. The fact that a subject's knowledge concerning her propositional attitudes is defeasible by behavioural evidence places others in as good a position as she to know what those attitudes are.

One might suppose that one or the other of the two epistemic criteria under consideration can be extended to cover all mental phenomena by means of the 'trick' used earlier in this section to show that linguistic versions of the intentionality criterion qualify any event as mental. However, in this case the trick won't work. Recall that any event could be shown to be mental by linguistic versions of the intentionality criterion assuming only that there is some (intentional) mental event spatiotemporally related to every event. Suppose that we were to attempt something along these lines with the epistemic criterion in order to extend it to cover propositional attitudes, assuming instead that there is some phenomenal mental event spatiotemporally related to every event. In contrast with the intentionality criterion, we are not able to conclude that all events are mental: the description '$(\iota x)(Px$ & x bears spatiotemporal relation R to John's throbbing pain)' (where 'Px' is a purely physical predicate) does not count as mental by Levison's first criterion for an event's being mental, for it does not satisfy the condition that it must be logically possible for a subject S to be *de re* directly aware of x. In this case x is not an event which could be necessarily as it appears to be. Similar reasoning can be used to show that propositional attitudes do not qualify as mental by either of Levison's criteria or by Kim's criterion. Take '$(\iota x)(Mx)$' to be a description of the event or state which is John's realization that the earth is round. Despite the fact that we can describe that event in terms of its spatiotemporal relation R to an event which does satisfy the criterion of *de re* direct awareness (viz. as '(ιx) $(Mx$ & x bears spatiotemporal relation R to John's throbbing pain)'), that event itself satisfies neither of the two versions of the epistemic criterion for the reason just cited: x is not an event which could be necessarily as it appears to be.

Of the two types of criteria of the mental canvassed here, linguistic versions of the intentionality criterion emerge as the more satisfactory. This is perhaps surprising given that they only cover the sensations in virtue of the fact that they cover any event whatsoever. However, what is crucial from the point of view of mind-body identity is that they cover all of what is intuitively deemed mental. And this they appear to do. Epistemic criteria, on the other hand, evidently have more difficulty covering the propositional attitudes and so serving as adequate conceptions of the mental. The fault seems to lie in the notion of direct awareness. While being suited to the sensations, it has little application, if any, to a large number of propositional attitudes, particularly to beliefs, expectations, and the like. As long as epistemic criteria take this to be the earmark of the mental, there is little hope of extending them to cover all of what is mental.

2. Type-Type Identity Theories and the Objection From Phenomenal Properties

A vast amount of literature produced on mind-body identity today is indirectly due to the work of J.J.C. Smart. In his seminal paper, 'Sensations and Brain Processes', Smart argued for what he called a 'strict' identity of sensations and brain processes, an identity no different in kind from that of lightning and electric discharges (or from any theoretical, empirical identity). His thesis was one of the stronger ones in the sense that it asserted the existence of general identities between types or kinds of brain processes (e.g., C-fibre stimulation) and types or kinds of sensations (e.g., having pain). Statements asserting such identities were held by him in addition to be contingent, not necessary.

The importance of Smart's work, however, lies less in the kind of identity thesis he argued for than in his answers to objections raised against the thesis. Talk of identifying aches, pains, and after-images with brain processes suggests that there are such *things* as aches and pains. This, combined with the claim that the relation between sensations and brain processes is one of 'strict' identity, generates what is known as the objection from phenomenal properties.

A defining feature of strict identity is that the terms of the relation (or objects related) satisfy what is known as Leibniz's Principle of the Indiscernibility of Identicals. According to this, if, for any objects (events) x and y, x is identical with y, then x and y share all properties (i.e., $(x)(y)(x = y \rightarrow (Fx \leftrightarrow Fy)))$. Thus, if 'John's pain at t' and 'John's Brain State α at t' pick out the same object or event, then any (usually non-modal, non-intensional) property truly attributable to the referent of the former expression must also be truly attributable to the referent of the latter one. The objection from phenomenal properties is commonly understood as stating that there are certain properties, like that of being dull, sharp, or throbbing, that are truly attributable to pains, after-images, and the like, but falsely attributable to any brain process.

Smart was one of the first to suggest a novel manoeuvre for avoiding this objection. He proposed that we give up talk of mental objects such as pains and aches in favour of talk of mental events, processes, or states. He then proposed to handle the objection in the following way:

> if it is objected that the after-image is yellowy-orange, my reply is that it is the experience of seeing yellowy-orange that is being described, and this experience is not a yellowy-orange something. So to say that a brain process cannot in fact be yellowy-orange is not to say that a brain process cannot in fact be the experience of having a yellowy-orange after-image. There is, in a sense, no such thing as an after-image or a sense-datum, though there is such a thing as the experience of having an image.[17]

If, the suggestion goes, the objection from phenomenal properties requires supposing that there are such things as pains, after-images, and the like, then the way to avoid it is to deny that there are such things.

Smart's suggestion has since been pursued by a number of identity theorists for a variety of reasons. The most obvious of these is, of course, that it does appear to avoid the objection from phenomenal properties in its original form. While Sue's pain may be dull and throbbing, her having of a pain is not (though we return to this below). There are other, perhaps less obvious, reasons in favour of the suggestion too. First, an event-identity thesis accords with our intuitions regarding certain mental phenomena; for instance, pains, tingles, thoughts, and desires. Intuition tells us that when a person is in pain or is thinking, something is happening to her. It is therefore misleading to speak as if such phenomena are objects that a person possesses when what is meant is that a change is occurring whose subject is a person. Second, the suggestion avoids the possible charge of category error, since it requires viewing the identity of mind and body as one holding between mental and physical phenomena rather than as one holding between mental objects and physical phenomena. Mental and physical phenomena are given the same ontological status; when the identity is viewed as one holding between mental events of a person and physical events of that person's body.

Finally, talk of mental phenomena avoids, at least at the outset, certain problems of location. While it may be true that a person locates his pain in his knee, the event which is his having of a pain may not be located where the feeling of it is. Just as one can have a yellow after-image and the having of it fail to be yellow, one can have a pain and the having of it fail to be in the knee. If pains do not exist but the havings of them do, then the having of a pain has a real location, e.g., in the body, and also a phenomenal location, e.g., in the knee. The phenomenal location, i.e., the location of the feeling, may or may not coincide with the location of the event.

As these last remarks may indicate, however, there is more to the objection from phenomenal properties than might meet the eye. Smart's strategy might be termed 'the adverbial manoeuvre': instead of construing mental phenomena as particular objects possessing phenomenal properties to which persons are related, they are construed as complex properties of persons (if conceived of as types) or as instancings of such properties in persons (if conceived of as individual token events).[18] Thus construed, the phenomenal aspect of any sensation becomes an integral part of the phenomenon itself. The result is that there are no phenomenal properties conceived of as properties either of sensation types (such as the type, having pain) or of sensation tokens (such as Sue's having of a pain at time t). There are only phenomenal mental types or properties themselves, e.g., the property of having a throbbing pain, or phenomenal mental tokens, e.g., Sue's having of a throbbing pain at t. Nevertheless, the fact that sensations are acknowledged to have phenomenal *aspects* invites fresh attacks. These have taken a number of forms in recent literature. However, they have a common source, viz. the assumption that, whereas it is of the essence of any type of sensation that it have a felt, or phenomenal, aspect or quality, it is not of the essence of any physical type of phenomenon that it feel in any way at all to its subject. We consider three versions of this objection below.

3. Rejoinders to Smart: Nagel, Jackson, and Kripke

The first is voiced by Thomas Nagel. Stripped of details, his argument is that the quale (the qualitative, or felt aspect) of any type of sensation or experience is essentially accessible from only a single (subjective) type of point of view, whereas physical properties or types are accessible from indefinitely many types of points of view. Since the quale of any type of sensation is essential to it, no sensation type can be identical with any physical–state type. Bats, for example, have experience: there is something that it is like for them to be them. This something – what Nagel calls 'the subjective character' of experience – is accessible to bats but inaccessible to humans.[19] The point is not that experience is private to its subject: the subjective nature of a bat's experience is not such that it is inaccessible to every other organism. However, it is accessible to others only to the extent that they too can undergo it (i.e., undergo experiences type-identical with it) or imagine what the quality of that experience is on the basis of the quality of their own. The more closely others' experience approximates to that of bats, the more able others will be to imagine what it is like to be a bat.

Nagel's point evidently is not simply that the manner or *way* in which sensations are experienced or known differs from the way in which physical properties are experienced or known. This formulation would in any case suffer from the objection (see Section 1) that epistemic contexts of the form '*x* is known by *S* to be *G*' or '*x* is experienced by *S* to be *G*' are non-extensional, in which case failure of intersubstitutivity of, say, 'pain' and 'C-fibre stimulation' for '*x*' in '*x* is experienced by *S* essentially subjectively' does not show that pain is not identical with C-fibre stimulation. Rather, it is that the way in which sensations are know*able* or experience*able* differs from the way in which physical properties are knowable or experienceable.[20] Construed in this way, Nagel's is an argument concerning the nature of what is known rather than one concerning the manner in which it is known.

Nagel's argument has suffered from two major objections. The first is that, viewed as an argument about the nature of what is known, it avoids the opacity problem but contains a false premiss. The argument is that sensation types are knowable subjectively only; physical types are knowable from indefinitely many points of view; so sensation types cannot be physical types. But issue can be taken with both the first premiss and the second. Against the first it might be objected that the most that Nagel is entitled to is the claim that sensations are known subjectively only, not that they are knowable subjectively only. Suppose that pain is indeed C-fibre stimulation (an issue that should be open at this stage of the argument). Then, being a physical type, it is (if the second premiss is true) knowable, if not known, from other points of view. It will not do to try to block the objection by saying that '*x* is knowable by *S* to be *G*' is non-extensional. The point of modalizing the argument is to *avoid* the opacity problem. Short of begging the question against the identity theorist, then, the first premiss must be amended to read: sensations are knowable subjectively.

Read in this way, it can be seen to conflict with the second premiss only if that premiss is taken to imply that what is physical is *not* knowable subjectively. But this too is questionable, and for the same reason: to assume that what is physical is not knowable from a subjective point of view is to beg the question against the identity theorist. It is true that what is physical is typically known in ways that are not subjective. But it does not follow that at least some physical states aren't knowable in ways that are subjective. One might just as well try to argue that heat isn't molecular motion because heat is knowable by tactile sensing and molecular motion is not knowable by tactile sensing. Since heat *is* molecular motion, one or the other of these premisses must be wrong. Since knowability is meant to concern the nature of what is known and not the manner in which it is known, the fault must lie with the second premiss: molecular motion is knowable by tactile sensing, despite the fact that it may not be known *as* molecular motion.[21]

The second main objection to Nagel's argument is that it equivocates between two different senses of 'subjective' and 'objective'.[22] Crucial to the argument is the claim that the essential nature of a given type of sensation is revealed in a certain type of epistemic situation; put differently, that the nature of a sensation type is revealed by the distinctively subjective manner in which it is known. Now, on one way of reading 'subjective', subjectivity is a property of a method or manner of knowing (as when, for example, one knows something *from* a certain point of view). Read in this way, one cannot infer from 'sensation types are knowable from a subjective point of view' and 'physical types are knowable from many points of view' that sensation types aren't physical types. For 'knowable' here means 'knowable from point of view p'; and the (supposed) fact that the physical point of view is not the only point of view does not show that *what* is knowable from other points of view cannot be known from the physical perspective also.

A second way of reading 'subjective' and 'objective', however, does entitle one to make such inferences. Here subjectivity is understood to be a property of what is known (as when, for example, one knows that what is subjective essentially involves a certain point of view). The knowability of a type of phenomenon is subjective in this second way, not merely in the sense that it is knowable from a subjective point of view, but also in the sense that being knowable from a subjective point of view is an essential property of it. Construed in this way, it concerns the nature of what is known.

The conclusion that sensations are not physical types requires that the premises be read in the second, not in the first, way, since only this reading will sustain the claim that sensations can *only* be known subjectively. The difficulty is that the only support available for the premises interpreted thus is that the manner or method of knowing qualia is distinctively subjective. The conclusion evidently requires one to accept the move from viewing subjectivity or objectivity as a property of a method or manner of knowing to viewing it as a property of what is known. But identity theorists will not accept this move.

It may be that Nagel's version of the knowledge argument does not (or at least need not) involve this kind of equivocation. One might wish to argue, for example, that the premises of the argument are to be understood in the second of the two ways outlined above, this reading being both intuitively plausible and in need of no further support.[23] But it can hardly be held that the claim that what is knowable in the case of sensations is knowable *only* from a single subjective point of view requires no support. What is intuitively plausible and needs no support, perhaps, is the weaker claim that what is knowable (sensations) is knowable subjectively. However, this claim will not suffice to generate the conclusion that sensation types aren't physical types for reasons already given. Consequently, even if the argument skirts objections based on the supposed equivocation between different senses of 'objective' and 'subjective', its premises evidently cannot sustain readings of sufficient strength to generate the desired conclusion without begging questions against the identity theorist.

Nagel's argument is very like a second version of the objection from phenomenal properties based on knowability, viz. that advanced by Frank Jackson.[24] This too is an argument, not about the manner in which we might come to know qualia, but rather, about the nature of what is known. However, there is a notable, and crucial, difference between the two, which turns on Nagel's emphasis on the subjective nature (hence the inaccessibility to others) of the quality of one's own experience. As Jackson sees it, Nagel's argument rests on the dubious claim that one cannot know what it is like to have a sensation unless one either has it or can imagine what it is like on the basis of sensations that one does have. This makes knowability heavily dependent on one's imaginative powers. But physicalism – the view that all objects, phenomena, properties (types and tokens) are physical – is primarily an ontological thesis, not a conceptual one. It need not make any special claims on behalf of our imaginative powers. Physicalists should concede that no amount of information or knowledge we can have about the experiences of others can yield knowledge about their experiences *as they experience them*. We are not them and so cannot experience their experiences as they do.

Jackson's claim is that it is not how experiences are undergone by a subject that poses a problem for physicalism, but rather, the qualities or properties of the experiences had. The problem is that no amount of physical information can reveal the nature of a person's experiences – either 'from the inside' *or* 'from the outside'. This is illustrated by way of the example of Mary, a brilliant scientist who is shut up in a black and white room and forced to view the world from a black and white television monitor.[25] Being a specialist in the neurophysiology of vision, Mary has at her disposal all the physical information there is to be had about what goes on when people have visual experiences such as seeing ripe tomatoes or the sky etc. Despite this, she learns something upon her release from the room about the world (not just about her experiences, but also about others') that she did not know before. Since she possesses knowledge of all matters physical about experiences prior to her release and yet acquires knowledge of her (and others') experiences after her release, there must be something knowable about experiences which no amount of physical information can provide. Inasmuch as there is, physicalism must be false.

Jackson is anxious to dissociate his argument from Nagel's, but his examples are apt to cause confusion. Mary's knowledge about the qualia of sensations is obtained by introspective awareness of her own. And, in another example, Fred's red_1 and red_2 experiences are held to be unknowable by us until such time as we all undergo operations that reproduce in us Fred's optical workings and consequently experiences that are type identical to Fred's.[26] It is natural to assume on the basis of such examples that the point of the argument is to show that the quale of any type of sensation is essentially accessible from only a single point of view, hence that it is vulnerable to the same objections as Nagel's.

In fact, however, the argument does not require the claim that the quale of any type of sensation is essentially accessible from only a subjective point of view. The problem posed for physicalists concerns the quale of any sensation type, not the subjective nature of any subject's experience of it. It may be true that knowledge of qualia is typically obtained 'from the inside'. But this is not to say that what is knowable from that point of view is not knowable from other points of view. The crux of the argument is that, *irrespective* of whether what is known is knowable 'from the inside' or 'from the outside', no amount of physical information can yield knowledge of qualia.

For this reason, the argument escapes the kinds of objections to which Nagel's falls prey. However, it is vulnerable to others. Specifically, the charge might now be made that it equivocates, not between different senses of 'subjective' and 'objective', but between different senses of 'physical information'.[27] On one way of understanding it, physical information is information described in a certain way, i.e., described in overtly physical terms. Interpreted in this way, it follows trivially from 'Mary knows everything physical there is to know about experiences' and 'Mary does not know all there is to know about experiences' that there is something knowable about experiences that physical information cannot provide. To say that there is something knowable about experiences that physical information cannot provide is to say no more than that mentalistic descriptions do not belong to, nor do they follow from, any complete and adequate physical account of human experiences.

This represents no real victory over the physicalist, however. Physicalism is primarily an ontological thesis, not a conceptual one. Just as it need make no special claims on behalf of our imaginative powers, it need make no special claims about the conceptual resources of physical theory. In order to refute physicalism, the knowledge argument must invoke a different sense of 'physical information' – one according to which information is physical just in case it concerns objects, properties, and phenomena that fall within the domain of physical theory (we may call this 'ontologically physical information').[28] The objection is, however, that the argument is fallacious because it moves from premises about overtly physical information to a conclusion about ontologically physical information.

An obvious response to this is to say that, irrespective of whether Jackson himself makes use of the first sense of 'physical information' (the sense in which it is overtly physical information), the argument need not. Just as Nagel's argument can be modalized in order to block objections based on the non-extensionality of contexts of the form 'x is known by S to be G', Jackson's can proceed with only the ontological sense of 'physical information'.

But now a different objection can be voiced. On the second reading of 'physical information', it might be argued, the argument, though valid, contains a false premiss, viz. 'Mary does not know all there is to know about experiences'. No physicalist will concede that Mary might have all the physical information there is to be had about experiences in this second sense and yet fail to possess all the information there is to be had about experiences. What Mary acquires when she is released from her black and white room, it will be maintained, is a new manner or way of knowing experiences, not an increase in her stock of things known. For qualia are physical aspects of physical properties.[29]

In order for this objection to succeed, we need to be able to suppose that the nature of any quale can be specified independently of how it is felt or experienced. It is as though qualia, or felt qualities, are qualities that just happen to be undergone by their subjects in typical, i.e., felt, ways. The felt aspect of any quale, on this way of understanding qualia, is not to be considered as intrinsic to or as part of the content of the quale. If it were to be considered so, we would be forced to conclude, in the case of Mary, that there *was* something knowable about experiences which physical information could not provide.

Now, this attempt to distinguish the nature of a property from the way in which it might, or typically does, affect things (e.g., human visual experiences) may be plausible in certain cases. For example, in cases of colour properties, for which physical bases exist, it is plausible to suppose that the nature of such properties can be given in purely physical terms independently of any reference to how instances of such properties are typically experienced by humans. (Being red, for instance, can be described in terms of having a certain triplet of electromagnetic reflectance efficiency.) However, the distinction that needs to be seen as plausible here is not that between the nature of a colour property and a subject's colour experience, but rather, that between the nature of a colour *experience* and *how* it is experienced. It is utterly unclear how we are to conceive of the nature of an experience in terms which are independent of the way that that experience is had, how it appears to its subject. The difficulty is that its very nature is itself phenomenal, or felt.

This point is illustrated vividly by cases of sensation types like pain. It is both natural and extremely plausible to think that it is at least part of the essence of these types that they feel in a characteristic way to their subjects. Nothing, one wants to say, could be of the type 'having pain' without feeling a certain way. The feel of a sensation just is its quale; it is part of its nature, not how it is felt. If it were not intrinsic to a sensation type that it feel a certain way, we could conceive of that type being instanced in a person without its characteristic feel (indeed, without feeling any way at all). But if a phenomenon were to lack a characteristic feel, it simply would not be pain. Unlike the colour property/ colour experience case, there is here no place 'between' what is felt and how it is felt in which to drive a wedge.

The knowledge argument can seem to be less effective than it is because cases of visual experiences fail to bring out forcefully enough the fact, which lies behind all versions of the objection from phenomenal properties, that it is essential to certain types of mental phenomena that they feel in characteristic ways to their subjects. In cases of visual experiences, we seem able to imagine having an adequate account in physical terms of what the experience is (i.e., the nature of the type of experience) because we suppose ourselves able to identify this independently of how the experience is typically had or undergone by its subject. But if we consider types of visual experiences alongside types of sensations like pain, then, in contrast with cases of colour properties and their experiential effects on subjects, it is not clear that the supposition is warranted. Experiential, phenomenal, properties evidently are not, as colour properties are, capable of possession by subjects that lack consciousness – subjects whose experience of such properties in part constitutes the means by which those properties are individuated. To say that the quale of an experience type could exist without feeling in a characteristic way (or in any way at all) to its subject is to come dangerously close to denying what is peculiarly and distinctively mental about certain mental properties or types, viz. their felt aspect. Whether any theory of the relation between the mental and the physical which makes this claim deserves to be called an identity theory rather than a form of eliminative materialism is doubtful.

A comparison with what Kim has to say about the 'disappear-ance' form of the identity theory might help to illustrate this. This version of the identity theory was originally motivated by the concern to avoid the objection from phenomenal properties; and did so by denying the existence of mental phenomena altogether, hence of any entities that could serve as candidates for the possession of phenomenal properties. The trouble is that it avoids the objection at the cost of denying the most fundamental tenet of the identity theory, viz. that mental phenomena are legitimate entities in the world.

In spite of its rather short history, the identity theory does have some fairly clear-cut features that identify it as a well-defined position on the relation between mind and body. As I see it, the fundamental tenet of the theory is that it is a *physicalist monism that retains mental events as legitimate entities in the world*. That is both its central attraction and the source of its gravest difficulties. And it may prove to be the cause of its downfall. But if you take it away, you take away the identity theory.[30]

It is no solution to the problem of how phenomenal mental types such as the type 'having pain' can be identical with physical types to be told that the qualia of such types can exist without being felt. For it is precisely this feel – the way in which such types are experienced – which makes them distinctively mental types. It is one thing to identify mental and physical types; another altogether to eliminate them.

Evidently, the strategy of insisting that qualia are physical aspects of physical properties will not succeed if one's aim is to be an identity theorist as opposed to an eliminative materialist. Jackson's objection thus stands undefeated. The only other obvious avenue of defence open to a type-type identity theorist pursuing the adverbial manoeuvre in the light of it is to insist that qualia are physical aspects of physical properties *and* that it is of the essence of certain physical types that they have a characteristic feel. However, this flatly contradicts any plausible conception of what it is to be a physical type or property. Our understanding of physical properties is such that their possession does not require, presuppose, or entail consciousness. To say that it is of the essence of certain types that they have a characteristic feel is tantamount to claiming that it is of the essence of certain physical types that they be *mental*. But no physical type is such that it could not exist if it did not feel some way or other to its subject. To insist upon it is to beg the question in favour of physicalism (see earlier discussion of criteria of the mental).

A third and final version of the objection from phenomenal properties is voiced by Saul Kripke.[31] His objection to type-type identity theories of the mental and the physical stems from his more general semantical views; in particular, from the view that identity statements involving rigid designators are, if true, necessarily true (a designator being rigid just in case it names whatever it does not only in this world but in every possible world in which that object exists). It is his contention that mental terms such as 'pain' (more generally, any natural-kind term such as 'water', 'tiger', 'heat', etc.) are such designators; and that consequently any identity statement expressed by means of them is, if true, necessarily true. This is incompatible with the so-called 'Cartesian intuition' that pain might have existed in the absence of any physical type of phenomenon. For if it is true that pain is identical with a given physical type, say, C-fibre stimulation, it is necessarily true: it cannot be possible that it should fail to be identical with that state. The Cartesian intuition challenges the truth of any supposed identity statement linking mental types and physical ones by challenging its necessary truth. What it effectively challenges is the supposition that terms like 'pain' (and 'C-fibre stimulation') could not fail to name the same type of phenomenon in every world in which they name anything at all; and it does this by challenging the supposition that the relation between any mental type and any physical type is a necessary one. It is this that brings the intuition into sharp conflict with the view that identity statements involving rigid mental designators are, if true, necessary.

This objection might appear to rely essentially on the truth of the principle (sometimes referred to as 'Kripke's Principle') that identity statements involving rigid designators are necessarily true if true at all (i.e., the principle that if α is rigid and β is rigid, and $\ulcorner \alpha = \beta \urcorner$ is true, then $\ulcorner \Box(\alpha = \beta) \urcorner$ is true). However, the objection can be put without appeal to this principle. Independently of it, we can prove the necessity of the identity relation (i.e., the principle, $(x)(y)(x = y \rightarrow \Box (x = y)))$.[32] This latter principle, combined with Leibniz's Principle of the Indiscernibility of Identicals and the Cartesian intuition, undermines the claim that identity statements involving terms for mental kinds are even true by suggesting that the relation between mental and physical kinds is not a necessary one. The argument is that if pain is identical with some physical type, it is necessarily identical with that type $(p = b \rightarrow \Box (p = b))$. Thus pain has the property of being necessarily identical with b. But, given the Cartesian intuition, it is possible that pain should exist where no corresponding physical type does, i.e., pain has the property of being possibly distinct from any physical type $(\Diamond \sim (p = b))$. But then, by the application of Leibniz's Principle, p has a property that b lacks; hence p and b are distinct. Kripke's Principle nowhere appears in this argument; and so objections to it based on that principle (in particular, the objection that terms like 'pain' are not rigid designators) go by the board.

This argument is a version of the objection from phenomenal properties inasmuch as its efficacy requires the twin theses of (*a*) the necessity of identity and (*b*) the Cartesian intuition. For (*b*) requires appeal to phenomenal properties. Suppose that the identity theorist responds to the challenge by rejecting (*b*). Then she must also reject the basis for that intuition, viz. the belief that what makes a given type of phenomenon pain is that it feels a certain way to its subject – that it is both necessary and sufficient for a type of phenomenon to be pain that it possess a certain felt quality. In cases of such phenomena as heat or such substances as water, we can explain the appearance of contingency associated with the true but necessary 'Heat = molecular motion' and 'Water = H_2O', not by supposing that the type of phenomenon that is heat or the substance that is water might have existed apart from molecular motion or H_2O respectively; but rather, by supposing that some distinct but qualitatively indiscernible (indiscernible by means of felt, or perceived, qualities) type of phenomenon or substance might have existed apart from molecular motion or H_2O. That is to say, we can explain the air of contingency associated with such statements compatibly with the mooted identities by showing the real possibilities thought (incorrectly) to be associated with them to be associated (correctly) with distinct but qualitatively indiscernible types of phenomena and substances (e.g., the phenomenon which heat-presents; the stuff that looks and tastes like water). For it evidently is really possible that the substance which looks and tastes like water should exist apart from H_2O, and that the phenomenon which heat-presents should exist apart from molecular motion. Not so in the case of pain: whatever presents itself as pain *is* pain; whatever feels like pain is pain.

The basis for the objection is thus revealed at root to be a metaphysical view concerning the nature of pain, viz. that it is the sole essence of pain, as a type of phenomenon, that it be felt or be experienced in a certain way by a sentient organism. It is this that justifies the supposition that *that* type of phenomenon might exist in another world apart from any physical type or property of an organism. And it is this that presents such a formidable obstacle to the identification of any phenomenal mental type with any physical type.

There are at least two ways of attempting to meet Kripke's challenge. One is to argue that his assumption that the only way that one can explain away the illusion of contingency associated with such statements as 'Pain = C-fibre stimulation' is by showing them to be confused with others which represent real and not merely epistemic possibilities is too strong. Illusions of contingency, it might be held, can be explained without reference to any other possibility, real or imagined. One needs only to distinguish *ways* of conceiving things or phenomena from *what* is conceived, and to maintain that in general the former provide incomplete information or knowledge of phenomena. The illusion of contingency associated with 'Pain = C-fibre stimulation' can then be explained, not as the result of confusing the possibility of pain existing where C-fibre stimulation does not with some other real or imagined possibility, but rather, as the result of supposing oneself to be conceiving something one does not know to be impossible (viz. that pain can exist where C-fibre stimulation does not) on the basis of the manner of conceiving it. If pain is identical with C-fibre stimulation, then *what* one supposes oneself to be conceiving is not possible. The impossibility one mistakenly supposes oneself to be conceiving is due to the fact that one's ways of conceiving pain or C-fibre stimulation, or both, are incomplete.

It is important to see that this strategy is not necessarily the same as that canvassed against Jackson's argument. Here it is not being held that the way in which pain presents itself does not provide knowledge as to its nature; only that the manner of conceiving it provides *incomplete* knowledge of its nature. This strategy does not entail that the feel of a sensation type is extrinsic or inessential to it. However, it is vulnerable to another difficulty. In order to succeed compatibly with the mooted identities between phenomenal and physical types, we must suppose that the feel of a phenomenal mental type is such that its nature (unbeknownst to us) is physical. But this is objectionable for reasons given earlier: it is no part of the essence of any physical type that it feel in any way to its subject. For a type of phenomenon to be physical is for it to be such that its attribution does not require, presuppose, or entail consciousness. Phenomenal mental types do, however, require consciousness in just this sense. One can of course avoid this difficulty by relegating the feel of a phenomenal mental type to the status of a way of conceiving it only. But then all of the problems that arose in connection with Jackson's argument will surface again here.

A second strategy for dealing with the challenge is to argue that one *can* explain away the illusion of contingency associated with such statements as 'Pain = C-fibre stimulation' by showing them to be confused with others which represent real and not merely apparent possibilities, but not in the way Kripke envisages. Kripke supposes that the identity theorist will attempt to meet this challenge by assimilating the case of pain to other cases of natural kinds of phenomena and substances, such as heat and water. However, there is another way of meeting that challenge, viz. by supposing that the *physical* type with which pain is identical, say, C-fibre stimulation, might be confused with a distinct but qualitatively indiscernible phenomenon (something which C-fibre stimulation-presents), say, the stimulation of strands of grey fibrous tissue distinct from C-fibres.[33] The illusion of contingency associated with such statements as 'Pain = C-fibre stimulation' would here be explained as the result of confusing C-fibre stimulation with something distinct which C-fibre stimulation-presents and supposing it possible that pain might exist while this latter type of phenomenon did not. Since this possibility evidently is real and not merely apparent, the challenge is effectively met.

Notice that this strategy does not suffer from the problems associated with the first. It is utterly conceivable in cases of physical types of phenomena that there should be a gap between the nature of that type of phenomenon or substance and how it presents itself to a sentient subject. Fool's gold and gold are distinct substances despite being indiscernible with respect to qualitative properties accessible to the naked eye; distinct, despite the fact that fool's gold gold-presents. It is plausible for this reason to suppose that we should be confused as to the real nature of a given type of physical phenomenon concerned and so suppose (incorrectly) that some type of phenomenon with which it is identical (e.g., pain) might exist apart from it.

Nevertheless, there is a difficulty with this strategy too. Put generally, the Cartesian intuition is not just that pain (and any other phenomenal mental type) might exist apart from any particular physical type with which it might be supposed to be identical. It is that pain might exist apart from any physical type of phenomenon at all. For this reason it is arguable that the illusion of contingency associated with any type-type identity statement between the mental and the physical is no mere illusion. The objection to the above line of reasoning is apt to be that it is really possible that pain should exist where C-fibre stimulation does not just because it is really possible that pain should exist apart from *any* physical type: for whereas it is of the essence of a phenomenal mental type that it feel a certain way to its subject, it is not of the essence of any physical type that it feel in any way to its subject. This intuition, and the challenge it presents to any type-type identity theorist, is not met by the above line of reasoning.

Evidently, neither of the two ways here considered of accommodating the characteristic feel or quale of a sensation type alongside type-type identities between mental and physical phenomena is successful. Relegating qualia to the status of manners or ways of conceiving sensations as opposed to what is conceived invites objections of one kind, while insisting that qualia are physical aspects of physical properties raises objections of another. Until such objections are met, both Jackson's and Kripke's challenges to type-type identity theories remain undefeated.

4. *The Problem of Variable Realizability*

Phenomenal-property objections present one major problem for type-type identity theories. But this is not the only problem they face. They also face objections based on what is often referred to as the possibility of variable realization: the possibility that a given mental type or property might be realized by different subjects (or by the same subject at different times) in physically diverse ways.[34] The intuition underlying this objection is that the attribution to a creature of a mental property, whether phenomenal or intentional, is so tied to introspection and intentional behaviour that the fact that two creatures may differ radically in their internal physical constitution could not thereby prohibit their possession of such properties. This intuition is incompatible with the belief that mental types or properties are identical with physical ones. For suppose that pain were to be realized in a given creature by the physical property or type, C-fibre stimulation. Then any creature whose physical constitution differed to the extent that it did not possess C-fibres *could* not exemplify the property of being in pain.

Many find this result unacceptable, the reason being that the commonsensical basis upon which the attribution of mental properties is typically made, viz. introspection and (intentional) behaviour, is one that we cannot seriously suppose to be replaceable by any other basis.[35] To suppose that this basis might be replaced by some other is effectively to suggest that we might regard creatures as different psychologically when their behavioural dispositions are indiscernible. But what could possibly ground this belief? Our day-to-day attribution of mental properties to creatures is so intimately bound up with the physical properties of their bodies and their environments that we could have no reason to discern a difference in mental properties where there was no corresponding difference in such physical properties. For mental properties are causally efficacious with regard to the physical world. Our conception of causality is such that we expect like causes to have like effects and vice versa; and this, given causal interaction, has the consequence that where organisms differ in their mental properties, this must make a potential physical difference. Such physical differences as might occur within the confines of a creature's body alone could not ground the belief that they differ psychologically. For first, we typically do not have access to these in our day-to-day attributions of mental properties. But second and more important, we would not deem such differences significant even if we did have access to them if they did not effect corresponding introspective and (intentional) behavioural differences. Attributions of mental properties are constrained by principles of rationality, consistency, and coherence; consistency and coherence between the properties themselves (including beliefs based on introspection) and between these and the intentional behaviour their instances cause (for more on this, see Chapter Three). Ultimately, it seems, only such differences as would make for an intentional behavioural difference (i.e., a difference in physical behaviour, intentionally described) could ground the belief that creatures differ psychologically.

Variable realizability is incompatible with type-type identities between the mental and the physical precisely because it suggests that the relation between mental and physical types is one/many, whereas the relation required for identity must be one/one. Nor can it be reconciled with such identities by supposing that they are species-specific (hence, for example, that it is pain for humans that is identical with C-fibre stimulation, and so on). The problem arises within a single species also. Even if it were to be *de facto* true that pain is realized in all human beings by the same physical type or property, still, if a human being were to differ in her physical constitution from others of the same species, she would not thereby be prohibited from possessing mental properties.

Variable realizability appears to be an unavoidable consequence of constraints that must attend the ascription of mental properties to persons. However, it is open to a type-type identity theorist to insist that this is compatible with a somewhat different account of the nature of psychophysical type-type identities. Variable realizability ensures that the relation between mental and physical types is possibly one/many, and this very possibility alone is enough to generate conflict with the view that mental types are identical with single physical types. Given the thesis of the necessity of identity (i.e., $(x)(y)(x = y \rightarrow \Box \, (x = y)))$, if a given mental property or type – say, pain – is in fact identical with a given physical type – say, C-fibre stimulation – then it cannot be possible that pain might be identical with any other physical type. Nevertheless, the possibility of variable realization *is* compatible with the supposition that mental types are identical, not with single physical types, but rather, with disjunctions of such types.

This encourages the suggestion that the physical types with which mental ones are identical are ones compounded by Boolean operations of conjunction, disjunction, and complementation, from the indefinitely (perhaps infinitely) many (first-order) physical types that might realize those mental types in any given organism.[36] The suggestion, that is, is that statements identifying mental and physical types are to be viewed, not as of the form 'Pain = Brain State α', for any first-order physical type (first-order because it is a property of organisms), but rather, as of the form 'Pain = Brain State B_1 v Brain State B_2 v . . . v Brain State B_n'.

However, this suggestion faces at least two major difficulties. The first has to do with both the size and the heterogeneity of the envisaged disjunctions, and it raises the issue of whether such disjunctive properties are *bona fide* ones. Can we seriously contemplate the supposition that the nature of any and every single mental type is to be one or the other of an indefinite (perhaps infinite) number of heterogeneous physical types? That the nature of a mental type such as pain is to be a physical – but no particular physical – type? Worse still, that its nature is to be any of a potential infinity of such types?

Given variable realizability, we can at least expect the number of physical-state types that might qualify as disjuncts in such a disjunction to be indefinitely many (indeed, there is no clear *a priori* reason to think that there should not be infinitely many). Given also that Boolean operations permit the formation of infinite conjunctions and disjunctions of properties, the fact that the envisaged disjunctions of first-order physical properties or types may be infinitely long does not in itself show that such properties are not *bona fide* in some sense. What it is for a property to be *bona fide* or real as opposed to merely apparent is in any case problematic. Of course, the supposition – which some may feel an obligation to make good if we are to take seriously the suggestion that properties like these exist – that we (or those within the scientific community among us) might discover and articulate the envisaged disjunctions will not be viable if they are infinite in length. And this poses a problem for those type-type identity theorists (as well as causal-role identity theorists like Lewis and Armstrong: see Chapter Two) who, like Smart, believe that empirical science may one day establish that mental types are physical types.

More worrying is the fact that these disjunctions must, in the light of variable realizability, be seen to be heterogeneous in nature. Since membership in the list of disjuncts is fixed by no single feature we must suppose each disjunct to possess (not even a causal power, as is the case in the causal-role identity theory: see Chapter Two), there is effectively no limit to the number of distinct physical types that could serve as disjuncts in such a disjunctive property. That any of a potential infinity of physical types could realize, in distinct individuals at the same time or in the same individual at distinct times, one and the same mental type offends the intuition that mental types are unitary ones – that distinct individuals in pain have something in common in virtue of which they are both in pain. If this suggestion is correct, the nature of a given mental type is not unitary and our intuition that distinct individuals in pain are undergoing events of a single type is in an important sense wrong.

This intuition may of course be misguided. However, there is a deeper concern connected with it, which is that these envisaged disjunctive properties are properties in an extended sense only.[37] The worry can perhaps best be expressed by contrasting the case of pain with properties like that of being green or being square. Typically, attributions of these latter types of properties to two or more distinct individuals proceed by way of discerning certain relevant similarities in them – similarities that make for the possession of the single common property of being green, or being square. Characteristically, these attributions are grounded in the intuitive belief that individuals with common properties share them because of other features that they possess – features similar to one another in ways that make for the possession of those properties.

One need not be realist with respect to properties to appreciate this intuition. However, disjunctive properties of the sort envisaged by this strategy for endorsing type-type identities between the mental and the physical do not appear to conform to it. Distinct individuals in pain may be so in virtue of instancing properties which have nothing in common with one another in the way that individuals that share the property of being square do. They may be undergoing events of no common type in virtue of which they are in pain. Despite instancing properties of a common, disjunctive type, they are undergoing the same type of event in only a nominal sense. This is what is meant by saying that disjunctive properties are properties in an extended sense only.

A different but related point might be made by considering for a moment these infinitely long disjunctions of physical properties and asking what the criteria might be, not for *inclusion* in any such disjunction, but for *exclusion* from it. Here the problem is not that the same mental type might be realized in distinct individuals by events of types that have nothing physically in common, but rather, that intuitively different mental types might have associated with them disjunctive physical types that have too much in common (i.e., are physically indiscernible). It is tempting to suggest that physiological theory will determine which of the various possible candidates are more likely to realize a given mental type. However, this alone will not do the job in the light of the twin theses of variable realizability and the necessity of identity. The possibility of variable realization counts equally against the truth of type-type identity statements of the form 'Pain = Brain State α' and those of the form 'Pain for humans = Brain State α'. Given this, discovering which physical types among a potential infinity are most likely to serve as (certain of the) disjuncts of the disjunction with which a given mental type is to be identified will not circumvent objections from the same source as that to type-type identities expressed by sentences of the form 'Pain = Brain State B_1 v Brain State B_2 v . . . v Brain State B_n'. For variable realizability has to do with logical and not merely with physical possibility. Since the constraints on the sorts and number of physical types that might serve as members of the disjunctive type with which a given mental type is to be identified are not themselves physical (indeed, it is uncertain what these constraints might be), there seems to be no limit to the number and kinds of physical states that might serve as disjuncts. On pain of compromising the supposed identity between mental and disjunctive physical types, no physical type for which it is logically possible that it serve as a member of a disjunctive physical type can be excluded from *any* of the disjunctions with which mental types are to be identified (for surely, it is logically possible that a given mental type might in one individual be realized by an event of one physical type while it is realized in another individual by an event of a distinct physical type). But then the identity theory, if viewed as type-type in this way, is threatened with triviality: not only may no physical type for which it is even logically possible that it serve as a member of a disjunctive type with which a given mental type is to be identified be excluded from the list of its disjuncts, but no physical type for which it is logically possible that it occur in the disjunctive type associated with one mental type can be prohibited from occurring in the disjunctive types associated with any other. Mental types themselves threaten to collapse into one another – an inadmissable result for any type-type identity theorist.

Suppose, despite these doubts, that someone were to insist upon the *bona fide* nature of these disjunctive physical types. Then there would be a second major problem for this strategy to contend with. It is doubtful whether every property constructible from a physical property by Boolean operations of infinite conjunction, disjunction, and complementation, is itself a *physical* property.[38] To assume so is to assume that the set of properties constructible by such operations is closed under them. But it can be argued that this assumption is false. It requires one to suppose that the properties in a given set $S*$ (where $S*$ is the set of maximally consistent conjunctions of S-properties and their negations for any set S of properties) are mutually exclusive *and* that they jointly exhaust the domain of discourse D associated with $S*$ (in this case, the domain of physical objects). However, the members of S will only satisfy this requirement if negation is construed as exclusive negation. Consider the example of a set S containing two properties, P and B, where P is the property of being pink and B the property of being blue.[39] Then $S* = \{PB, -PB, P-B, -P-B\}$, the set of maximally consistent conjunctions of S-properties and their negations. Under exclusive negation, neutrinos have the property $-P-B$. Under choice negation, they don't even have this property since they are colourless. If this is right, then there is no way of ensuring that the infinite disjunctions of first-order physical types and their complements with which mental types or properties are envisaged as being identical are themselves physical properties – again, an unacceptable result for any type-type identity theorist.

This exhausts the avenues of defence open to type-type identity theorists against the thesis of variable realizability given the thesis of the necessity of identity. Neither single nor disjunctive physical types are plausible candidates for ones with which mental types might be identified in the light of these two theses. Variable realizability thus presents a second formidable obstacle to type-type identity theories of the mental and the physical.

Chapter Two

In the last chapter, one kind of type-type identity theory of the mental and the physical was discussed. However, many think that this is neither the only nor the most plausible kind of type-type identity theory that there is. Our concern in this chapter is with a second kind of identity theory which is often thought to be both type-type and capable of avoiding objections from phenomenal properties while accomodating variable realizability, viz. the causal-role identity theory.

Strictly speaking, functionalist theories are not identity theories of the mental and physical. However, they are typically held in conjunction with some sort of identity thesis (specifically of a physicalist kind), and in this form they may be considered together with the positions of causal-role identity theorists such as Lewis and Armstrong. In particular, the functional specification theory, which we address below in Section 4, is virtually indistinguishable from the Lewis/Armstrong type of position. Both can be roughly characterized by their commitment to (*a*) the causal-role, or causal-functional, specification of the nature of any given mental-state type, and (*b*) the truth of identity statements linking the mental with the physical. Despite this, there is considerable confusion regarding the details of the causal role/functional specification (CR/FS) theory; and one of the primary aims of this chapter will be to disentangle various theses that are often associated with it.

One major confusion concerns whether the theory does in fact entail the existence of type-type identities between the mental and the physical in addition to token-token ones. Variable realizability will be seen to present obstacles to the view that the CR/FS identity theory is a type-type identity theory. Of the four possible kinds of type-type identities considered in Section 3 to which the theory might be seen to be committed, only one will be found to be compatible with the twin theses of variable realizability and the necessity of identity. Ultimately, it will be argued, type-type identities of even this kind ought to be eschewed by the CR/FS theorist, since they are incompatible with the theory's physicalist commitments. The CR/FS identity theory is thus best construed as a token-token rather than as a type-type identity theory.

Construed in this way, the theory avoids Kripke's version of the objection from phenomenal properties in its original form. However, there is a residual issue to be addressed (in Section 4) as to whether it avoids that objection when construed as a token identity theory given that it identifies the essences of mental types with causal-functional properties. If variable realizability threatens the theory's commitment to type-type identities between the mental and the physical, phenomenal property objections dog its commitment to the causal role/functional specification of the nature of any given type of mental phenomenon. These present a formidable obstacle to the supposition that the essence of any given mental type consists in its causal role, with the consequence that the first step in the CR/FS theorist's argument for the identification of particular mental events with particular physical ones cannot be taken. By way of introduction to all of these problems, we begin in Section 1 with Armstrong's early position, which differs somewhat from his later view and from Lewis's position (addressed in Section 2).[1]

1. Armstrong's Early View

Armstrong's concern to develop a plausible theory of mind was originally dominated by two beliefs: first, that materialism must, in some form or other, be true; and second, that any acceptable version of it must be couched in terms that are topic-neutral. This second belief was dictated in part by the view, which Armstrong shared with Place and Smart, that statements identifying mental with physical phenomena are contingently true if true at all. Being contingently true, such statements were to be established *a posteriori*. Evidently, Smart and Armstrong thought that in order to ensure the possibility of type-type identity, mental terms must be shown to be co-referential *a priori* with topic-neutral expressions. Otherwise it would be difficult to avoid the conclusion that the referents of mental and physical terms differ in their modes of presentation and hence that there are irreducibly mental properties.[2]

Armstrong's commitment to topic-neutrality, combined with a deep attraction to behaviourist theories of mind, eventually led to a 'two-tiered' account of the mental. This account consists of two quite separate components. The first is conceptual, a 'logical analysis' of mental concepts. The second is empirical, a thesis about the nature of mind. The identity of mental and physical phenomena hinges on the second of these two components. The first component, on the other hand, makes possible the contingent identifications endorsed by the second, since it preserves the topic-neutrality of mental and physical descriptions.

According to the first component, it is an essential part of our concept of the mental that what is mental is apt for the production of certain types of behaviour; or, in cases of certain mental phenomena (e.g., pain), that it is apt for being caused by certain sorts of characteristic stimuli. Of course, any given mental event (token) may occur without actually being caused by or causing phenomena of the types definitive of the mental state (type) of which it is a token; and so we must distinguish between the causal relations a given token may actually have with regard to its physical stimuli and behavioural effects, and the relations it is *apt* to have with regard to phenomena of those types. Although our concept of the mental is of states which are essentially relational (identified and individuated by physical, behavioural, and other mental types from which they are distinct), it is no part of that concept that a given mental event *could* not occur apart from events, types of which are involved in the definition of the mental type of which it is a token. In short, our concept of the mental is of states which are dispositional; ones with causal powers which may or may not be actualized in any given token. Just as a substance may be soluble without ever realizing that capacity, so too a given mental state may dispose its subject to engage in a certain type of behaviour without that (or any other) subject ever actually engaging in behaviour of the relevant type. Mental states are, according to this account, 'pure' dispositions.

The causal-role analysis of mental concepts is concerned with concepts of *types* of mental phenomena, not with concepts of tokens. It is true that causal relations are most naturally conceived of as holding in the first instance between particular, token, occurrences or events, and only derivatively of the types (or properties) of which they are tokens (or instances), where the latter are often conceived of as abstract and capable of multiple instantiation. Nevertheless, it is types of mental phenomena, concepts of which are the subject of analysis in terms of causal roles, that are of interest to causal-role identity theorists. They are not concerned simply to analyse the concept of Jones's pain at *t*, or of Sue's sudden desire at 3 p.m. on Tuesday, 2 July 1985, for an ice-cream cone, inasmuch as these are concepts of non-repeatable, dated occurrences. For their interest is primarily to provide an account of those concepts that are embodied in our commonsensical talk about the mental; and this requires talk of pain as a general concept – as a concept that can attach unambiguously to any number of different organisms at any number of distinct times. There is, of course, good reason for this: the less general this first component of the overall theory is, the weaker (more likely to fail in its account of all mental phenomena) and less plausible (in its suggestion that the concept of pain as it attaches to a given person at a given time differs from the concept of pain as it attaches to another at that or at any other time) the resulting theory will be.

Thus, the type, 'pain', is defined as that state, instances of which are apt to be caused by events (tokens) of certain (physical and mental) types and apt to cause phenomena of certain (mental and behavioural) types. Mental types in general are defined by relation to other, distinct, types; but the causal relations that any such type is apt to bear to other types it is so disposed to bear by virtue of its instances possessing such capacities. Lest one confuse the first component of the causal-role account with the second, however, the definitions provided by the first are concerned with mental concepts rather than with the states (types and/or tokens) to which they attach. This being so, they are silent on the *ontological* issue of whether any identities that might exist between the mental and physical are merely token-token as opposed to type-type. In short, the first, conceptual, component of the causal-role identity theory is neutral with regard to the question of whether mental/physical identities are token-token or type-type, and this despite the fact that it is concepts of mental types that it sets out to define. Indeed, as we shall see when we later turn to functionalist theories of mind, it is neutral as between identity and dualist theories of mind altogether.

We have not yet touched upon the second, empirical component of the causal-role identity theory. One might nevertheless wonder how the theory thus far considered differs from behaviourism, the view that mental states (types) can be defined in terms of (or 'reduced to') their relations to characteristic stimuli and behavioural effects (where these contain no ineliminable reference to other mental types). One fundamental difference should be apparent from the start: whereas behaviourism identifies a mental state with its causal role with respect to physical stimuli and behavioural responses, the causal-role account does not. According to it, the concept of the mental is of a state which *mediates* between stimulus and response. Thus, mental states, while *having* causal roles, are not identified (i.e., held to be identical) with such roles. The mental is accorded an ontological status frankly denied it from the outset by the behaviourist. This is sometimes expressed by saying that the causal-role account does, whereas behaviourism cannot, recognize the existence of pure dispositional mental states, i.e., states that have but do not consist in their causal roles.[3]

There is another, equally apparent, difference between the two theories, however, and that is that behaviourism is, whereas the causal-role account is not, a *reductive* account of the mental. That is to say, the former does while the latter does not prohibit reference to distinct mental types in the characterization of any given mental concept. The aim of the first component of the theory is to give a topic-neutral analysis – one which does not entail that mental phenomena are purely physical phenomena. Since a reductive account would entail just this, however, the causal-role theorist must be non-reductionist.

While nothing in the first component actually entails the truth of materialism – the thesis that everything is not only physical but material – it does make materialism more plausible. One of the major stumbling-blocks faced by all forms of dualism arises from the appearance of causal interaction between the mental and the physical. It is a major strength of materialist theories, and of identity theories in particular, that they hold the promise of making more intelligible than their dualist rivals the phenomenon of causal interaction between the mental and the physical. They do so, of course, by relegating the relatively obscure mechanism of psychophysical interaction to the (purportedly) more familiar status of physical/physical interaction.

The first component of the causal-role identity theory thus paves the way for the second, in which it is argued, on empirical grounds, that only physical states of organisms in fact play the causal roles in terms of which mental states are defined. The first component makes possible the contingent identification of mental and physical phenomena by characterizing each in terms logically independent of the other, while the second establishes the physical nature of the mental. Together they form the premises of an argument whose form is held to be roughly this:

(1) Mental State M = The occupant of causal role R (by logical analysis of the concept M)
(2) Brain State B = The occupant of causal role R (by theoretical empirical hypothesis)
(3) Mental State M = Brain State B (by the transitivity of =)

(where the terms flanking the identity sign are intended to be ones referring to types or properties).[4] It is in virtue of (2), it should be stressed, that the status of psychophysical identity statements is held to be contingent. The physical state – say, Brain State B, which we might in fact discover to be the state which plays the causal role definitive of mental state M (for any subject s) might have played some *other* role (or none at all); conversely, some other brain state, distinct from B, might have been the state which plays causal role R. As Lewis puts the point, 'Pain might not have been pain', i.e., the occupant of the causal role definitive of pain might not have occupied it (we return to this below).[5]

As Armstrong and Lewis intend it, the causal-role identity theory is a type-type identity theory: it purports to establish the truth of statements identifying mental-state types with physical-state types (where this plainly requires talk not merely of meanings, of mental concepts, but of the entities which make statements involving them true). That this should be so is not, however, apparent from the first premiss and its ground alone, since this concerns mental concepts and is intended to flow solely from contemplation of our ordinary commonsensical talk of persons and their mental properties. Why Armstrong and Lewis should profess themselves to be type-type identity theorists, and whether the causal-role account of mind requires such commitment, are major problems associated with the theory, and we shall investigate them further shortly.

2. Lewis's Position

This completes our description of Armstrong's early position, which, as stated earlier, differs in certain ways from his later view, as well as from Lewis's. Such differences as are of interest here do not affect the form of the argument as set out a few paragraphs back. They do, however, raise issues that will emerge as important when we turn to criticisms of the causal-role account.

It is evident from the early view that the analysis of mental concepts is meant to proceed in an *a priori* fashion quite independently of any empirical investigation into the nature of the entities that serve as referents of mental terms. That is to say, the definitions provided by the first component of the causal-role account are intended to be read as analytically true; and this in turn presupposes a distinction in kind between analytic and synthetic truths. Lest one be tempted to reject the account on the (Quinean) grounds that there is no distinction in kind between truths deemed analytic and those deemed synthetic, however, Armstrong later points out that the first component need not be developed along precisely these lines.[6] One way to view it is as part of a scientific theory wherein mental terms are introduced into discourse by way of descriptions of the causal-roles played by their referents. Such a theory would, of course, need to be viewed as of a more commonsensical, general sort than the kind of theory envisaged in the second component of the account; for the latter envisages a scientific community as discovering the real nature of mental phenomena, of which those familiar with the truths expressed by the first component of the theory are ignorant.

This is precisely the view held by Lewis.[7] According to it, psychophysical identities are theoretical identities implied by the empirical theories that make them possible. One such theory will be a term-introducing theory of mental phenomena, the aim of which is to define those phenomena by reference to their causal roles – the relations they are apt to bear to physical stimuli, other mental states, and behaviour. The other, a physiological theory, will imply psychophysical identities in conjunction with the first by establishing that a certain n-tuple of physical entities realizes, or satisfies, the first theory suitably purged of all of its mental terms. It is thus that we may discover empirically that the referents of mental terms are physical states.

Lewis too is committed to the topic-neutrality of the analysis of mental concepts. His strategy for defining mental terms in such a way as to meet this constraint is to treat all of the commonsensical platitudes of folk psychology as a term-introducing scientific theory whose mental terms may then be eliminated as follows. First, we conjoin all of the truths of folk psychology, obtaining one very long sentence in which all mental terms appear as names. In this sentence there occur certain *T*-terms, whose referents are specified in terms of their causal relations to each other and to other entities named by other (*O*-terms) in the sentence. This single sentence we call the postulate of *T*, which we write thus:

$$T\langle t_1 \ldots t_n \rangle$$

Replacing each occurrence of a *T*-term with a variable, we may obtain a formula in which only *O*-terms appear; and by prefixing this with existential quantifiers, we obtain the *Ramsey* sentence of *T*. This says that there is at least one n-tuple of entities which realizes *T*.[8]

The importance of this method of defining mental terms for the issue of mind-body identity cannot be underestimated. Armstrong's analysis of mental concepts proceeds by relating synonym to synonym in a system of concepts whose relations to other, non-mental concepts is never purged entirely of reference to mental ones. This non-reductionist commitment is part and parcel of the commitment to topic-neutrality in the characterization of any given mental state. But now another problem threatens the theory; and that is the threat of circularity in the analysis of mental concepts. This undermines the thesis, to which causal-role identity theorists are committed, that mental states just are physical states, by undermining the view that a complete account of mind can be given in terms that utilize only physical and topic-neutral language. The Ramsey technique illustrates perspicuously and simply how one might proceed to define mental terms in such a way as to meet the constraint of topic-neutrality while avoiding the threat of circularity.

There is a second difference between Armstrong's early and later work about which Lewis has much to say, and this has to do with the commitment to type-type identities between the mental and the physical. The early work explicitly assumes that the kinds of identities postulated by the second component of the theory as holding between mental and physical phenomena hold between single mental- and physical-state types; and that these identities hold across species rather than merely within them. It thus assumes that empirical science might establish the truth of such statements as 'Pain = C-fibre stimulation', where the terms flanking each side of the identity sign are taken to refer to single types of phenomena. However, there is a formidable objection to this version of the identity theory, as was noted in the last chapter: the variable realizability or plasticity of any given mental state prevents the identification of it with any single physical type. Even if it were to be true that pain is in fact realized in all creatures by the same type of brain state, we would not be prepared (nor should we be, according to the first component of the causal-role account) to prohibit attribution of mental properties to persons whose brain states differed from ours provided such states occupied (in them) the causal role definitive of pain. The possibility of variable realization of any given mental state just is the possibility that some state, distinct from the physical state that in fact occupies the causal role definitive of, say, pain, might occupy that role. Since, *ex hypothesi*, the envisaged states are distinct from one another, this possibility is incompatible with the supposition that both might be identical with pain. Armstrong's later work explicitly attempts to countenance this objection.

3. The Causal-Role Identity Theory and Type-Type Identities

There are a number of ways for a causal-role identity theorist to attempt to meet objections based on the variable realizability of any given mental state. One, which we will consider at length in Section 4 below, is to reject type-type identities outright and insist on a token identity causal-role theory (call this Strategy 1). However, there seem to be at least four other ways for a causal-role identity theorist to attempt to accommodate variable realizability *without* eschewing commitment to type-type identities of some kind or other. One, considered at length in Chapter One, is to identify single first-order mental types or states such as pain, not with any single first-order physical state type, but rather, with the disjunction (perhaps infinite) of such types (call this Strategy 2). We will briefly re-examine this strategy shortly. Another (Strategy 3) is to identify single *second*-order types, such as the property of fulfilling or having a certain causal role (say, causal role *R*) with single *second*-order mental types, such as the property of being pain.[9]

Finally, there are two others, both of which are intended to be compatible with full commitment to type-type identities between the mental and the physical.[10] The first (Strategy 4) is to maintain that single first-order mental properties or states (such as pain) are to be identified, not with single first-order physical types (such as C-fibre stimulation), but with (second-order) properties possessed by such states, viz. properties like that of fulfilling a certain causal role (the causal role definitive of a given mental type). Since the states themselves are types, the properties with which mental types are to be identified according to this strategy are not first-order, but second-order, physical types. Thus, pain is to be identified, not with any of the *occupants* of, or states which fulfil, a given causal role, but rather, with a single (common) property possessed by all such occupants, viz. the property of fulfilling, or being occupants of, that causal role. We will return to this suggestion shortly. The second strategy (Strategy 5), which both Armstrong and Lewis favour, is to insist that mental terms such as 'pain' refer to, or pick out, properties (or states) of organisms *via* theoretical or abstract descriptions of those properties, viz. ones specifying that they fulfil certain causal roles definitive of the mental types associated with the relevant terms.[11] Thus 'pain' is effectively to be construed as a predictable of states that fulfil or play a certain causal role. Since such descriptions can be satisfied by any of a number of states in the same or different organisms, the identities expressed by terms linking mental with physical types are compatible with the hypothesis of variable realization.

Let us consider the final four strategies first, beginning with the fifth. Exactly what are we being invited to accommodate consistently with the possibility of variable realization? The truth of an indefinite number of statements identifying the same mental type with distinct physical types? No, since this is plainly incompatible with the supposition, given the transitivity of identity, that such statements are both true and genuine identity statements. It seems, rather, that we are being asked to entertain the suggestion that mental terms like 'pain' are ones whose references are fixed by descriptions which at different times and in different organisms can be satisfied by different physical state types. Just as a description like 'The head of Fairweather Enterprises' can be satisfied by different people at different times in different places, so too, it might be thought, 'pain' (as defined by 'the occupant of causal role R') can be satisfied by different physical states at different times in different organisms. Similarly, just as the truth of such statements as 'The head of Fairweather Enterprises in June 1988 = Sue Gleam' need not compete with the equal truth of 'The head of Fairweather Enterprises in April 1987 = John Bluster', despite the fact that both are instances of a *single*, more general, type – the type, 'head of Fairweather Enterprises' – so too, one might think, the truth of identity statements such as 'Pain for O at t = Brain State α' need not compete with the equal truth of 'Pain for S at t' = Brain State β' or 'Pain for S at t = Brain State γ' ($\alpha \neq \beta \neq \gamma$), despite the fact that all are instances of the more general type, the type 'pain'. In short, we are being invited to suppose that the possibility of variable realization can be accommodated alongside psycho-physical type-type identities by supposing that mental *terms* have variable reference.

But there is a major difficulty here, as the analogy itself makes plain. Despite the fact that the description, 'The head of Fairweather Enterprises', is of a position whose occupants are identified by their role with respect to other individuals in a certain context (and in this it does resemble fairly well the causal-role analysis of terms like 'pain'), it may at any given time be satisfied by *only* one individual if sentences containing it are to turn out true, and so (on the condition that it refers at all) it can be seen to function as a proper (uniquely identifying) definite description. Not so with mental terms such as 'pain' on the causal-role account: the occupants of the causal role definitive of pain may not only differ as between individuals at different times, but they may differ between distinct individuals at the *same* time quite compatibly with the truth of sentences of the form 'Pain = C-fibre stimulation'. The description by which the reference of 'pain' is fixed is not a proper one given that the possibility of variable realization covers both differences in physical (realizing) states in distinct (as well as identical) organisms at distinct times *and* differences in such states in distinct organisms at identical times. Uniqueness of reference is thus *not* presumed to be secured by descriptions that fix the references of mental terms in the mental/physical case. This point is sometimes put by saying that there is no such state as *the* occupant of the causal role definitive of pain.[12]

This is not, it should be noted, simply the point (which Lewis, Armstrong, and others stress) that concepts like that of pain are non-rigid concepts and that terms like 'pain' are non-rigid designators.[13] To say that a term, specifically, a singular term, is a non-rigid rather than a rigid designator is to say that its reference may vary from one possible world to another; that it is possible that what it in fact refers to in this world should both exist and fail to be the referent of that term in any (or every) other possible world. Thus, suppose that Sue Gleam is in fact the sole referent of the description, 'The head of Fairweather Enterprises', in this world. Still, she might have failed to satisfy that description (if, for instance, she had decided to train to be a doctor), and someone else might have satisfied the description instead. Typically, those who maintain the rigid/non-rigid designator distinction hold that most definite descriptions are (unlike proper names such as 'Sue Gleam') non-rigid (the exceptions being ones which identify an individual (or a natural kind) by means of a property essential to it in the sense that that individual could not cease to possess that property without thereby ceasing to exist altogether).[14]

The present point is not simply the point that terms like 'pain' are non-rigid. For it is evident to proponents of the rigid/non-rigid designator distinction that definite descriptions can be both rigid and non-rigid. And while it is true that the rigid ones cannot fail to secure uniqueness of reference if they refer at all, it is not true that at any given time, all non-rigid ones must *fail* to uniquely identify an individual. The description, 'The head of Fairweather Enterprises', is a case in point, for though its reference may vary from time to time and from one world to another, it purports to and may nevertheless succeed in uniquely identifying a given individual at a specific time. This is not so with improper definite descriptions, which, even at a specific time, do not purport to secure uniqueness of reference and so may be satisfied by any number of distinct individuals. In short, the class of non-rigid designators include both proper *and* improper definite descriptions. But it is the fact that mental terms are ones whose references are fixed by improper and not merely non-rigid descriptions, ones such as 'the occupant of causal role R', that causes problems for causal role theorists committed to type-type identities between single mental and single physical states. (These descriptions ought not to be confused with ones such as 'the property of having causal role R' or 'the property of typically mediating between inputs I and outputs O', for it is the occupants of such roles, the state types that have properties referred to by the latter descriptions, whose identity with physical state types are at issue here. Such descriptions as 'the occupant of causal role R' are thus to be associated with Strategy 4, not Strategy 5. See p.49 above.)

If this is right, then attempting to accommodate the possibility of variable realization by invoking the rigid/non-rigid designator distinction will not resolve the tension for those who wish to maintain that there are true statements identifying mental with single physical types. Even if such identity statements as 'Pain = C-fibre stimulation' are relativized to times, the possibility of variable realization ensures that an indefinite number of distinct physical states may simultaneously occupy, in distinct organisms, the causal role definitive of pain. The case is yet worse, since variable realization, if it is a valid possibility at all, holds equally for specific organisms at specific times and for distinct individuals (whether at the same or at distinct times). If the possibility that a

physical state, β, distinct from a given state, α, might nevertheless occupy the causal role definitive of pain counts against the
truth of the sentence, 'Pain = Brain State α', because it is
effectively to suppose that one state might be two, then equally
the possibility that a physical state, β, distinct from a given state,
α, might occupy the causal role definitive of pain for O at t counts
against the truth of 'Pain for O at t = Brain State α'. The upshot
would seem to be that there is in general no such thing as *the*
occupant of the causal role definitive of pain even for a specific
organism at a specific time. To suppose that there is is to suppose
that the possibility of variable realization might hold in the
general case of pain and other mental types but not in the case of
more specific mental types, such as the type, 'pain for O at t.' But
there is no reason why it should not be thought to hold in the
latter when one is prepared to endorse it in the former.[15]

It is tempting to respond to this line of reasoning by claiming
that it equivocates between the necessity or contingency of
statements identifying mental and physical types, on the one
hand, and the necessity or contingency of the identity *relation*, on
the other. What's being envisaged here, it might be held, is not
that one thing might be two, but rather, that a term that in fact
picks out a specific neural state in this world (a state which is
necessarily self-identical) might, in some other world, pick out a
distinct (necessarily self-identical) state. What makes identity
statements linking single mental with single physical types
contingent has to do, not with the metaphysical relation of
identity concerning the types referred to, but rather, the semantic
functioning of the terms appearing in such statements. To
suppose that because the statements are contingent, the identity
relation must also be contingent (and hence that it is possible that
one thing be non-self-identical), is to equivocate between the
two.

But this, though correct, is beside the present point. The point
here concerns, not the contingency of statements identifying
single mental with single physical types, but rather, their truth.
And though this does have something to do with the issue of
whether terms like 'pain' pick out the same first-order properties
or types of states from one world to another (in its suggestion
that the descriptions by which the references of mental terms are
fixed are not proper ones and so cannot purport to secure

uniqueness of reference even in this world), it plainly goes well beyond it. At root it is a metaphysical issue having to do with the twin theses of (*a*) the necessity of identity and (*b*) the possibility of variable realization. (*a*) tells us that if a given mental type – say, pain – is identical with a given physical type – say, Brain State α – then it could not be that pain (however it is picked out) is identical also, at any time, in any organism, with a state – say, Brain State β – distinct from α. This is because, given the transitivity of identity, the supposition would amount to the hypothesis that two distinct states be one. Now (*b*) tells us that pain might in one creature at one time be realized by one type of state of the brain – say, Brain State α – and that that very mental type might also, at that or some other time, be realized by another, distinct state of the brain, say, Brain State β. These two theses are plainly incompatible with the supposition that identity statements of the form 'Pain = Brain State α' and 'Pain = Brain State β' are both true and relate single first-order physical and mental types.

The claim that the descriptions by which the references of mental terms are fixed are improper is of a piece with this issue. It is true that many definite descriptions (indeed, the vast majority) appear in true identity statements whose truth is in no way compromised by the fact that those descriptions might have picked out entities other than the ones they do. As long as they in fact happen to pick out a single entity, identity statements involving such descriptions may be true. It is tempting to think that a similar point holds for the descriptions by which the references of mental terms are fixed. But what emerges here is that these latter are improper, not because they in fact pick out more than a single type of state (it may so happen that in this world only a single physical type of state of the brain occupies the causal role definitive of pain), but because they cannot purport to pick out one such state. Just as an indefinite description such as 'A head of Fairweather Enterprises' might in fact be satisfied by a single person (say, because the business goes bankrupt within weeks of starting out) despite having no claim to secure uniqueness of reference, so too might the descriptions by which the references of mental terms are fixed. However, the former do not purport to secure uniqueness of reference. Nor can the latter; and the reason has to do with the possibility of variable realization.

Evidently, variable realizability cannot be accommodated along with the fifth strategy for endorsing type-type identities between the mental and the physical. This leaves, apart from the suggestion that type-type identities between the mental and the physical be eschewed altogether (Strategy 1), three further options. One is to identify first-order mental types such as pain with second-order physical properties (Strategy 4), and we shall pursue this strategy shortly. Another (Strategy 3) is to identify *second*-order mental types, such as the property of being pain, with second-order physical properties. Finally, there is the possibility, to which we now briefly turn, of identifying first-order mental types like pain with what one might call *disjunctive* physical types (Strategy 2).

Discussion of Strategy 5 showed that the relation between mental and first-order physical states (states or properties of organisms rather than properties of those states) is a one/many relation. This might encourage the suggestion that type-type identity commitments are compatible · with the possibility of variable realization provided that the physical types with which mental ones are held to be identical are viewed as compounded by the Boolean operations of conjunction, disjunction, and complementation out of the indefinitely (perhaps infinitely) many first-order physical types that might realize those mental types in any given organism. Recall that this strategy was canvassed in connection with straightforward type-type identity theories but rejected for two reasons. The first was that it is doubtful whether the envisaged disjunctive physical types or properties are properties in any more than an extended sense (hence whether they are *bona fide*); and the second was that it is doubtful whether every property compounded by Boolean operations of disjunction, conjunction, and complementation from physical properties is itself a physical property. The second doubt plainly counts equally against the causal-role identity theory. However, the first might be thought to be less compelling in the case of the causal-role identity theory than it was in the case of the straightforward type-type ones, and so is worth a brief re-examination.

Crucial to the question of whether the disjunctive physical types with which mental ones might be held to be identical are *bona fide* was that there appear to be no principles, either of inclusion or of exclusion, by which to determine, from the indefinitely many physical types that might serve as disjuncts in any such disjunctive type, membership in the list of disjuncts associated with that type. Any and every physical type concerning which it is logically possible that it occur as a disjunct in any such type had, it seemed, an equal claim to be included in every disjunction with which any mental type might be associated. The causal-role identity theory might appear to provide a way around this difficulty, since although the disjunctions with which mental types are to be identified may be *physically* heterogeneous according to the theory, there is a principle of inclusion and exclusion associated with every such disjunction. The causal-role account has it that physical types can only realize pain for any individual if they have or fulfil the causal role definitive of pain. Hence, no two individuals could realize the property of being in pain without possessing a number of features that make for the possession of that property – in particular, in the case of pain, of engaging in relevantly similar behaviour.

However, this, though correct, misses the crux of the issue. Pain, as defined by the causal-role identity theory, is to be identified, not with a certain causal role had by various first-order physical states, but with the states that have that causal role. It is true enough that distinct individuals cannot, if the causal-role account is correct, share the property of being in pain without having features that are similar in ways that make for possession of that property, since no physical state can realize pain for a given individual unless it fulfils the causal role definitive of pain. However, it is the states that fulfil that role that realize pain for distinct individuals; and it is the heterogeneity of these first-order physical states (and not the homogeneity of the second-order physical property, viz. that of fulfilling a given causal role, possessed by all such states) that presents the major worry here. Other, behavioural states may be relevantly similar; but what makes for pain in distinct individuals may nevertheless be states which themselves have nothing physical in common. To put the point another way: the causal role which is held to be essential to pain suggests that pain is a unitary kind; but the disjunction with which it is held to be identical, being heterogeneous in the essential properties of its disjuncts, suggests not. The intuition that distinct individuals in pain share a single common type of experience is importantly wrong if the disjunctive nature of mental states is accepted.

Connected with this is a second major concern, which can perhaps best be brought out by contrasting the case of pain with cases of other properties, like those of being red or being rectangular. There is a crucial difference between the kinds of features distinct individuals may be expected to have in virtue of which they share a property like that of being red, or being rectangular, and those properties that first-order physical states may be expected to have in virtue of which they are disjuncts in the physical disjunctions with which mental types are held to be identical. In the former case, the features that make for similarities in ways that are relevant for being red or being rectangular are expected to be themselves first-order properties of the individuals possessing such properties – having a certain chemical constitution, perhaps, or having a certain spatial distribution of molecules. Not so in the latter case: the properties in virtue of which each and every disjunct is a member of the disjunction with which pain is to be identified are *second*-order properties – properties possessed by the states that serve as the occupants of the causal role definitive of pain, where these states are themselves types. To suppose that such second-order properties might alone ground the belief that distinct first-order states have features that are relevantly similar in ways that make for them being pain is rather like supposing that distinct individuals share the property of being red by virtue of the possession by *that* property (the property of being red) of a further property, viz. the property of being the property of being red.

It is the conjunction of these two points – that a mental type like pain on the causal-role account is to be identified, not with the causal role by means of which it is defined, but with the entities that have it; and that the only property that these entities can be expected to have in virtue of which they all qualify as pain is a second-order, rather than first-order, property – that seriously compromises the view that the disjunctive properties with which mental types are to be identified are properties in any but an extended sense. Evidently, this second suggested strategy for accommodating type-type identities between the mental and the physical consistently with the possibility of variable realization is no more viable in the case of the causal-role identity theory than it was in the case of the more straightforward type-type identity theories considered in Chapter One.

However, the preceding discussion suggests that Strategy 4 might be plausible. This is the suggestion that mental types such as pain are to be identified, not with the *occupants* of the causal roles definitive of such types, but rather, with the common property possessed by all such states in virtue of which they fulfil those roles (viz. that of occupying, having, or playing the causal roles definitive of those types). A mental type such as pain is thus to be identified with the (causal-functional) property expressed by the causal-role description by which the term 'pain' is defined – a description satisfied by all occupants of that causal role, in virtue of which they all have the property of being occupants of that role.

It is instructive to note that Armstrong himself rejects this strategy on the grounds that such second-order properties cannot be conceived of as having causal efficacy.[16] Certainly, there are difficulties accommodating it within the confines of the causal-role identity theory as envisaged here. The reason will perhaps be seen more clearly in the context of our discussion of functional-ism in the next section; but it is implicit in what has already been said about the causal-role account. Pain, on this account, is construed as a first-order mental property or state of organisms – a type, instances of which are undergone by sentient beings. It is that type of state, instances of which are apt (perhaps in conjunction with instances of other mental state types) to be caused by certain characteristic stimuli and apt (in conjunction with instances of other mental types) to cause characteristic behaviour. This being so, it can only be a confusion to suppose that anything but a first-order physical state of an organism can be identified with pain, i.e., can occupy that causal role. States of organisms may *be* types, but the properties that such states possess are plainly distinct from those states themselves. In particular, properties like that of being an occupant of, or being a state which typically plays, a given causal role (the causal role definitive of pain, say) are distinct from and attach to a number of distinct physical states rather than themselves being states which play such roles. It is perhaps this consideration that lies behind the claim that second-order properties like that of occupying or fulfilling the causal role definitive of pain could not be causally efficacious. Being second-order properties, they could not bear the causal relations to physical stimuli, other mental states, and behavioural output that first-order mental types like pain do.

There is nevertheless a strategy to be salvaged from this suggestion, and that is to hold that type-type identities between *second*-order mental and second-order physical types follow from the causal-role identity theory (Strategy 3).[17] It seems quite possible for a causal-role identity theorist to maintain, consistently with the denial of the truth of *all* statements identifying any first-order mental state (such as pain) with either a single or disjunctive first-order or a second-order physical type, that second-order type-type identity statements between the mental and physical are true. Indeed, commitment to the latter would seem to be a necessary consequence of the causal-role account. The account, it may be recalled, defines first-order mental types like pain in terms of their causal role: whatever occupies the causal role definitive of pain *is* pain. Thus, to be pain is to be such as to fulfil the causal role by which pain is defined. From this alone certain second-order type-type identities evidently follow, since anything which is pain (and thus has the property of being pain) has the causal role definitive of that type. This encourages the thought that it is the property of being pain, rather than pain itself, that is to be identified with the second-order property possessed by all occupants of the causal role definitive of pain, viz. the property of having, fulfilling, or occupying the causal role definitive of pain. The suggestion, that is, is that causal-role identity theorists are committed to *no* first-order type-type identities between the mental and the physical, but are rather committed to the truth of statements identifying second-order mental states or properties, like that of being pain, with second-order physical ones like that of fulfilling the causal role definitive of pain (i.e., to the truth of statements of the form 'Being pain = Having causal role R').

If causal-role identity theorists are committed to any type-type identities between the mental and the physical, these would seem to be the most likely. For these alone appear to be both consistent with the first component of the theory and with the twin theses of variable realizability and the necessity of identity.

The second-order properties envisaged here seem plainly capable of possession by any number of distinct physical (first-order) states, no one (nor any disjunction) of which is identical with a given first-order mental state like pain. But there is a real question as to whether causal-role identity theorists should endorse commitment to *any* type-type identities between the mental and physical, these included. For there are other, crippling difficulties that attend this commitment. These emerge with particular clarity in connection with functionalism, a doctrine with which the causal-role identity theory has a great deal in common and to which we now turn.

4. *Causal Role/Functional Specification and Type-Type Identities*

Functionalism in the philosophy of mind is, broadly construed, the doctrine that mental states (types) can be exhaustively characterized and uniquely individuated by their functional properties – by the relations that they are apt to bear to certain characteristic types of physical stimuli, other mental states, and behavioural responses. Construed in this way, it bears more than a passing resemblance to the causal-role identity theory. Indeed, the logical analyses of mental concepts or definitions of mental terms with which the first component of the causal-role account is concerned are virtually indistinguishable from the functionalist analyses or definitions of mental terms advanced by certain kinds of functionalists. viz. functional specification theorists.[18] Of the wide variety of doctrines that go under the name of functionalism, those associated with the functional specification view and one other only (viz. the functional-state identity theory) will serve as the basis of the discussion of functionalism to follow.

It is no accident that Lewis and Armstrong are often said to be functionalists, since many functional-specification theorists favour Lewis's method of defining mental terms.[19] Despite clear affinities between functionalism of this sort and the causal-role identity theory, however, care must be taken not to assimilate the two. The latter *combines* claims of identity between the mental and the physical (at least of the token-token sort, and probably of the type-type sort as well) with a causal-functional analysis of mental concepts. It is thus committed on both an ideological and an ontological plane. Strictly speaking, however, it is no part of the functional specification doctrine (nor of the functional-state identity thesis) to hold that mental states are physical states (a point that will emerge as important when we come to discuss the differences between the two functionalist doctrines). Both are compatible with psychophysical dualism. This is sometimes put by saying that functionalism employs a physicalist ideology while remaining neutral on the issue of ontology.[20] What it is committed to is a claim about the definition and/or characterization of mental states. It says that they can be specified in terms that employ only physical and topic-neutral language (along the lines of the Ramsey-type sentences envisaged as obtainable from the commonsensical platitudes of folk psychology described in Section 2 of this chapter).

Of course, many functional specification theorists do in fact go beyond the commitments engendered by adherence to this particular variety of functionalism by conjoining claims of functional specification with some sort of psychophysical type-type identity thesis. In this form, the view is effectively the same as the Lewis/Armstrong type of position (but see Note 18). It is this functionalist position, rather than the functional-state identity theory, with which we shall be concerned in the remaining sections of this chapter.

Functionalists of the two sorts just described have been known to differ in their allegiance to materialism, and, in particular, in their allegiance to the truth of some sort of identity theory of the mental and the physical, despite the fact that both profess to be identity theorists of mind and body. The reason is not easy to see, but can perhaps be made clear with the help of points made earlier regarding possible type-type commitments open to the causal-role identity theorist. Recall that one strategy (Strategy 4) that was briefly canvassed for accommodating type-type identities between the mental and physical within the confines of the causal-role account was to hold that first-order mental types like pain are to be identified with second-order properties possessed by the occupants of the causal roles definitive of those mental types (e.g., the property of having causal role R). This strategy was rejected in favour of the suggestion (Strategy 3) that *second*-order mental types such as that of being pain (second-order because it is the property of being the state that fulfils or occupies a certain causal role; a property of a state – pain – which is itself a first-order type) be identified with the envisaged second-order (causal-functional) properties possessed by those physical states. The former strategy was rejected because it was incompatible with the causal-role account. What it was incompatible with was the functional specification doctrine embodied in the first component of that account.

This should provide an idea of what differentiates functional specification theorists who are also identity theorists with regard to the mental and the physical and functional-state identity theorists. The fourth strategy, with which the causal-role identity theory was held to be incompatible, describes the commitments of a functional-state identity theorist. Accordingly, first-order mental states or properties such as pain are held to be functional properties; properties which, like having or fulfilling a given causal role, are possessed by first-order states (which may or may not themselves be physical) and so are *second*-order properties of such states. Many proponents of this account are inclined to reject identity theories of the mental and physical of any sort simply because they do not consider functional properties of the sort envisaged to be physical properties. Such properties, they hold, may conceivably attach not only to first-order physical states but also to non-physical ones.[21] In short, functional-state identity theorists, being committed only to the identification of mental states or properties with second-order functional properties, are neutral with regard to the physical or non-physical nature of the first-order states possessing those properties.

While the two sorts of functionalist positions under discussion differ in their commitments to materialism (and *a fortiori* to any mind/body identity theory), they both profess to be committed to type-type identities (albeit of very different kinds). However, it is evident that the functional-state identity theory is not, strictly speaking, a version of the mind/body identity theory at all. Inasmuch as it is not, it falls outside the scope of this discussion. The functional specification theory is another matter. Being virtually indistinguishable from the causal-role identity theory, it ought (for all of the reasons outlined in the previous section), if it is committed to type-type identities of any sort, to be construed as being committed to the truth of statements identifying single second-order mental with second-order physical types. Below we consider the implications of that commitment for the two theories taken together under the name 'causal-role/functional-specification (hereafter, CR/FS) identity theory'.

It is at least partly because of the apparent commitment to type-type identities between the mental and the physical that the CR/FS identity theory suffers from a variety of well-known difficulties. One has already been considered at length – that of accommodating type-type identities consistently with the possibility of variable realization given the necessity of identity. There is, however, a second major objection to consider, viz. the objection from phenomenal properties. We have seen how a version of this objection (voiced by Saul Kripke) applies to theories committed to the truth of statements identifying single first-order mental with single first-order physical physical types. Equally, a version of this objection may appear to apply to the CR/FS identity theory.

Kripke's objection, it may be recalled, stems from a certain metaphysical view concerning the nature of pain, viz. that it is of the essence of pain, as a type of state, that it feel or be experienced in a certain way by a sentient organism, or that it have a certain phenomenological or felt quality. This view fosters the belief that *that* state could exist in another world apart from any physical state of an organism (the Cartesian intuition). Combined with the thesis of the necessity of identity, it presents a formidable obstacle to the identification of any mental state type with any physical state type.

A familiar strategy for attempting to meet this objection is to maintain that terms like 'pain' are not rigid designators, and that, consequently, statements identifying mental with physical types do not express necessary truths. However, discussion of the possible type-type commitments open to a CR/FS identity theory in the preceeding section of this chapter has shown that contingency is purchased at the cost of truth. The suggestion that mental terms such as 'pain' are non-rigid is compatible with the Cartesian intuition because such terms may, in another world, pick out states other than the ones they in fact pick out. It is thus compatible with the supposition that statements identifying pain with distinct physical state types (or with some non-physical state type) may be equally true from one world to another (or indeed, even within a single world). What it is *not* compatible with is the thesis of the necessity of identity. The fact that 'pain' may pick out distinct physical states in this or other possible worlds will not resolve the tension generated by the supposition that whatever it does in fact pick out is necessarily self-identical. For this implies that whatever in fact happens to be pain – say, Brain State α – *could* not be another brain state distinct from Brain State α. The identity relation is a necessary one and so carries across possible worlds; and this point is untouched by the realization that a term like 'pain' might pick out a state other than the one it in fact picks out. In short, treating mental terms as non-rigid may avoid Kripke's objection, but for reasons quite other than those intended. For if identity statements of the form 'Pain = Brain State α' are uniformly false (and false because treating mental terms as non-rigid is incompatible with the necessity of identity), then CR/FS identity theorists have no option but to reject commitment to the sorts of type-type identities between the mental and the physical that lie at the basis of Kripke's attack (those endorsed by Strategy 5).

However, discussion of the possible type-type commitments open to causal-role identity theorists also revealed that, irrespective of whether they endorse type-type identities of the form 'Pain = Brain State α', they are very likely to be committed, if they are committed to type-type identities at all, to the truth of statements identifying second-order mental with second-order causal-functional types, i.e., to type-type identities of the form 'Being pain = having causal role R' (Strategy 3). Moreover, expressions like 'being pain' evidently are rigid even if ones like 'pain' are not.[22] Indeed, it would seem to follow from the very definition of mental terms on the CR/FS view that, though the occupants of the causal role definitive of a given first-order mental type like pain may vary from organism to organism in this or in any other world, what makes it the case that all such occupants are pain is that they all possess *that* causal-functional property. If to be pain is to have that causal-functional property, it cannot be possible in any other world that 'being pain' should pick out a property distinct from that expressed by 'having causal role R'. While distinct physical state types may have that property, it had better be *that* property that all such states have; and if that property is the property of being pain (= having causal role R), then 'being pain' would seem to be rigid.

Does, then, a version of the Kripke objection apply to type-type identities of the form 'Being pain = having causal role R'? Again, it would seem not. Suppose that it is true that being pain = having causal role R. Then in any world in which terms rigidly designate this property, it is true that being pain = having causal role R. Now, the Cartesian intuition is simply the intuition that pain, or any other mental state (any state that has the property of being pain) might exist independently of any single physical state, and indeed, independently of all physical states. In the context of the CR/FS identity theory, this threatens any identification of any mental state possessing the property of being pain with any single or disjunctive physical state (even if infinite in length) possessing the property of having causal role R. But all of this is utterly compatible with the supposition that being pain = having causal role R. The reason is, of course, that having causal role R is a *causal-functional* property of first-order physical states, and it is conceivable that such a property might attach to states other than physical ones.

But now there is another problem for the CR/FS identity theorist to contend with. If Kripke's objection poses no threat to the sorts of type-type identities envisaged here, it is because the truth of these is compatible with the Cartesian intuition. If, however, type-type identities of the form 'Being pain = Having causal role R' are compatible with dualism – compatible with mental types such as pain being realized in different creatures by non-physical types of state – in what sense is this theory an identity theory of the mental and the physical? In what sense can it even be supposed to be a *physicalist* account of mind? This is precisely the problem faced by functional-state identity theorists, who frankly concede that the truth of their theory shows materialism to be very probably false.[23] But this concession is not equally an option for the CR/FS identity theorist. It is an essential part of his theory that functional specification be conjoined with an identity thesis of mind and body. Such identities as 'Being pain = having causal role R' are incompatible with that theory because they countenance the possibility of dualism. They are therefore incompatible with the view, to which CR/FS identity theorists are committed, that their theory is itself an identity theory of the mental and the physical (in particular, that it is a physicalist account of the mental).

Evidently, the CR/FS identity theorist has the resources to emerge unscathed from Kripke's objection. In so far as the strategy of treating mental terms as non-rigid designators succeeds in avoiding the objection as it applies to certain sorts of type-type identities (viz. those expressed by sentences of the form 'Pain = Brain State α'), such identities do not hold and the identity theorist must reject them. And in so far as the truth of type-type identity statements of the form 'Being pain = having causal role *R*' is compatible with the truth of the Cartesian intuition, the CR/FS identity theorist must also reject them. Either way, the CR/FS identity theorist is able to avoid one version of the objection from phenomenal properties. For he ought, if he is to be consistent with the basic tenets of the theory, to commit himself to no more than token-token identities between the mental and the physical.

5. *The CR/FS Identity Theory and Token-Token Identities*

This may deal with Kripke's objection in its strongest form. Evidently, however, a version of the same objection can be generated with regard to any *token* identities that might be entailed by the CR/FS identity theory. Suppose that we attempt to counter the Kripkean charge by insisting that the theory is committed only to the truth of token-identity statements of the form '*S*'s pain at *t* = *S*'s Brain State α at *t*'. The rejoinder will be that the Cartesian intuition has it that *any* pain, type or token, might exist apart from *any* physical state, type or token.[24] Indeed, if pain, as a type of state, might exist apart from any physical state type, then every instance or token of the former might exist apart from any token physical state. The air of contingency associated with token identity statements linking the mental with the physical is no more illusory than that associated with type-type ones: no amount of empirical information about brain events (or state tokens) could show that this particular pain event now could not but be a brain event. For whereas it is of the essence of any token pain state that it be felt in a certain way by its subject, it is not of the essence of any physical state token that it be felt in any way at all. The situation is yet worse for the token-identity theorist, since if, as seems evident, a state type like pain has its characteristic felt essence in virtue of its tokens instancing a phenomenal or felt property, the force of the Cartesian intuition attaches more firmly to token than to type identities between the mental and the physical. If it is obvious that nothing could count as being the type 'pain' if it did not have associated with it a characteristic feel, it is still more obvious that nothing could count as being an instance of that type – say, being Jones's pain at t, or being my pain now – if it did not now feel a certain way. In short, this objection cuts across the mental/physical type/token distinction; and so it will not do to attempt to circumvent it merely by eschewing type-type commitments.

Kripke's objection evidently presents obstacles to any attempt to identify mental with physical phenomena, irrespective of whether such phenomena are taken to be types or tokens. It therefore presents obstacles to the CR/FS identity theory even when construed as a token identity theory. The objections we are about to consider count as versions of that objection since they are to the effect that mental state types such as pain have essentially certain felt properties not had by any causal-functional state, with the consequence that no mental state token can be identical with any token of any causal-functional state type (irrespective of whether the latter is physical). In effect, this is to say that it cannot be the sole essence of any mental state token that it occupy a given (any given) causal role, and hence, that the first premiss in the CR/FS identity theorist's argument for token identity of the mental with the physical is false. It counts against any token identities that might be licensed by the CR/FS identity theory since, if nothing can be an instance of the type 'pain' unless it feels a certain way, and any causal-functional state token can exist or occur without feeling a certain way, then no mental state token can be identical with any causal-functional state token.

Recent discussions of the CR/FS identity theory have centred on two types of case (or thought experiment) that present phenomenal-property problems for the theory. They are known respectively as the inverted qualia objection and the absent qualia objection.[25] Both presume that certain mental phenomena (types), viz. the sensations and perceptions, have associated with them characteristic qualia (i.e., phenomenal content), variations concerning which are perfectly conceivable amongst tokens of such types despite supposed identity of causal-functional roles. Specifically, the inverted qualia objection supposes that two (token) mental states – say, perceptions – might vary in their visual qualia (one having the qualitative content of red, perhaps, while the other has the qualitative content of green) yet remain invariant with respect to their associated causal-functional roles. (Another case focuses on pain.) The absent qualia objection goes further and supposes that two token mental states might be identical with regard to causal-functional role, yet differ to the extent that one has qualitative content (has qualia) while the other lacks it altogether. If either or both of these suppositions are correct, then, since the quale of any type of sensation is essential to it, no token of that type can be identical with any token of any causal-functional state type.

As stated, these objections fall squarely within the domain of traditional phenomenal property objections, since they focus on *felt* qualities of phenomenal mental state tokens rather than on features of thoughts or propositional attitudes. It is worth noting, however, that a similar objection can be generated with regard to the latter.[26] Given that the identity of any individual thought is fixed in part at least by its content (that which it is 'about'), it can be argued that the causal-functional role of two token thoughts may remain invariant while their contents vary. The reason given will of course differ from that cited in the case of sensations. In the latter, the guiding consideration is that sensations differ when their felt qualities do, and that this escapes (as it must) causal-functional characterization. Since thoughts are not felt in this characteristic way by their subjects, qualia cannot figure in any argument concerning them against the CR/FS identity theorist. On the other hand, it seems plain that the content of any thought is as essential a part of its identity as is the quale of any sensation to its identity. Given that it is, the objection is that causal-functional role specification, being sensitive to differences only in causal role, extensionally characterized, between phenomena, cannot capture differences in mental phenomena due to content, these being non-extensionally characterized and logical rather than (merely) causal in their relations to other mental phenomena. That is to say, no mental phenomenon could count as a thought unless it were to possess a content, deductively (and not merely causally) related to other thought contents and behaviour in such a way as to answer to the constraint of rationality. Taking the sensations and propositional attitudes together, the charge against the CR/FS identity theorist is that differences in qualia and/or contents of experiences and/or thoughts are possible which cannot be captured in causal-functional specifications and which constitute part, at least, of the nature of such phenomena.

It is tempting to respond to this line of attack by simply denying the intuitions upon which the objections are based. This is in fact the strategy favoured by many functionalists with regard to the absent qualia objection. Those sympathetic to the absent qualia hypothesis (and its propositional analogue) presume that it is conceivable (i.e., logically possible) that two token mental states should be functionally identical, or identical with regard to their causal role, yet differ with regard to their contents. But the CR/FS identity theorist will deny that this *is* possible. That it is presumed to be so may itself be considered question-begging by such a theorist.[27]

This strategy might be backed up by arguing that the absent qualia objection underestimates the importance to the CR/FS identity theorist of qualia, presuming that only causal-functional properties matter to the theory. The CR/FS identity theorist is in no way committed to denying either the existence of qualia or its importance in a proper causal-functional characterization of mental state types, tokens of which are held to be physical. Such a theorist can acknowledge that experiences are discriminated by their subjects, not on the basis of their causal-functional characteristics, but rather, on the basis of features *intrinsic* (non-relational, monadic) to them. Nor is it any part of such an account to deny that occupants of causal roles definitive of mental state types have other, intrinsic properties beyond their causal-functional ones. What is and must be denied is that any *particular* intrinsic properties are essential to the identity of any mental state token. In short, the CR/FS identity theorist can insist that qualia both exist and have a proper role to play in a satisfactory account of the nature of mental phenomena by maintaining that they are those intrinsic features of sensations, perceptions, and the like, whose introspective detection by subjects are apt to cause belief tokens of certain types. For instance, *S*'s sensation of heat is one whose intrinsic features are such that introspective awareness by S of them is apt to cause S to believe that he has/is having a sensation-of-heat. The upshot of the defence is that absent qualia are logically impossible because the presence or absence of qualia *would* (and must) make a causal-functional difference; in this case, a difference to the introspective subject.[28]

The inverted qualia objection is typically handled rather differently by the CR/FS theorist. Rather than deny the intuitions upon which the thought experiment is based, the strategy favoured in this case is to concede the possibility of two mental state tokens being identical with regard to causal-functional role, yet differing with regard to qualia; and then attempt to show that this is consistent with a causal-functional specification of the nature of mental phenomena. Suppose that two subjects, S and S', undergo visual experiences of exactly the same types in exactly the same circumstances, the only difference between these experiences (apart from their subjects and perhaps times of occurrence) being that S experiences greenly where S' experiences redly, i.e., the qualia of these supposedly functionally identical states are 'inverted'. Then the obvious move for the CR/FS identity theorist to make is to argue that though inverted qualia are indeed possible, they pose no threat to the theory because the nature and identity conditions of mental state types are fixed, not by qualia, but by the causal-functional roles of states which happen to have them. What that theorist must insist upon is that inverted qualia pose no threat to the theory because, though it is of the essence of a given mental state type, if it *is* a qualitative state, that it have qualia of some sort or other, it is *not* of the essence of any such state that it have any specific quale. Shoemaker, for example, contends that while particular qualitative state types (such as that involved in my seeing blue, or my being in pain) may not be definable in causal-functional terms, the *class* of qualitative state types is.[29] His strategy is thus to concede that it may be of the essence of any mental state token that it have some quale or other (where this can be accounted for in causal-functional terms) but not that it have the particular quale it does.

The strength of this way of accommodating the possibility of inverted qualia within the confines of a causal-functional account of the nature of mental types lies in the fact that it frankly concedes that it is of the essence of a qualitative state that it have qualitative character. Crucial to the strategy is the claim that it is of the essence of any qualitative state token that it have a quale which is qualitatively similar to and different from the qualia of other qualitative state tokens; and that a causal-functional account of qualitative similarity and difference can be given for the class of qualitative states as a whole in terms of relations of qualitative similarity and difference which hold between tokens of such states. Specifically, the class of qualitative states as a whole is held to be definable in terms of similarities and differences between a person's qualitative state tokens, on the one hand, and the aptness of such tokens to cause that person to believe that certain objective similarities and differences exist in the world outside his experience, on the other. Thus, what makes a relation one of qualitative similarity is that it plays a certain causal-functional role *vis-à-vis* perceptual beliefs about objective similarities and differences, ones held to exist independently of experience.

The main difficulty with this response is that it requires one to concede that it is not of the essence of any qualitative state token that it have any of the intrinsic features it has; that whereas the causal-functional role such features have with regard to qualitative properties (e.g., the redness) of objects outside the experiencing subject, on the one hand, and that subject's qualitative beliefs and behavioural responses, on the other, is essential to that token state's identity, its intrinsic properties are not. The response requires supposing that the nature and identity conditions of qualia (e.g., the felt quality of pain, the experienced colour of one's perceptual experiences) can be fixed in causal-functional terms. But this goes against the strong intuition that the felt quality of any qualitative state token is both essential and intrinsic to it in the sense that it could exist apart from any causal role that token state may be apt to play *vis-à-vis* physical input, other mental state tokens, and behavioural output.[30] Since the account of qualitative similarity acknowledges the impossibility of providing a causal-functional definition of particular qualia, it is not only unclear how it can account for differences in qualia amongst certain *types* of sensations, such as pain and pleasure; it is also unclear how it can account for differences in qualia between types of sensations, e.g., pain and pleasure, on the one hand, and types of perceptions (e.g., perceptions of blue things), on the other. Since it is no part of the essence of any qualitative state token that it have any particular quale, nor indeed any particular *type* of quale, such a token could count as a pain event in virtue of having pleasure qualia, or, worse still, in virtue of having colour qualia. But this seems absurd.

Of course, reasons can be and have been given for thinking that the above intuition, though strong, is groundless. For instance, it might be argued that the inverted qualia objection rests on the assumption that the *only* factors necessary for determining the identity of any mental state token are its intrinsic, directly introspectible features – in particular, its qualia. This assumption derives from the intuition that what makes a given mental state token what it is must be something uniformly possessed by all tokens of the same type; that, for example, what makes this particular experience a pain experience must be some one feature possessed by all pains. This is in turn encouraged by the suggestion that mental kinds (such as pain) are natural kinds (like tigers, water, or heat), since natural kinds of substances and phenomena are often thought to have associated with them underlying uniform essences empirically discoverable, whose possession by members of those kinds is considered to be both necessary and sufficient for them to be of such kinds. Given the intuition and the thought that lies behind it, it is natural to suppose that it is the quale of any sensation that constitutes its essence. But both the assumption and its associated intuition, it might be argued, are wrong.[31]

It has been suggested that just as it is an empirical matter whether tigers or heat are natural kinds (where this turns on whether there *is* a single underlying essence, empirically discoverable, definitive of the kind in question), so too is it an empirical matter whether mental kinds are natural kinds. In fact there are reasons for thinking that mental kinds such as pain are *not* natural kinds. The phenomenon of variable realization prevents taking any single *physical* underlying essence as definitive of a mental kind such as pain. To assume that there must be some underlying non-physical essence possessed by all tokens of such states is to beg the question against the CR/FS identity theorist outright.

To the view, founded on introspection, that the quale of any (token) sensation constitutes its essence, it can be pointed out that many of the perceptible, qualitative properties by which substances and phenomena are identified and individuated in everyday discourse have turned out not to figure in the identity conditions of such entities, i.e., not to be essences of them. Take the stripes of tigers, the colour of gold, etc. Why should this not also be so in the case of sensations?

However, the response in this latter case is weak. The reason why it is often thought that it is not possible for experiences to exist without their qualia, and in particular, without qualia of certain kinds associated with the types of which those experiences are tokens, is that it seems plain that, for sensations at least, their *esse* is *percipi*: their very existence consists in their being felt, and in certain characteristic ways. This cannot be the case for physical phenomena, for it is plausible that no physical phenomenon is one whose existence depends on its being perceived or experienced in any kind of way by any subject. It is this intuition that serves as the basis for both the Kripkean charge and the objection from phenomenal properties in general. The case of pain is not analogous to the case of other physical objects and phenomena. For whether sensations such as pain are natural kinds or not, it does seem to be of the essence of such kinds that they be felt (in a way in which, e.g., perceptions and other kinds of mental phenomena are not). The above response to the inverted qualia objection fails to convince precisely because it requires one to view the relation between sensations and their qualitative character as of the same kind as the relation between physical objects and their qualitative features. But it is not; and simply to insist that it is is tantamount to denying what is distinctively mental about certain kinds of mental phenomena. To do so is to blur the boundaries between a genuine form of the identity theory and one which, like eliminative materialism, is not a form of the identity theory at all. Sensations such as pain may or may not be natural kinds; but if they are, their essences cannot be such as to conflict with their characteristic felt quality.

Despite this weakness in the rationale for the strategy for handling the inverted qualia objection, the strategy itself has seemed to many to be promising.[32] In contrast, the favoured response to the absent qualia objection has failed to meet with similar success. One danger in acknowledging the possibility of inverted qualia is that it lends credence to the supposition, upon which the absent qualia objection is based, that if two token experiences can differ to the extent that their qualia are inverted relative to one another yet remain invariant *vis-à-vis* causal-functional role, then any two such experiences can differ to the extent that one has qualia while the other lacks it altogether. The favoured response to the latter is to deny that it is possible. But this response is open to objections based on cases of what Block and others call 'ersatz' pain.[33]

According to these objections, the supposition of absent qualia is just the supposition that there could be a mental state token, identical in causal-functional role with a token of what is *genuine* pain, but which lacks, where genuine pain has, qualitative content. This is ersatz pain. CR/FS theorists who maintain that absent qualia are logically impossible are apt to defend their view along the lines pursued by Shoemaker, viz. by assuming that some kind of causal theory of knowledge is true and then arguing that if absent qualia are possible, the absence or presence of qualia would make no difference to a token mental state's causal role. Since this would make the qualia of mental phenomena unknowable, and since we do have such knowledge, absent qualia are impossible.[34]

However, Block takes issue with the first premiss of the argument, viz. the claim that if absent qualia are possible, then the presence or absence of qualia would make no causal role difference.[35] He argues that it is ambiguous between two readings, both of which are false. The first, weak, reading has it that there could be a token state identical in causal role with a given pain token but differing in lacking qualia. This reading allows us to concede that it is crucial to genuine pain's being pain that it have qualia, since it is not part of the supposition that what is in fact pain could exist without qualia. It is nevertheless false because, while it is true that if absent qualia are possible, ersatz pain (i.e., state tokens functionally identical with token pain states but lacking in qualia) is possible, it does not follow that it is possible that two token states, one of which is pain and the other of which is ersatz pain, should have identical *causal* roles. That is to say, two token mental states may differ in their total causal roles and yet be functionally identical – a possibility which must be countenanced by the CR/FS identity theorist if the possibility of variable realization is to be countenanced. (We must suppose here that, whereas every functional difference entails a difference in causal role, not every difference in total causal role entails a functional difference, i.e., that there are causal role differences that are not causal-functional differences. See Note 18 in the previous section.) One might hold, for instance, that ersatz pain could only occur in a being which is physically very different from one in which pain occurs. Indeed, if, as Block points out, one holds a 'minimal physicalist' position, i.e., a token identity thesis with regard to the occupants of causal roles definitive of mental types such as pain combined with a supervenience thesis with regard to the mental types themselves (a doctrine to which CR/FS identity theorists are evidently committed), then one is forced to reject Shoemaker's first premiss weakly read. For it would be incompatible with the (supervenience) thesis that two token states cannot differ mentally (i.e., with regard to qualia) without differing physically. If every token mental state *is* a physical state token, then there can be no mental difference without a physical difference. And any physical difference, on a thoroughgoing functionalist account of the nature of mental types, will at least entail a difference in causal roles (we will return to this).

The second, strong, reading of Shoemaker's first premiss has it that what is in fact genuine pain might exist without any qualia. This is false according to Block because the most that one can conclude from the absent qualia argument is that ersatz pain is possible, not that genuine pain could exist without qualia. The difference here is that between supposing, for any genuine pain with its qualia and causal-functional role, that it might exist without its qualia, and supposing that there might be a state token, distinct from any given actual pain, identical in causal-functional role with it but lacking in qualia. It may in fact be crucial to any given genuine pain's causal-functional role that it have qualia. If so, then the strong reading is also false.

Block's arguments are decisive against the kind of defence against absent qualia objections given by those such as Shoemaker only if they succeed in establishing that both the strong and the weak reading of the first premiss of that defence are false. However, it is doubtful whether his argument against the weak reading succeeds. That argument trades on the distinction, important enough to the CR/FS identity theorist, between a given state token's total causal role and its causal-functional role. It then attempts to show that it is possible for two token mental states to be identical in causal-functional role, yet differ in total causal role. To the reply – that if such causal role differences are relevant to the presence or absence of qualia, then it is possible to *construct* an adequate functional definition of a given mental state type which does not fail to include them – Block rightly points out that inasmuch as such causal-role differences turn on differences in physical state tokens that may serve as occupants of the causal roles definitive of mental types, this would be incompatible with the possibility of variable realization. Moreover, Shoemaker points out that such a reply, if generalized, would prove too much, since if it is right, it would be impossible to show by counterexamples that a given state is not definable in causal-functional terms; only that it can contribute to the construction of a more complete functional characterization.[36] It thus appears from Block's argument that, while the presence or absence of qualia may well make a difference to the total causal role of a given mental state token, it need not (and if variable realizability is to be countenanced, it should not) make a difference to that event's causal-functional role.

However, there is a response to this line of reasoning; and that is to insist that if there *is* a difference in total causal role between genuine pain and ersatz pain, then it must be one which not only subjects of genuine pain can discern, but also one which subjects of ersatz pain can discern. Now what difference might this be? Block suggests that it might consist in discernible differences in physical state tokens that serve as occupants of the causal role definitive of pain. We are to imagine that subjects of ersatz pain may learn what humans as subjects of genuine pain may learn from these physical differences, viz. that ersatz pains lack qualia while genuine pains do not.

But this is utterly implausible. The most that one can reasonably conclude, given acknowledged causal-functional identity, is that ersatz pain tokens do not feel the same to their subjects – their qualia are not the same – as genuine pain tokens. After all, we are to assume that the causal-functional characterization of pain is satisfied by both genuine and ersatz pain tokens. We have no grounds at all for concluding that the subjects of ersatz pain feel nothing at all. In short, such causal-role differences as make no difference to causal-functional role could not enable one to distinguish genuine from ersatz pain in the sense of enabling one to tell which is genuine and which is ersatz. Only those which make a difference to functional role could enable one to do this.

If this rejoinder is correct, some emendation of the first premiss of the defence provided by Shoemaker is called for. Rather than state that if absent qualia are possible, the presence or absence of qualia in pain would make no difference to its causal role, it should be read as stating that if absent qualia are possible, then the absence or presence of qualia in pain would make no difference to any aspect of its causal role that would enable one to distinguish genuine pain from ersatz pain.[37] Read in this way, Block's argument against the weak reading of the first premiss is not decisive against it.

However, there is a further objection to consider here, and this has to do with the CR/FS identity theorist's equal commitment to the causal-functional specification of mental state types and to token identities between the mental and the physical. Recall that the favoured strategy for blocking the absent qualia objection is to hold both that it is essential to any sensation token that it have some quale or other, and that the presence or absence of qualia makes a difference to its causal role (ultimately to its causal-functional role if it is true that no non-functional differences in causal role could enable one to tell, of two token pains identical in causal-functional role, which is genuine and which is ersatz). On the other hand, any CR/FS identity theorist must hold that it is a contingent feature of any physical state token which may occupy the causal role definitive of a given mental state type that it have any phenomenological feel, or qualia. This is because it cannot be of the essence of any physical state token that it feel in any way at all to its subject. But this is a disastrous result for the CR/FS identity theorist. It cannot be that it both is and is not of the essence of any given state token that it feel a certain way.

This objection is plainly a version of the objection from phenomenal properties. It is in fact the objection that was voiced earlier when considering the ramifications of Kripke's objection for any token identities that may be licensed by the CR/FS theory. We shall consider this objection again at length in Part II.

Here it is important to see the difficulty it presents specifically for any CR/FS identity theorist committed to the view that absent qualia are impossible because the presence or absence of qualia would make a difference to a qualitative state token's causal-functional role. If it is essential to a state type such as pain that it have some quale or other, no phenomenon which is an instance of that type can fail to instance or possess some felt quality or other. If instances (tokens) of mental types just are instances (tokens) of physical types, then no physical event which is (i.e., is identical with) a pain event can fail to instance or possess some felt quality. Since it cannot be of the essence of any physical state token that it feel in any way at all, the CR/FS identity theorist's strategy for blocking the absent qualia objection is incompatible with the theory's commitment even to token identities between the mental and the physical.

These objections, if correct, are crippling to the CR/FS identity theory, since they rob it of an adequate response to the objection from phenomenal properties. Between them, they have the consequence that either mental types cannot be defined in causal-functional terms (as the absent qualia objection implies), or that, if they can, no tokens of those types can be physical. Finally, however, there are objections other than phenomenal property ones to the CR/FS identity theory – specifically, to its attempt to accommodate causal-functional role specification of mental state types with identity of physical and mental state tokens. These objections have to do with doubts about the necessity of any mental state type having any characteristic causal antecedents or consequences (a point that was briefly made when discussing the inverted qualia objection), on the one hand, and the compatibility of this supposition with token identity, on the other. One is that the CR/FS identity theory (specifically, Lewis's version of it) is effectively a 'disguised description' view of the way in which mental terms derive their meaning, i.e., one by which each mental term is elliptical for some one definite description; it is wrong for essentially the same reasons.[38] It has the consequence, as does the description theory of names, that a person who uses a name to refer to an object which fails to satisfy the description by means of which that name is defined but which satisfies some other (uniquely identifying) description has false beliefs about a certain object (one which he or she intends to be but is unsuccessful in referring to) but true beliefs about some other object to which he or she in fact refers and which satisfies that description. Terms of a falsified theory would, if this view were correct, be denotationless; but this is a radically implausible account of the development of science in general and of the development of theoretical and/or folk psychology in particular. It would have the consequence that there could not be two theories, one succeeding the other, both of which contain the same theoretical term with the same denotation, but where the latter corrects specifications of the denotation of the term in the former. The objection is that the causal role that any given mental event may have is not necessarily but only contingently possessed by it; and if this is true, every such event might exist without any characteristic relations to stimuli, other mental phenomena, and behavioural output.

Another objection is that the view, to which CR/FS identity theorists (specifically Lewis again) are committed, that the nature (essence) of any mental state type is functional ultimately undermines that theory's commitment to token identities between the mental and the physical.[39] The main source of the difficulty with the theory is its commitment to the thesis that it is essential to any given mental state token that it have a causal role – a role *typically* played by instances of the type of which it is a token. This allows for an event's being, say, an instance of the type 'pain' while failing to play the role typical of the type of which it is a token. However, the theory is unable for precisely this reason to accommodate cases like those of a total paralytic or a perfect deceiver (cases for which Lewis's account was specifically constructed). Construed only as a token identity theory, we cannot say that the total paralytic is in pain because he is in *the* state which in him typically plays the causal role of pain. There is no such state. However, we are also prevented from saying that because he is in *whatever* state – some state or other – which in him occupies at that time the causal role definitive of pain, he is in pain. For no state is in him at that time *playing* the role definitive of that type. The result is that, in cases where only token identities are entailed by the theory and the causal role definitive of a given mental type is not actually being played by any token of that type, we have no basis whatever for claiming that the subject is in a mental state of that type. We have no physical basis because no physical state is such that any instance of it is both necessary and sufficient for the occurrence of any mental state token of the relevant type. And we have no mental basis because the role typically played by instances of the mental type in question is not in this instance being played. In short, because the essence of any mental type on a CR/FS identity theory is dispositional, in cases where the relevant disposition is not realized and only token identities between the mental and the physical are entailed by the theory, there is no basis at all for the claim that a person is in a mental state token of a certain type.[40]

The reason why this poses such a problem for the CR/FS identity theorist is that it seems obvious both that total paralytics and perfect deceivers could nevertheless have mental states and, because it does, there must some basis for that intuition. Since the CR/FS identity theory construed as a token identity theory provides no such basis, we are effectively in the same position as that of a logical behaviourist – we must either deny that these cases are possible, or show that, appearances notwithstanding, there is some physical basis for thinking that persons in such circumstances are undergoing mental states (one which makes a difference to the causal roles definitive of those states).

One way of attempting to accommodate cases like those of the perfect deceiver and the total paralytic within the confines of the CR/FS identity theory would be, of course, to insist that the identities entailed by the theory are not token-token but rather type-type. Evidently, however, commitment to type-type identities is ultimately incompatible with the claim that the nature of any given mental state type is causal-functional. According to Lewis, it is open to empirical investigation whether a given physical state type occupies the causal role definitive of a given mental state type. It is incompatible with the supposed identity in the actual world of certain physical with certain mental state types that, in other possible or hypothetical worlds, a physical type *other* than that which occupies in this world the causal role definitive of a given mental type – say, pain – should occupy that role. For the fact is that, having discovered which physical types are identical with which mental types, we have now discovered a physical basis – states with their own physical essences or natures – for the mental types in the actual world. Having discovered this, we have no reason whatever for thinking that *different* physical state types might in other worlds occupy the causal role definitive of a given mental type. The identity relation is a necessary relation, and so type identity of physical with causal-functional states is incompatible with the supposition that causal-functional essences (of mental types) and physical essences (of physical types) might vary independently of one another. Given this, the natural and most plausible line to take is to maintain that the physical states which empirical investigation may discover as occupying the causal roles definitive of mental types provide the essences of such types; that the causal role definitive of a given mental type may fix the *reference* of that type, but it does not provide its essence.

That type-type identities are incompatible with the CR/FS identity theory should come as no surprise in the light of arguments presented earlier in the present chapter. What may be surprising is that commitment to token identities also suffers at the hand of the CR/FS identity theorist. The second objection voiced above brings out clearly the consequence of attempting to combine commitment to causal-functional essences of mental state types with the view that no single physical essence is possessed by any of the physical tokens that may occupy the causal role typically played by instances of those types. It is to undermine the claim that mental events are physical events in cases like those of the total paralytic and the perfect deceiver, where we wish to say that the subjects concerned may undergo mental states despite the fact that their experiences do not in them play the causal role definitive of the mental types in question. We could avoid this by insisting that the theory be committed to the stronger, type-type, identities, but at the cost of having to reject the causal-functional role specification part of the theory. Commitment to token-token identities between the mental and the physical also effectively leads to the rejection of that part of the theory; for it leads to the rejection of the view that it is of the essence of any mental state token that it be apt to play the causal-functional role definitive of the type of which it is a token.

These objections to the CR/FS identity theory, even when construed as a token identity theory, are formidable if not decisive. They suggest, time and again, that the major difficulty with the theory is with its attempt to combine causal-functional specification of mental state types either with type-type or with token-token identities between mental and physical phenomena. The obvious move for any identity theorist to make in the light of this is to reject the functional specification part of the theory. In the next chapter we will consider two token identity theories which do not construe the essences of mental types as causal-functional.

Chapter Three

We turn now to a third and final group of identity theories, commonly known as token identity theories of the mental and the physical. These assert the existence of particular identities between individual tokens of mental and physical types (or between instances of mental and physical properties), as in, for example, the identity between John's pain at time t and John's C-fibres' firing at time t. Often the existence of such identities is held to be compatible with the irreducible distinctness of mental and physical types or properties themselves. For this reason token identity theories are thought by many to be the most plausible of the identity theories of the mental and the physical: they appear to avoid both phenomenal property objections to the identification of mental and physical types and objections based on the variable realizability of any given mental type. In fact, whether such theories do avoid commitment to type-type identities and the associated objections depends on the metaphysical theory of events with which they are associated, as we shall see.

At least three types of position go under the name of token identity theory. The first, which we have dealt with at length in the previous chapter and will have no more to say about here, is the causal-role identity theory. The second and third are, respectively, non-reductive monism and nomological monism. The purpose of the present chapter is to outline, compare, and contrast these latter two theories. Part II constitutes an extended defence of the former as against the latter theory in the light of a certain metaphysical theory of events.

1. Non-Reductive Monism

Roughly speaking, non-reductive monism is the view that each individual (token) mental event is a physical event despite the fact that mental types or properties are neither reducible to nor nomologically correlated with physical ones. Its most notable proponent is its originator, Donald Davidson.[1] Davidson calls his position 'anomalous monism', where full mental anomalism is understood to require the absence of any kind of nomological connection between mental properties or types and *any* other property or type. Davidson holds not only that there are no psychophysical causal or correlation laws, but also that there are no purely psychological laws, laws linking psychological properties with one another. However, the argument for token identity requires only the weaker thesis that there are no *causal* laws linking mental properties with others. The use of the term 'non-reductive' here is intended to capture that aspect most relevant to Davidson's position, the claim that there are no psychophysical or psychological causal laws.

The position results from an attempt to reconcile three apparently inconsistent principles. The first is the Principle of Causal Interaction (PCI) – the thesis that there is causal interaction between mental and physical events, where the causal relation is understood as holding between individual events in extension. The second is the Principle of the Nomological Character of Causality (PNCC) – the thesis that events causally related instantiate (universal) laws (but only under certain descriptions). And the third is the Anomalism of the Mental (AM) – the thesis that there are no (causal or other) laws linking mental events. The apparent inconsistency arises from the fact that the first two principles imply what the third appears to deny, viz. that causally related mental and physical events instantiate laws. This appearance of inconsistency persists when the third principle (AM) is replaced by the weaker Principle of Psychophysical and Psychological Causal Anomalism (PAM).

Davidson suggests that these three principles can be reconciled by adopting the further thesis that each particular token mental event is a physical event. Since it is understood that to be a mental or physical event is to be described in a certain way (i.e., in the vocabulary of propositional attitudes), this thesis amounts to the claim that every mental event has a physical description and hence instantiates a physical causal law. Davidson further suggests that a sound argument can be constructed from those principles to that thesis. His argument, and the reconciliation it effects, depends crucially on the issue of whether there can be laws linking the mental with the physical. A major part of 'Mental Events' is therefore devoted to arguing, not for full mental anomalism, but for psychophysical anomalism. Since the argument is in essence one for non-reductive monism, attention will focus in what follows on this position.

The argument for non-reductive monism seems to work because of the extensionality of the causal relation and the intensionality of nomologicality. If e and e' are causally related events, they are so no matter how they are described. However, any causal law under which e and e' may be subsumed is a law in part because of the descriptions embedded in it. Thus if mental and physical events causally interact and pairs of events causally related instantiate causal laws, then there must either exist causal laws in which mental descriptions are embedded, or mental events must possess further descriptions in virtue of which they instantiate such laws. If the argument for non-reductive monism is correct, there are no causal laws embedding mental descriptions. Hence mental events must possess physical descriptions which instantiate physical causal laws, which is to say that mental events are physical events.

A number of preliminary points need to be made about this argument. First, although it plainly proceeds at the linguistic level, it need not be formulated in these terms. Davidson himself works with a linguistic formulation of the intentionality criterion of the mental (see Chapter One, Section 1); events are held to be mental inasmuch as they are describable in the vocabulary of propositional attitudes.[2] Similarly, events are held to be physical just in case they have physical descriptions; and laws are deemed to be so at least in part because of the descriptions embedded in them. However, the argument could proceed equally effectively at the level of events and their properties. Suppose that an event is mental just in case it is an exemplification of an intentional mental property in an object at a time, physical just in case it is an exemplification of a physical property at a time in an object. Then the argument can be seen as moving from the claim that mental events which interact causally with physical events must be exemplifications of properties that figure in causal laws (laws here being construed as consisting in relations between properties) to the conclusion that, since mental properties do not figure in causal laws, mental events that interact causally with physical events must be exemplifications of physical properties and so must be physical events. For ease of exposition only we shall follow Davidson's formulation in the remaining sections of the present chapter.

Second, while there is no doubt that Davidson endorses non-reductive monism, the argument offered in 'Mental Events' is in one way stronger, and in another way weaker, than the argument just sketched. Non-reductive monism requires the Principle of Psychophysical and Psychological Causal Anomalism (PAM). But the argument in 'Mental Events' is for full psychophysical anomalism and only for psychophysical anomalism. It is silent on the issue of whether there can be purely psychological causal laws (though Davidson addresses this issue elsewhere); and it purports to establish not only that there can be no psychophysical causal laws, but that there can be no psychophysical correlation laws.[3] In fact, this latter claim is probably needed in order to rule out the possibility that psychophysical causal laws might be derivable from psychophysical correlation laws in conjunction with purely physical causal laws given the thesis that correlation laws license substitutions of terms embedded in them in others where one or the other of those terms appear.[4]

Even supposing that the argument in 'Mental Events' can be bolstered by an independent argument against the possibility of purely psychological laws, it falls short of what is required for non-reductive monism in at least two ways. First, the premiss that is evidently needed by the position is that the only causal laws that there can be are physical laws, for only this would appear to ensure mental/*physical* token identity (but see pp. 97–8 below). However, the argument in 'Mental Events' ignores the possibility that there might be non-physical causal laws (e.g., laws of the ectoplasm), in which case causally related mental and physical events might be held to instantiate causal laws without instantiating physical causal laws.[5] (Whether this possibility is ruled out by considerations which tell against the possibility of psychophysical laws is a matter to which we return in Section 2 below.) Second, the argument works to establish token identity of the mental and the physical only for those mental events which (*a*) interact causally with physical events, and (*b*) are intentional. In fact, (*b*) is not a serious problem, since, as the discussion of linguistic formulations of the intentionality criterion of the mental (Chapter One, Section 1) shows, any event (and so any intuitively non-intentional mental event) can be seen to have a mental description by that criterion given minimal assumptions about spatial (and/or temporal) connectedness of events. The more serious problem is with (*a*). The argument for non-reductive monism can only be generalized across all mental events if we are allowed to assume that all mental events have causes or effects (or both). To what extent this assumption may be justified is an issue taken up in Part II (Chapter Four).

Finally, the argument works only to the extent that it is justified in assuming a nomological conception of causality – the view that true singular causal statements linking events entail that there is a law subsuming those events under certain of their descriptions. This view is contentious not so much because of its implications for the domain of the mental but because of its implications for the domain of the physical. Specifically, the assumption that every pair of causally related physical events instantiates a physical law under some description is contentious. This issue is also taken up in Part II (Chapter Five).

2. Causal Anomalism of the Mental

What is the argument for psychophysical anomalism, and to what extent does it support the stronger claim that the only causal laws there can be are physical ones? In brief outline, the argument is that laws connect terms that we can tell *a priori* are suited to one another, but psychophysical generalizations connect terms that we can tell *a priori* are unsuited to one another, so psychophysical generalizations cannot be laws. They can be true; but they cannot be laws. This argument is fleshed out by way of the concepts of homonomic and heteronomic generalizations. The former draw on concepts formulated within the same conceptual domain, i.e., are ones 'whose positive instances give us reason to believe the generalization itself could be improved by adding further provisos and conditions stated in the same general vocabulary as the original generalization'.[6] The latter, in contrast, are generalizations whose instances give us reason to think that there is a law operating, but one that could only be expressed in another vocabulary. This is because they draw on concepts from a system which is 'open' rather than 'closed', and consequently, refinement under the terms of the system is not possible.

Psychophysical generalizations are held to be heteronomic rather than homonomic in character because of a disparity between the mental and the physical domains in the constitutive principles that govern them. These are *a priori* synthetic generalizations which govern the application of mental and physical concepts and their associated properties to things. They have to do with what Davidson calls the 'evidential sources' and 'conceptual commitments' associated with each domain, which constrain the kinds of explanations that can be given of the phenomena within them.[7] It is characteristic of the physical that physical occurrences can be explained by reference to (causal) laws connecting them with other occurrences physically described, whereas attributions of beliefs, desires, and the like draw on further concepts from the mental domain. Because these two sorts of explanation operate under different constraints – in particular, because psychological explanation operates under the constraints of rationality, consistency, and coherence, which have no clear place in physical theory – generalizations connecting predicates from the mental and physical domains have no hope of refinement. Davidson's conclusion is that 'there cannot be tight connections between the realms if each is to retain allegiance to its proper source of evidence'.[8]

Many have been puzzled as to how precisely this argument is supposed to show that there can be no lawlike connections whatever between mental and physical predicates or properties even if it does show that there cannot be tight connections in the sense of reductive explicability.[9] In fact, its efficacy requires a certain conception of what it is to be a law. The conception which Davidson takes to be at stake in the argument for non-reductive monism is that of a *strict* law, where a strict law is homonomic: it draws on concepts from a single conceptual domain, a system which is both comprehensive and closed. We may define a theory or system T as comprehensive just in case every event in T's domain instantiates (under some uniquely satisfiable description) a causal law of T which is both as explicit and exceptionless as possible.[10] Defining closure for a system, however, is more problematic.

Davidson explicitly claims in certain of his works that what makes for a system's being open rather than closed is that its phenomena interact causally with phenomena outside its domain. Thus, the mental system is held to be open because 'too much happens to affect the mental that is not itself a systematic part of the mental'.[11] The problem with this conception of closure is that it cannot be presumed in the argument for non-reductive monism without begging questions. In order for it to work to establish token identity, we must suppose that mental events are physical events because they fall under strict physical laws, i.e., laws connecting phenomena within a domain which is closed. Now if physical theory *is* closed, then any event that causally interacts with a physical one is itself physical. But the question is whether physical theory is closed. Just as one might hold with Davidson that the mental system is open because its phenomena interact causally with phenomena outside its domain, one might insist against him that physical theory is open because its phenomena interact causally with mental phenomena, *i.e.*, with phenomena falling outside *its* domain. To assume that physical laws are homonomic on this conception of closure is to assume that every event with which a physical event interacts causally is itself physical. But we need an independent argument for this.[12]

One way of dealing with the difficulty here is to define closure for a domain of a theory T in a way that is neutral on the issue as to whether the phenomena that fall within it interact causally with phenomena falling outside it. Thus McLaughlin defines a theory T as closed∗ if and only if, [for any space-time regions, r and r', an event occurring at r is a cause (or effect) of an event occurring at r' just in case a T-event occurring at r is a cause/effect of a T-event occurring at r'].[13] (Intuitively, T is closed∗ if and only if any two events occurring in spatiotemporal regions r and r' causally interact when and only when two T-events occurring in r and r' causally interact.) On this conception of closure, physical theory comes out as closed∗ but psychology does not.

However, there is another way of handling the difficulty which is arguably both more desirable and consistent with remarks made by Davidson himself. The difficulties that are held to attend any attempt to render psychophysical generalizations lawlike have to do, not with events in extension (and hence with causal interaction between events), but rather, with (nomological) causal *explanation*, where the explanation relation is understood as holding between events when described in certain ways only. That is to say, the relation that holds between events referred to in the explanandum and explanans in any nomological explanation holds in virtue of certain but not all of their descriptions (or only in virtue of certain but not all of their properties), and so is intensional rather than extensional. This suggests that what makes for a theory's being open or closed has to do, not with whether the *phenomena* within its domain interact causally with phenomena outside its domain, but rather, with whether nomological causal *explanations* can be given of phenomena within the theory's domain invoking only the vocabulary and associated properties of that theory. Thus Davidson remarks that it is characteristic of the physical that 'physical change can be explained by laws that connect it with other changes, physically described'; and that the failure of the mental system to be closed 'is due to the irreducibility of psychological concepts and to the fact that psychological events and states often have causes that have no psychological descriptions'.[14] Here the failure of psychological theory to be closed is held to be due, not merely to the fact that mental events causally interact with non-mental ones, but to the fact that the descriptions and associated concepts and properties by which such events are identified and individuated as the relata of causal explanations are not part of psychological theory. This indicates that closure amounts to closure under nomological causal explanation. A theory T counts as closed in this sense just in case the phenomena within its domain are capable of nomological causal explanation using the predicates and associated concepts and properties of T. Since it is part of the purpose of physical theory to provide causal explanations of phenomena within its domain, it follows that if physical theory is closed, then all the phenomena within its domain subject to nomological causal explanations must be subject to such explanations using only physical vocabulary (and associated concepts and properties).

If this conception of closure is to work without begging questions in favour of token identity between mental and physical events, it must not be possible to generate the conclusion that mental events are physical ones simply by supposing (*a*) that mental events causally interact with physical events, and (*b*) that physical theory is closed. And evidently it is not possible to do so. It does not rule out the possibility of causal overdetermination of physical events by both physical and mental ones, and so does not ensure, from the fact that every physical event has a nomological physical causal explanation, that mental events with which physical events interact are physical. Overdetermination must be ruled out on other grounds. Moreover, the thesis that physical theory is closed under nomological causal explanation whereas psychological theory is not is independently plausible. It amounts to the claim that physical theory is capable of generating nomological causal explanations for all its causally related phenomena whereas psychological theory is not. The reasons which favour this claim can no doubt be traced to the belief that physical phenomena have adequate physical causes whereas at least some psychological phenomena have non-psychological causes. But this belief falls short of the question-begging claim that physical phenomena have *only* physical causes, and so skirts the difficulty associated with the conception of closure as closure of causal interaction of events within a single domain.

To see why the notion of nomological causal-explanatory closure is more desirable than the neutral conception of closure∗ mentioned earlier, one needs to ask what work is being done by the notion of closure∗ in the argument for psychophysical anomalism. Recall that, according to it, a theory T is closed∗ if and only if any two events occurring in spatiotemporal regions r and r' causally interact just in case any two T-events occurring in r and r' causally interact. The point of introducing it was to ensure that physical theory may be closed∗ (while psychological theory is not) irrespective of whether phenomena within its domain interact with phenomena outside its domain, closure∗ having to do with the fact that there must be causal interaction between events in the domain of physical theory where-and-whenever there is causal interaction between *any* two events. But what has this got to do with the claim that psychophysical generalizations cannot be laws because they connect predicates that we can tell *a priori* are unsuited to one another? *This* claim is compatible with the thesis that mental and physical predicates have, as a matter of fact, the same extension. It is therefore compatible with the suggestion that events within the domain of physical theory interact causally only with other physical events. Davidson's point is that, even supposing that this suggestion is true, *still* psychophysical generalizations could not be laws. Couple this with the further claim that psychophysical generalizations cannot be laws because of the disparity between physical and psychological theory in conceptual commitments and evidential sources, and it is a mystery why the fact that psychophysical generalizations are heteronomic to the extent that they draw on concepts from a theory which is not closed∗ should explain, even in part, why they cannot be laws. It is utterly unclear why, from the fact that whenever two events occurring in spatiotemporal regions *r* and *r'* causally interact it does not follow that two *p* (psychological) events *r* and *r'* causally interact, we are allowed to conclude that there can be no (causal or correlation) laws connecting pairs of events one of which is a *p* event and the other of which is not. The problem is that, however neutral it may be as regards the issue of causal interaction between events from distinct domains, closure∗ has only to do with events in extension, whereas nomologicality, like the explanation relation, concerns events under certain descriptions only.

Still, we need to see why it is that the failure of psychological theory to be closed under nomological causal explanation *does* explain, at least in part, why psychophysical (correlation or causal) generalizations cannot be laws. The idea seems to be that psychophysical causal explanation can only proceed by way of generalizations connecting predicates from distinct theories. However, there is nothing in this to indicate why such generalizations cannot be laws. In order to see why generalizations connecting predicates from physical and psychological theories cannot be laws, it needs to be shown that some feature or features of those theories prohibits nomic connections between them.

This is where the idea of constitutive principles governing the application of predicates within a theory comes in. Recall that a closed system is one which is closed with respect to conceptual sources and evidential commitments. The claim is that the application of psychological predicates, like the application of physical ones, is answerable to constraints imposed by principles which govern the theories of which they are a part. Beginning with the idea that the mental system is holistic in the sense that the ascription of any psychological predicate is possible only against the background of other psychological predicate ascriptions, the argument proceeds to show that the features that characterize this holism are different in kind from any which might characterize any holism that might attach to physical theory. It may be true that physical theory too is holistic; the ascription of length predicates to an object, for instance, is answerable to principles which govern the measurement of length within the physical domain (e.g., transitivity of 'longer than').[15] But the type of holism that characterizes the physical system is of a different kind from the type of holism that characterizes the mental system.

The holism of the mental is characterized by the features of rational coherence and consistency. Accordingly, the constitutive principles from which psychological holism arises are ones having to do with standards of rational coherence and consistency in the ascription of psychological predicates (specifically, it must be noted, of propositional-attitude ones). Such principles are normative in the sense that they have to do, not with what an agent will believe (think, desire) or do in such-and-such circumstances given other attitudes, but with what an agent ought rationally to believe (etc.) or do in such circumstances given other attitudes.[16] That is to say, the ascription of propositional attitude predicates to agents is constrained by the condition that they make sense of the (intentional) behaviour of those agents; and this condition cannot be met without supposing a minimal standard of rational coherence and consistency to apply to the domain of propositional attitudes as a whole. By 'minimal standard' is meant, for example, absence of logical inconsistency and the use of inductive and deductive principles of reasoning, as well as internal coherence in an agent's preference system (e.g., that it meets the transitivity requirement) and coherence of such preferences given an agent's probabilities with her decisions, etc.[17]

This condition of what a subject ought rationally to believe or do given other attitudes has no parallel in physical theory, whose constitutive principles are not themselves normative. Here there is no counterpart of rational coherence, of logical consistency and inductive and deductive rationality. On the contrary, physical theory is distinctive in its total absence of rationality constraints in the application of physical predicates. Of course, this alone does not explain why there can be no lawlike connections between psychological predicates and physical ones. All it shows is that we can tell *a priori* that psychological and physical predicates have *distinct* ascription conditions. What is needed to show *a priori* impossibility of nomic connection is that psychological and physical predicates are *a priori* unsuited to one another.

One appealing and persuasive way of going about showing this would be to argue that nomic connections between psychological and physical predicates would bring the constitutive principles and corresponding ascription conditions associated with the systems of which they are a part into conflict with one another.[18] According to this strategy, to say that psychological theory is essentially characterized by rationality is effectively to say that psychological properties have no non-rational conditions of ascription. To suppose that there might be psychophysical laws (specifically, correlation laws), however, is to suppose that the rational conditions that govern the ascription of psychological predicates might be superceded by or replaced with non-rational ones. Since psychological theory is essentially rational, this is impossible: rationality lies at the very heart of what it is to be a contentful intentional psychological property. Hence there can be no nomological connections between psychological and physical predicates.

This strategy requires the view that laws express more than mere *de facto* regularities – that nomological generalizations are possessed of a certain modal force. Given this, however, and the claim that rationality constitutes the essence of the psychological (to the extent that it constrains the ascription of psychological predicates to agents), an argument against the possibility of psychophysical correlation laws is easily constructed as follows (the argument is Kim's). Suppose, that two psychological predicates or properties, m_1 and m_2, are such that the principles of rational coherence and consistency warrant us in attributing m_1

over m_2 to an agent; and suppose that m_1 and m_2 are nomically correlated (coextensive) with two physical predicates – say, p_1 and p_2. We may assume that p_1 and p_2, no less than m_1 and m_2, have conditions of ascription associated with them: call these conditions C_1 and C_2 respectively. Then, given

(a) $N(C_1 \rightarrow p_1)$

and the psychophysical correlation law

(b) $N(p_1 \leftrightarrow m_1)$

we can infer

(c) $N(C_1 \rightarrow m_1)$

(and similarly $N(C_2 \rightarrow m_2)$ for p_2). Assuming that the relation between a mental/physical predicate and its ascription condition is one of logical necessity and that logical necessity entails nomological necessity, the consequence of supposing there to be nomological correlation laws between psychological predicates and physical ones is to transmit conditions of ascription from physical theory to psychological theory. But this is impossible. To suggest that psychological predicates might have non-rational conditions of application is to suggest that they might not, after all, be *psychological*. And this, as Davidson suggests, simply amounts to 'changing the subject':

> By changing the subject I mean here: deciding not to accept the criterion of the mental in terms of the vocabulary of propositional attitudes.[19]

If this is right, we have an explanation of why it is that the failure of psychological theory to be closed under nomological causal explanation prohibits treating psychological generalizations as laws. Psychological causal explanations must proceed by way of generalizations connecting predicates from theories with distinct evidential sources and conceptual commitments, where these are fixed by constitutive principles governing the ascription of predicates within them. In the case of psychological theory, these ascription conditions are rational, whereas in physical theory they are non-rational. Nomic connections between theories transmit conditions imposed by such principles from one theory to another. So if psychophysical generalizations are to be laws, psychological predicates must acquire non-rational conditions of ascription. Since it is of the essence of psychological properties to be rationally consistent and coherent, such transmission of ascription conditions is unthinkable. Hence psychophysical generalizations cannot be laws.

The mere fact that physical and psychological predicates have different ascription conditions does not suffice to explain why nomic connections between them cannot be tolerated. The conditions must be such as to conflict with one another; and this can only be so if the features of rational coherence and consistency are conceived of as essences of, or as specifying the nature of, psychological properties themselves, i.e., are features that they could not cease to possess without ceasing to exist altogether. It is part of the point of the argument that we do not just happen to identify, individuate, and ascribe contentful psychological properties by way of such features in the way that we might happen to identify a substance such as salt or fool's gold by its colour or texture. A property could not count as a contentful intentional property if it did not possess the features which govern its ascription and hence the application of its associated predicate. These features are what makes intentional mental properties peculiarly mental; and to suggest that they might survive the loss of such features is effectively to suggest that intentional mental properties might have non-mental essences. For all of the reasons that were brought to bear against type-type identity theories in Chapter One, this suggestion is one that cannot seriously be entertained.

Construed in this way, the argument against psychophysical laws is both persuasive and highly plausible. Nevertheless, it needs bolstering in at least two ways if it is to work along with PCI and PNCC to establish token *physicalism*, the view that every event is a physical event. First, some analogue of it must be constructed to cover non-intentional mental phenomena, whose features are not (or not obviously) those of rational coherence and consistency. The attribution of sensation predicates and their associated properties (e.g., the property of having pain) to persons, for example, is not obviously constrained by principles of rationality. It will not do to say that these predicates are covered by the argument against psychophysical laws because they count as mental by the 'trick' mentioned in Chapter One, Section 1 (whereby any event can be shown to be mental in virtue of its bearing spatiotemporal, or merely temporal, relations, to some intentional mental event). For the fact that descriptions like '$(\iota x)(Px$ and x bears temporal relation R to $(\iota y)Iy)$' (where 'Px' is a sensation predicate and 'Iy' is an intentional mental predicate) cannot be nomically correlated with purely physical predicates because they embed intentional mental predicates does not show that the events which satisfy them do not satisfy other predicates (e.g., '$(\iota x)(Px)$') which *do* bear nomic relations to purely physical predicates. This latter possibility must be rules out if the argument against psychophysical laws is to work to establish token physicalism in full generality. We return to this issue in Chapter Four (Section 6).

Second, we need to see how the argument against psycho-physical laws thus generalized across all mental events supports the claim that the only causal laws that there can be must be physical, since it is this latter claim that is evidently required for token physicalism. It is not easy to see how an argument of sufficient strength might be constructed for this claim. However, the following will perhaps suffice to give a rough idea of how, in broad outline, such an argument might proceed.

Suppose that all the properties that there are can be grouped into two classes, the first containing as members physical properties, the second containing non-physical ones. The latter, we may further suppose, contains at least two proper subsets, the first consisting of mental properties, the second consisting of non-physical properties distinct from mental ones, say, properties of some non-physical substance, ectoplasm. Now the supposition that causes problems for non-reductive monism is that there might be causal laws governing mental and physical events which are neither psychophysical, nor purely psychological, nor purely physical, viz. laws which physical and mental events instantiate in virtue of possessing further non-physical, non-mental descriptions. If this is indeed possible, then the argument against psychophysical causal and correlation laws would appear not to suffice, given PCI and PNCC, to establish token physicalism.

This possibility can only be realized in one of three ways. First, mental and physical events might instantiate causal laws of pure ectoplasm in virtue of possessing ectoplasm descriptions/properties. Second, mental and physical events might instantiate causal laws embedding ectoplasm predicates and physical predicates. Finally, mental and physical events might instantiate causal laws embedding mental predicates and predicates of the ectoplasm. All three of these suggestions, however, are undermined by the thesis that physical theory is closed under nomological causal explanation. This thesis does not rule out the possibility that there might exist causal laws embedding physical predicates and non-physical ones. What it does is ensure that any such law will be redundant in the explanation of any pair of events whose effect event is physical. For the thesis is that every physical event has an adequate nomological physical causal explanation. Given this and PCI, there could be no reason to suppose that causal laws of the ectoplasm, in so far as these govern pairs of events at least one of which is physical, aren't ultimately reducible to those of physical theory.

Moreover, even if we did have some reason to think that such non-physical, non-psychological laws weren't reducible to physical causal laws, this would not in fact show that PCI, PNCC, and PAM do not suffice for token physicalism. It is only if one assumes that pairs of events, one of which is mental and the other of which is physical, instantiate causal laws of the ectoplasm *without* instantiating physical causal laws that the argument for non-reductive monism falls short of establishing token physicalism. But the closure of physical theory prohibits assuming that such pairs of events do not also instantiate physical causal laws. In order for non-reductive monism to be threatened by the possibility that there might exist non-physical, non-psychological causal laws, it would have to be the case that physical theory is not closed under nomological causal explanation. But this in itself is a plausible thesis which there is no clear reason to question.

We shall have nothing further to say about those features of non-reductive monism that have been addressed at length in this section. In particular, nothing further will be said in subsequent chapters about the argument against psychophysical and psychological causal laws apart from its possible extension to phenomenal mental occurrences (sensations, perceptions, and the like). Features of the position that have been left untouched in this section will surface again in Part II, where the position is defended at length. Meanwhile, we turn to the second of the two token identity theories mentioned at the beginning of this chapter, viz. nomological monism.

3. Nomological Monism

Nomological monism is the view that each individual mental event is a physical event, with the consequence that mental properties are nomologically correlated with physical ones. Although its originator, Jaegwon Kim, evidently no longer espouses the position, it is nevertheless worthy of discussion principally because its plausibility requires holding a certain metaphysical view of the nature of events.[20] The connection between theories of events and token psychophysical event-identity, made explicit in nomological monism, is by no means accidental. Token event-identity theories of the mental and the physical in general ultimately rely on some conception of the nature of events, however poorly articulated that conception may be. At the very least, they rely either implicitly or explicitly on some view of the identity conditions for events, being ontologically committed to them. As we shall see, any such view will dictate, at least in part, the nature of the position one can take with regard to psychophysical event-identity as well as the means, if any, by which that position is able to avoid objections from phenomenal properties. The principal virtue of nomological monism is that it makes this connection explicit, and in so doing shows clearly why non-reductive monism, if it is to be defensible, requires supplementation by an adequate conception of events. For nomological monism embraces a theory of events which, if correct, shows non-reductive monism to be false.

Kim's central concern in constructing a tenable mind-body identity thesis is to escape the objection from phenomenal properties.[21] As he sees it, no sound argument should be inconsistent with or threaten the validity of Leibniz's Principle of the Indiscernibility of Identicals in its strictest form. Thus, he rejects the suggestion that the principle should be waived, on the grounds that the effect would be to take from the identity theorist the central core of the identity theory, viz. the concept of identity.[22] If mental (i.e., phenomenal) properties are taken to be *bona fide* properties, and if events are taken to be *bona fide* entities in this world, then Leibniz's Principle should not fail to hold in its strictest form. To weaken or waive the principle would be to admit that there *are* properties 'over and above' physical ones that, e.g., the havings of pains can have; and this amounts to saying that the havings of pains are something 'over and above' physiological events. Such an admission could not be compatible with any form of the identity theory. Similarly, he rejects the suggestion that Leibniz's Principle should be retained in its strictest form while the existence of mental events is rejected, on the grounds that it eliminates mental events *in toto*, and so cannot count as a version of the identity theory either.[23] Effectively, both suggestions are incompatible with the identity theory. Arguments for the identity of mental and physical events rest on the assumption that there *are* mental events and that these are *identical* with physical events. The first suggestion undermines the concept of identity, whereas the second eliminates mental events altogether.

Because the objection from phenomenal properties is most forceful when pains, toothaches, and the like are conceived of as mental objects, Kim proposes to speak instead of mental and physical events, where these are viewed as exemplifications of properties at times in objects (a view known as the property-exemplification account of events). In simple cases of monadic properties they can be represented schematically by expressions of the form '$[x,P,t]$' (these being understood as singular terms referring to events), where x is an object, P a property instantiated in or exemplified by x, and t a time of P's instantiation in x. Their existence and identity conditions are accordingly stated thus:

(1) Event $[x,P,t]$ exists just in case the substance x has the property P at time t
(2) $[x,P,t] = [y,Q,t']$ just in case $x = y$, $P = Q$, and $t = t'$.

where x, P, and t are known, respectively, as the constitutive object, constitutive property, and constitutive time of the event $[x,P,t]$. An event is mental just in case P is a phenomenal property, physical just in case P is a physical property.[24]

Under this construal, there are no phenomenal properties

(e.g., throbbing) that pains have but physical objects lack, since there are no such objects as pains. What there are are things such as a person's having-a-throbbing-pain, where the 'property' of being throbbing is 'absorbed into the constitutive property of the event'.[25] Evidently, expressions like 'having-a-throbbing-pain' are intended to indicate that terms like 'throbbing' are not nominal, i.e., that there is no real property of throbbing which is truly or falsely attributable to the havings of pains. If there were, then, on the understanding that events are entities over which we can quantify, the objection from phenomenal properties might arise afresh (see Chapter One, Section 2).

Kim holds that phenomenal properties are constitutive of the events which are exemplifications of them. The question of psychophysical token event identity therefore depends crucially for him on whether phenomenal and physical properties are identical. Given that phenomenal events *are* physical events, it follows that certain phenomenal and physical properties are identical and an extensional correlation law, i.e., a law stating that their extensions coincide, is true. Indeed, Kim suggests that nomic coextensivity might be sufficient in general for psychophysical property identity.[26] If this is right, then the truth of any particular identity statement linking mental with physical events requires the truth of some psychophysical correlation law.

This consequence of nomological monism brings it into direct conflict with non-reductive monism, making it vulnerable to the argument outlined in the previous section against psychophysical laws. More importantly for present purposes, it likens nomological monism to the type-type identity theories discussed in Chapter One. For this reason, the position falls prey to all the objections found to be crippling to, if not decisive against, type-type identity theories of the mental and the physical.

Nomological monism requires the view that phenomenal properties are constitutive properties of the events that are the exemplifications of them. This view is ultimately responsible both for the conflict with non-reductive monism and for the commitment to type-type identities between the mental and the physical. However, nothing in the basic principles of the property-exemplification account of events entails this view. Of course, the property-exemplification account does make possible commitment to nomological monism, since it is capable of grounding the belief that there can be nomic connections between mental and physical properties in a way that token-identity theories of the mental and the physical based on other views of events are not (for more on this, see Chapter Four). But the account must be coupled with the claim that mental properties are constitutive properties of the events that exemplify them in order to generate the dual commitment to (*a*) psychophysical correlation laws and (*b*) type-type identities between mental and physical properties. Nomological monism thus requires the truth of both the property-exemplification account of events *and* the claim that mental properties are constitutive of the events which exemplify them. Whether either or both of these are true must be deferred to Part II, Chapter Four, where they will be considered at length. We may close the present chapter by considering Kim's reasons for thinking that mental properties are constitutive of the events which exemplify them.

4. Kim's View of Phenomenal Mental Properties

Kim's belief that mental properties are constitutive of the events that exemplify them has partly to do with his view of how canonical descriptions of events (i.e., descriptions of events in terms of their constitutive objects, properties, and times) are derived and partly to do with his concern to avoid objections from phenomenal properties. In general, canonical descriptions of events are derived from sentences attributing an empirical property to an object at a time. The property whose possession by the relevant object at the relevant time is a property of that object is constitutive of the event which is (i.e., is identical with) the exemplification of it by that object. Objects possess properties at times, but events *are* exemplifications of properties in objects at times. The properties whose exemplifications by objects at times are events are called 'generic events'; and these determine the event types or kinds into which particular events fall.[27]

In addition to being exemplifications of properties, events also have properties; and these are known as characterizing properties of events. Being an evil thought and being a momentous occasion, for example, are properties, not of persons, but of events (a thought, an occasion). Since the identity conditions for events require only the identity of their constitutive properties, times, and objects, no property identities are entailed by true event-identity statements expressed by means of descriptions which merely characterize the events in question, i.e., are non-canonical. For instance, no property identities are entailed by the (true) identity statement, 'The event Jones underwent yesterday = the most momentous event in Jones's life'.

The belief that phenomenal mental properties are constitutive rather than characterizing properties of events is due in part to the fact that terms for such properties typically figure in descriptions attributing those properties to persons at times. Sentences like 'Jones is in pain' and 'Sue has a throbbing headache' seem paradigmatically to be ones which attribute empirical properties to objects at times. Given the criterion for the derivation of canonical descriptions of events, it is natural to assume that the properties that figure in these sentences are constitutive of the events that exemplify them. In fact, it seems unavoidable. Recall that constitutive properties of events, or generic events, determine the event types or kinds into which particular events fall. They determine the very nature of the events which exemplify them in a way that characterizing properties do not, for they figure in the existence and identity conditions of events. It does not seem possible, given this, that the property of having pain is merely a characterizing property of events which are havings of pains, in the way that, say, being a momentous event is a characterizing property of Jones's realizing that the earth is round. For being a having of a pain (being an exemplification of the property, or type, 'having pain') seems to lie at the very heart of what it is to be an individual pain event.

Couple this with the view that phenomenal mental properties are essentially felt in a characteristic way by their subjects, and the belief that such properties are constitutive rather than characterizing properties is motivated by a second concern, viz. to avoid objections from phenomenal properties. There is no doubt that this concern also plays a part in Kim's rationale for the claim that mental properties are constitutive of the events that have them.[28] If phenomenal mental properties are allowed to function as characterizing properties of events, and if expressions like 'dull' and 'throbbing' are not nominal, then, it seems, they

must be 'absorbed' into the characterizing properties of phenomenal mental events. But then event-identity theories of the
mental and the physical evidently fall prey to familiar phenomenal-
property objections. Since identical events must share all
properties, if it is of the essence of phenomenal mental properties
that they be felt, and it is not of the essence of any physical
property that it be felt in any way at all, phenomenal mental
events cannot be physical events. An obvious strategy to pursue
in the face of this objection is to deny that phenomenal mental
properties are characterizing properties of events.

It is a puzzling feature of this rationale that it should be
thought that construing phenomenal mental properties as constitutive of phenomenal mental events avoids phenomenal-property
objections whereas construing them as characterizing properties
does not. Given that constitutive properties of events determine
their nature by determining in part their existence and identity
conditions, and given that phenomenal mental properties are
essentially felt, it is difficult to see how one can avoid concluding
that, since it is not of the essence of any physical property that it
be felt, no phenomenal mental property can be identical with any
physical one (hence that nomological monism is false). Be that as
it may, it remains to be considered (1) whether the property-
exemplification account of events is correct, and, if so, (2)
whether phenomenal (and any other) mental properties are
constitutive of the events that exemplify them. These issues will
be further explored in Part II, Chapter Four.

PART TWO

Chapter Four

The aim of the preceding chapters has been to survey certain well-known identity theories of the mental and the physical. It is evident from that survey that token identity theories are, on the face of it at least, far more plausible than type-type ones. The aim of this and subsequent chapters is to provide an extended defence of one such token identity theory, viz. non-reductive monism. To do so, some discussion of identity conditions and associated metaphysical theories of events is necessary.

Token event-identity theories of the mental and the physical both acknowledge the existence of mental events and assert the identity of these with physical events. Of course, switching from talk of mental objects to talk of mental events in order to avoid phenomenal-property objections to the identification of mental and physical phenomena has little point if talk of events is not taken to imply their existence. Identity theories are not versions of eliminative materialism. In the absence of other mental and physical objects, events must serve in these theories as the relata of the identity relation. In fact, those who favour token event-identity theories over others (e.g., Davidson, Kim) accept this and assume that such theories are ontologically committed to events construed as non-repeatable, dated, particulars. Further, they assume that this commitment can only be discharged by way of providing an adequate account of events. At the very least this requires an adequate criterion of identity, or statement of identity conditions, for events. Such an account is of particular importance here not only because of its ramifications for the question of whether there are events. As the discussion of nomological monism showed, one's conception of events will determine in an important way both the kind of token identity theory that can be endorsed and the means, if any, by which it is able to avoid objections from phenomenal properties. The details of any well-developed account of events will therefore have ramifications for the question of which, if any, token identity theory of the mental and the physical is more viable than others.

It is not part of the present concern to question either of the above assumptions. Rather, bearing them in mind, the strategy in Part II will be this. First, in the remaining sections of the present chapter, identity conditions and associated metaphysical theories of events will be discussed, and one such theory will be shown to be compatible with non-reductive monism. Section 1 addresses the issue of the purpose (*a*) of a criterion of event identity, and (*b*) of a metaphysical theory of events, and sets out conditions that must be met by each to be adequate. The evident failure of certain well-known candidates for criteria of event identity to meet their associated adequacy conditions strongly suggests the need for a metaphysical theory of events. Sections 2 and 3 examine and evaluate one version of the most celebrated of such theories, the property-exemplification account, in the light of the conditions set out in Section 1. Sections 4–6 examine and defend a second version of that account and show it to be compatible with non-reductive monism. Chapters Five and Six to follow take up the most notable and serious objections to non-reductive monism thus construed.

1. Identity Conditions for Events

It is commonly thought that the main purpose of a criterion of event identity is to specify identity conditions for events – to specify properties essential to them as entities of a kind and so to tell us something about their nature.[1] If we were to assume that events were the only kind of entities that there are, then Leibniz's Law, according to which, $(x)(y)(x = y \leftrightarrow (Fx \leftrightarrow Fy))$, would suffice as a criterion of event identity (note that this is not the Principle of the Indiscernibility of Identicals, though it entails that principle). However, in an ontological framework in which entities of more than one kind – say, physical objects and events – are assumed to exist, Leibniz's Law does not suffice as a criterion of identity for entities of either kind. The reason is not that it fails to be true in such a framework, but rather, that it fails to be either useful or informative. Because it fails to differentiate those properties which do, from those which do not, distinguish objects of distinct kinds (where neither of these forms a subcategory of the other), it cannot suffice for the purpose of settling issues of the sort that are of concern here. A criterion of identity must for this purpose be sort- or kind-specific; and being so, it must specify properties whose possession in some determinate form by any entity of the relevant kind suffices to ensure its numerical identity as an entity *of that kind*.

This in fact covers two conditions. The first of these is sometimes referred to as the requirement that a criterion of identity be *stronger* than Leibniz's Law; and the second is commonly referred to as the requirement that any such criterion be *minimal*.[2] The first emphasizes a feature of a criterion of identity which is crucial to it in any ontological framework where there are entities of more than one kind, viz. that the properties specified by it should be unique to entities of the kind to which it applies. The general idea behind this requirement is that, while it may be true that identical things must share all properties, not all things have the same sorts of properties. Here criteria of identity can be seen to serve the vital function of justifying claims to the effect that entities of a given kind exist. An event, for instance, couldn't share all properties with a physical object if events and physical objects are of distinct kinds. The minimality requirement emphasizes a rather different feature of a criterion of identity, viz. that the properties specified by it should be only those upon which the identity conditions of entities of the kind to which it applies depend and so should be only a proper subset of all those properties able to be possessed by them. The general idea behind this requirement is that many of the properties of entities of any kind are such that they are, even if unique to them as entities of that kind, ones without which they might nevertheless exist and so ones upon which their identity conditions do not depend. Many of the so-called relational properties of physical objects and events, such as being Caesar's widow, or being a shooting (of Lincoln), as well as ones that are not obviously so, such as wearing bi-focals, being round, or being a momentous event, are intuitively properties of this kind.

These two requirements ought not to be confused. At least

some properties essential to entities of one kind may also be essential to entities of another, and so fail to be unique to either. Events and physical objects, for instance, seem equally to be essentially spatiotemporal inasmuch as both are non-repeatable, dated particulars. Conversely, certain properties might be unique to entities of a kind without being in any intuitive sense essential to them, as the above examples indicate. This suggests that an acceptable criterion of identity for entities of any kind must specify a property or properties at least one of which is both essential and unique to entities of the kind for which it serves as a criterion. Nevertheless, the joint satisfaction of the two requirements by a criterion of identity should guarantee that any objects which satisfy the conditions specified by it in some determinate form (as when, for instance, being in London at 12 p.m. on Monday, 13 January 1988, is a determinate form of the determinable, being spatiotemporal) are thereby guaranteed to be alike with regard to all other properties; for any entity which satisfies those conditions satisfies the antecedent of the Principle of the Indiscernibility of Identicals.

In effect, this means that any acceptable criterion of event identity must specify properties necessary and sufficient (1) to individuate events from entities of any *other* kind, and (2) to guarantee the numerical identity of any entity *within* the kind, events. To do this, it must at least take the following form:

$$(x)(y)[\text{event } (x) \text{ \& event } (y) \rightarrow (x = y \leftrightarrow (\ldots x \ldots y \ldots))]$$

where what follows the biconditional is a specification of a property or properties essential to events, at least one of which is unique to them also, indiscernibility with respect to which in some determinate form is both necessary and sufficient for x to be the same entity as y.[3] But this is not all, since it must not be possible for two events to satisfy the conditions specified by it simultaneously in the same determinate form. If, for instance, events are identical just in case they share all the same causes and effects, then it cannot be possible that two events share precisely the same causal history (note that this is not to say that an event might not have had a causal history other than the one it in fact has – an issue concerning individual essences of events). An acceptable criterion of event identity for events must therefore have the form

□ $(x)(y)$[event (x) & event $(y) \rightarrow (x = y \leftrightarrow (\ldots x \ldots y \ldots))$].

If it did not, it could not ensure that any event(s) that satisfied it are identical: it could not discriminate between identity and exact qualitative similarity with regard to the properties of events it specifies.

Now, any criterion of event identity which is both stronger than Leibniz's Law and minimal will also be both informative and epistemologically useful. It will be useful at least to the extent that it specifies properties of events such that, if they are discernible with respect to these, then they are guaranteed to be distinct. An acceptable criterion can therefore be used to answer at least some questions of identity and distinctness regarding events (e.g., it can be used to individuate events from one another). It will also be informative to the extent that it says something about the nature of events – about what it is to be an event as opposed to, say, a physical object. In doing so, it enables us to see why it is that the way in which Leibniz's Law comes out false when x and y are taken to be entities of distinct kinds (say, x is a physical object and y an event) differs from the way in which it comes out false (when it is false) when x and y are both taken to be entities of the same kind. In the former but not the latter case, it does not just happen to be true that x and y do not share all properties: x being a physical object and y an event, they *could* not share the same properties.

It is plain from all of this that a criterion of event identity embodies at least some conception of the nature of events. How does this relate to a metaphysical theory of events? Intuitively, a theory of events ought to do what a criterion of event identity does and more. Specifically, it ought to entail an acceptable criterion of event identity but go beyond it by providing an account of what it is that is crucial to something's being an event so as to explain how it is that events have the kinds of properties they have and how they differ from particulars of other, kinds. Ideally, in the course of meeting this condition, it should explain the relation between events and (*a*) space, (*b*) time, (*c*) physical objects, (*d*) states and processes, if these differ from events, and (*e*) their subjects, if they have them. Both versions of the property-exemplification account to be considered in this chapter meet most if not all of these desiderata and so qualify as theories of events. That there is a need for such a theory is clear from the problems, well-documented, associated with various candidates for acceptable criteria of event identity.[4]

Token event-identity theories presume commitment to events construed as non-repeatable, dated, particulars. It follows from this that events, like physical objects, have positional, or spatiotemporal properties, and hence that spatiotemporal coincidence is a necessary condition for event identity. Three well-known candidates for criteria of event identity, viz. *de facto* spatiotemporal coincidence, necessary spatiotemporal coincidence, and sameness of cause and effect, all take spatiotemporal coincidence to be necessary for event identity. Only the first of these takes that condition to be sufficient as well. Nevertheless, all three criteria suffer from one or the other, or both, of two main objections. These have their source in the requirement, mentioned above, that any acceptable criterion of event identity must specify properties of events that are both necessary and sufficient (1) to individuate events as entities of a kind from particulars of other kinds, and (2) to individuate events from one another.

The criterion of *de facto* spatiotemporal coincidence has been said to fail to meet both of these conditions. The envisaged example of a sphere, suspended in space, which both continuously rotates and becomes continuously warmer throughout its existence, is often cited in support of this.[5] The criterion of necessary spatiotemporal coincidence has been said to fail to meet condition (1). This is supported by the fact that both the criterion of *de facto* spatiotemporal coincidence and the criterion of necessary spatiotemporal coincidence apply to events and to physical objects, which suggests that entities of the one kind are a subcategory of entities of the other.[6] Although it is true that in each case a different criterion applies minimally (see Section 1), this itself calls out for further explanation by way of an underlying theory of events. Finally, the causal criterion has been said to fail to meet condition (2). This seems evident from the possibility that there should be a single particle which is split by a process of fission and later reunited by a process of fusion.[7] It is further supported by the charge that the criterion is unacceptable because circular (not formally, but conceptually or logically).[8] The circularity objections are instructive, since they indicate that even if it is true that events and only events bear causal relations to one another, this, in addition to the fact that they are essentially spatiotemporal, cannot be the whole truth about their nature. Causal properties are relational; they require for their attribution the existence or occurrence of at least two entities. But then, on pain of circularity, they cannot suffice to individuate events from one another.

All three criteria evidently fail to suffice either to individuate events from one another, or to individuate them from physical objects, or both. These failures repeatedly point to the need for an underlying theory of events – an account of their nature in terms of which an acceptable criterion of event identity can be formulated. In the next three sections of this chapter we examine two such accounts, both of which are versions of the property-exemplification account of events, and their respective criteria of identity.

2. Kim and the Property-Exemplification Account of Events

As stated in Chapter Three, Section 3, the property-exemplification (hereafter, PE) account regards an event as an exemplification of a property at a time in a (physical) object. In simple cases of monadic properties (the only ones we shall be concerned with), it can be represented schematically as $[x,P,t]$ (this being understood as a singular term referring to an event), where x is an instantiating object, P a property instantiated in or exemplified by x, and time of exemplification. As espoused by Kim, the account makes use of two basic principles. The first of these states the identity conditions for events, and the second states the conditions under which an event occurs or exists, thus:

(1) $[x,P,t] = [y,Q,t']$ just in case $x = y$, $P = Q$, and $t = t'$.

(2) Event $[x,P,t]$ exists just in case the substance x has the property P at t.[9]

Evidently, while the first condition is indispensable to the theory, the second, as formulated, is not: the theory could proceed, for instance, by defining the predicate 'is an event' over ordered n-tuples of objects, properties, and times. In this case, the ordered triple, $\langle x, P, t \rangle$, would be an event if and only if x has P at t; and the principles of set theory would guarantee the existence of the triple (assuming, of course, that x, P, and t exist). Kim himself appears to favour the first method over the second. It is certainly the more interesting from a metaphysical point of view, and also from the point of view of the phenomenon of causal interaction between events, where this is assumed to entail their positionality. On the other hand, it leaves the nature of the complexes, represented schematically as $[x, P, t]$, unexplained. The operator, '$[,,]$', is left formally undefined by the theory; and though we know enough about these complexes to know that they aren't themselves objects, properties, or times, we know very little else about them. Kim does insist that although events *involve* other objects, they are different in kind from them, i.e., they cannot be reduced to these other objects. Unfortunately, because his formal explanation of the sense in which events involve other objects is repeatedly in the terminology of 'constitutive components', remarks like these are apt to mislead. Such terminology invites us to view events as somehow composed of objects, properties, and times, related to each other in something like the way that a chair or any other complex physical object is often viewed as composed of or constituted by its parts (that is, molecules) arranged in a certain way. This, coupled with a certain view of the way in which physical objects are related to their 'constitutive components' (viz. one which construes them as identical with their components), might tempt one to conclude that events are nothing 'over and above' their objects, properties, and times, related in a certain way.

What is misleading about such remarks is that the relation that holds between events and their so-called 'constitutive components' cannot be viewed as of the same kind as that which holds between other physical things and their constituents. The components of events cannot be construed as parts of them in the way that the constituents of, say, artifacts or biological organisms, might plausibly be construed as parts of them. This much is clear from the fact that the relationships which the components of an event bear to one another on this account are very different from the relations that the components of the physical things bear to one another. In the case of an event, one component is *exemplified by* another, *at* yet another; and it is clear that whatever the constituents of a biological organism or an artifact may be, they do not bear this relationship to one another.

At the basis of this tendency to construe the way in which events involve other objects as analogous to the way in which the constituents of other physical things compose them lies a confusion between the way that a canonical description of an event involves mention of other entities and the way that the event described involves the entities mentioned. We can see this clearly if we turn our attention for a moment to functional expressions like 'the father of x', which, when they combine with names or descriptions, produce complex or structured expressions that map offspring onto their fathers. In spite of the fact that such expressions as a whole literally contain as constituents expressions which refer to or mention other entities (or purport to), there is no temptation to suppose, on the basis of this, that fathers are in some sense composed of their offspring. To do so would be to assume, falsely, that the way in which complex referring expressions are structured is like the way in which the entities referred to are structured. A similar point holds in the case of events. It is true that canonical descriptions of the form '$[x,P,t]$' contain as constituents expressions referring, or purporting to refer, to objects, properties, and times. But it in no way follows from this that events themselves 'contain' or are composed of the entities referred to by the constituent expressions of such descriptions.[10]

If this is right, then we can see why the PE account has no clear reductivist consequences for events. However, if events *aren't* structured in such a way as to make it plausible to suppose that a reductivist thesis holds for them, then it is difficult to see how the claim that the components of events are constitutive of them can amount to anything more than the claim that they are essential to them. Indeed, Kim explicitly commits himself to some version of this claim. Canonical descriptions of events (i.e., descriptions of the form '$[x,P,t]$') describe them in terms of their 'constitutive components', and thus give (on the condition that these components are given 'intrinsic' descriptions) 'intrinsic' descriptions of them. At least one essentialist consequence is implied by this, viz. that events have essentially the structure they have. That is, events are essentially exemplifications of act or event properties at times in (physical) objects; and hence, for any event, *e*, being an exemplification of an act or event property at a time in an object is an essential property of *e*. Notice, however, that this would appear to follow from the two basic tenets of the PE account *alone*. For, irrespective of how the existence condition is interpreted, the mere existence of the relevant *x*, *P*, and *t* is not enough to guarantee the existence of an event. No entity *could* be an event, according to this account, unless it were the exemplification of a property at a time in a object.

To say that events have essentially the structure they have is at least to say that they have characteristics or properties, the very possession of which by them guarantees that they are entities of a certain *kind* – properties without which they would not, as entities of that kind, exist. Of course, not all characteristics able to be possessed by events are of this sort; if they were, there would be little point in claiming that certain of these are essential. And even of those that are, some will be such that they are capable of possession (perhaps essentially) by entities of other kinds as well (see Section 1 above). On the other hand, if events are to be both distinct and distinguishable as entities of an irreducible ontological category, not all of their essential properties can be possessed in conjunction by entities of any other category. This in turn suggests that the kinds of properties that the PE account needs to circumscribe must be essential to events in a way that includes their uniqueness to them (again, see Section 1).

The contrast between 'intrinsic' and 'extrinsic' descriptions of events, where the former describe events in terms of their 'constitutive components', thus turns out to be of double significance. A description of an event is intrinsic to it only if it both describes that event in terms of properties at least one of which is capable of possession by events alone *and* describes that event in terms of properties without which it could not exist. Examples of descriptions that are 'extrinsic' to events in this second sense might be 'the first clapping of hands at the concert last night' or possibly 'has causal relations'.

Let us call these properties real, or kind, essences, thereby distinguishing them from the properties Plantinga and others are interested in (these latter being ones that can be had essentially by some individuals of a kind but accidentally by others of the same kind, like being Socrates or Greek).[11] Then, following Lombard, we can characterize an essence which determines a kind as a property, φ, such that,

(1) it is necessarily true that, if some entity has φ, then it is necessary that if that entity exists, then it has φ;

(2) it is possible that there are entities that have φ; and

(3) it is in principle possible to provide a minimal criterion of identity for the entities that have φ,

where the sense of 'necessarily' in use is that employed in a Kripke-type semantics for quantified S5 in which the Barcan formula fails.[12] The first occurrence of 'necessarily' in (1) is large scoped, and is read *de dicto*. Its purpose in being there is to make plain the fact that essences are not, as Plantiga's essential properties are, the kinds of properties that some objects of a kind can have essentially while others of the same kind have them accidentally or not at all. The second 'necessarily' in (1) is, unlike the first, *de re*; and it needs to be if φ is to be an essence. For an essence, as here construed, is a property which an object of a kind *must* have in order to exist as an object of that kind.

Conditions (2) and (3) serve to restrict the range of properties for which φ stands proxy. Thesis (2), for example, rules out as essences inconsistent properties. And Thesis (3) serves to rule out as kind-determining essences properties which may be common to objects of more than one kind, like being an existent thing, or being a particular (i.e., being a (merely) spatiotemporal thing). While any property which meets conditions (1) and (2) is an essence of a class of objects, the idea behind the third condition is that no property φ can be an essence which determines a kind if it is not unique to entities of that kind.

3. Kim's Version Considered

This version of the PE account has been subjected to a variety of criticisms. Most of these have their source in the condition ((2)) that an acceptable criterion of event identity must suffice to individuate events from one another. One complaint centres on the fact that the account discriminates too finely between events that we wish to say are identical, such as Brutus's stabbing Caesar, and Brutus's stabbing Caesar at the Forum. If it is correct, the conditions required by the criterion entailed by that account cannot be necessary for event identity.[13] Another complaint centres on the fact that the criterion for event identity entailed by the account (and in fact by *any* version of the PE account) requires property identity, but that there appear to be no acceptable (i.e., sufficient) identity conditions for property identity. If it is correct, the conditions specified by the criterion are insufficient for event identity.[14]

In fact, neither of these criticisms by itself is decisive against this version of the PE account. Consider the first one. Because properties differ when their extensions do, and events are distinct when their constitutive properties are, the criterion of event identity has been said to have the consequence, amongst others, that no shooting can be a killing, no arm-waving a signalling, and no signing of a cheque a paying of a bill. Because verbs like 'shot', 'killed', etc., express act or event properties in sentences attributing an empirical property to an object at a time, they express properties which are taken to be constitutive of events.

However, such consequences are avoidable within the confines of the PE account. Indeed, Kim himself suggests two ways in which events like strolls and leisurely strolls, or swimmings and slow swimmings, might be accommodated by his version of the account. According to the first, properties like that of strolling or stabbing are construed as generic events, with expressions like 'leisurely' and 'with a knife' being construed as modifying, not the generic events themselves, but rather, the individual events which are exemplifications of them.[15] According to the second, events like Sebastian's leisurely stroll are construed as including events like Sebastian's stroll, with the consequence that while the two events are non-identical, they are not entirely distinct.[16] If one pursues the first of these strategies, it is even possible to accommodate the intuition that particular stabbings may be (identical with) killings or that particular signings of cheques may be paying of bills within the confines of the PE account by insisting that verbs like 'kills' and 'pays (a bill)' express characterizing rather than constitutive properties of events. (It must be noted, however, that this manouevre would require a criterion for the individuation of generic events which is far more discriminating than the one actually adopted by Kim. Furthermore, it is doubtful whether any suches criterion would be compatible with one of the most fundamental tenets of this version of the PE account – a point to which we return below.)

What, then, of the second criticism? Objections of this sort are important to consider because they embody the intuition, which some may feel strongly, that *any* version of the PE account of events is, if not unacceptable, incomplete because it lacks a criterion of property identity. The question is whether this intuition is justified; and there are two grounds for thinking that it is not. First, the PE account purports to distinguish at the very least between properties whose exemplification by physical objects are constitutive of events (generic events) and ones whose exemplification by such objects are not constitutive of events. As we shall see, the present version of the account fails ultimately to do this; but the second version of the account to be considered below does not so fail. If any residual question about the criterion of event identity based on the issue of property identity remains, it must have its source in the condition ((2)) that an acceptable criterion of event identity must suffice to individuate events from one another. However, this can only concern the question of whether any acceptable identity conditions for act or event properties are forthcoming, not the question of whether any such conditions are forthcoming for properties in general.

Second, and perhaps more important, this kind of objection, if correct, would entail that Leibniz's Principle of the Indiscernibility of Identicals is unacceptable because it claims that identical objects (of any sort) must have the same properties but fails to provide a criterion of property identity. But surely, no one would wish to take issue with *this* principle on such grounds.

In fact, the real difficulty with this version of the PE account has its source, not in condition (2) (though, as it was suggested above, the first criticism is indicative of a deeper difficulty in his account), but rather, in condition (1). If the PE account is correct, the one crucial difference between events and particulars of other sorts is that the former have the (essential) property of being exemplifications of act or event properties of objects. The truth of the claim that events have essences which determine them as an irreducible kind thus rests on the issue of which of their properties are said to be generic, i.e., ones the havings of which by a physical object imply that a change has occurred, is occurring, or will occur. In particular, it rests on the issue of how these properties are to be individuated from other properties, the havings of which by a physical object do *not* imply change. It is this part of the account that is most vulnerable to attack. Part of the problem with it is that the main, if not sole, criterion operated by its proponents for the identification and individuation of act and event properties is by reference to sentences which attribute an empirical property to an object at a time. This criterion cannot discriminate between properties constitutive of events, where these are narrowly construed as changes (such as the property of firing (a gun)), and ones constitutive of states or processes, where these are construed as including persisting conditions (such as being blue). Kim does indicate that generic events might also be adequately identified and individuated from other sorts of properties by means of the laws or lawful regularities of a favoured scientific theory. However, it is clear both from the kinds of properties he cites as figuring in such laws (for instance, colour properties, temperature properties, and weight properties), and from his remarks throughout various papers, that he intends any acceptable criterion to circumscribe not only those properties constitutive of events narrowly construed, but also those constitutive of states and processes.[17] This has the consequence of blurring the distinction, so crucial to the PE account, between properties whose possession by a physical object implies the existence or occurrence of events and those which do not.

A comparison here between Kim's position on events and a certain (essentialist) theory of particulars of another sort, viz. (natural) physical substances, may help to illustrate this. It is a familiar doctrine in metaphysics that substances, though 'other than' the mere sum or bundle of their associated attributes or properties (as the traditionally conceived bundle theory would have it) are (unlike bare substrata) essentially characterized individuals. It states, that is, that substances are to be characterized by some proper subset of the properties they are able to possess, without which they would not exist and whose possession in some determinate form entails that they form a kind. Typically, proponents of this type of view hold that substances themselves aggregate into kinds that are mutually exclusive of one another (as, e.g., plants, animals, and the like are normally conceived of as doing). Thus, each kind of substance is said to be essentially characterized by a distinct subset of properties (a substance-kind essence), the sharing of which, by particulars of that kind, ensures that they form the kind they do.[18]

This type of position plainly bears more than a passing resemblance to the conception of events embodied in the PE account. Suppose that it is correct. Then it is natural to suppose that substances have, as events do, an 'internal structure' – specifically, that they are exemplifications of certain kinds of properties (viz. substance-kind properties, such as being a horse, or being a tiger) in various spatiotemporal positions, and thus have associated with them the (essential) property of being exemplifications of substance-kind properties. (Indeed, it is properties of this latter kind, and not the so-called 'constitutive' properties of substances, such as the property 'horse' which deserve the name, 'kind-determining essence'.) Given the conception of essences articulated above, it follows that although some essences may be shared by substances of different kinds (as spatiotemporal properties are shared by both animals and plants), each kind of substance must have associated with it at least one (substance-kind) property which is such that (1) no object of that kind could exist without being an exemplification of it; and (2) being an exemplification of it, in addition to being an exemplification of certain spatiotemporal properties, ensures that it is of *that* kind and no other. Thus, kinds of substances, by possessing substance-kind properties that are exclusive of one another, like being an exemplification of the property 'being a horse' are themselves exclusive of one another. The sorts of properties that immediately suggest themselves as essential to kinds of substances in this way are those that would figure in their identity and persistence conditions. For these seem plainly to be properties without which a thing of a kind could not exist. In cases like those of animals and vegetables, such properties may themselves be determined by yet further subcategories of kinds of substances, like tigers and human beings, or trees and oranges.

Couple this with a corresponding view of events and a question naturally arises. Of all the properties, accidental and essential, that animals of a certain kind – say, horses – might possess, which of these can be determined by the kind of criterion for the identification and individuation of generic events that this version of the PE account works with to be ones whose exemplification it is of the essence of events or states to which they might be subject during their lifespan to be, as opposed to ones whose exemplification it is of the essence of horses themselves to be? If we were to restrict our attention to properties like being brown, or perhaps, having certain visible markings such as a white patch on a foreleg, this might seem a relatively simple matter to settle. For properties such as these are commonly considered to be accidental to an object like a horse on an essentialist account. Thus, they can easily be construed as being ones whose exemplification it is of the essence of states to which it might be subject without creating any tension in an essentialist account of the nature of these two supposedly distinct kinds of particulars.

But what about properties like those of being an exemplification of the property 'being a horse' or being an exemplification of the property 'being a human being'? These emerge on an essentialist account as *essences* of animals of certain kinds. Yet it is clear from what Kim has to say about events that the properties whose exemplification it is of the essence of such objects to be (viz. being a horse, being a human being) are no less indicative of states or 'unchanges' to which these objects are subject than are properties like those of being born. It is clear that a property like that of being a horse cannot be one whose exemplification it is of the essence of both a horse *and* an event to be if these are to constitute two distinct kinds of things. Yet a Kim-type criterion for the identification and individuation of act and event properties, encompassing as it does properties constitutive of states as well, cannot provide a means of clearly demarcating what are held to be two quite distinct ontological categories of particulars.

Proponents of a Kim-type view of events are apt to object to this, insisting that properties like that of being a horse are not ones that could be constitutive of both horses and events (or states that horses might be in). Such properties, they might say, are possessed *by* horses but are *constitutive* of events (where if a property, ϕ, is a constitutive property of an entity, x, then x is not φ). However, if a PE account of *substances* is a *prima facie* plausible one, an exemplification of a substance-kind property *is* the thing that has it, and the above principle is not, in general, true. The property 'being a horse' for instance, would seem to be both constitutive of Old Dobbin *and* a property of him, since Old Dobbin is an exemplification of the property 'being a horse' but he also has that property. In short, substances would seem to have at least some of their properties in virtue of being exemplifications of them. It is true that the same does not appear to hold for events. The property 'being a horse' may be constitutive of the state which is Old Dobbin's being a horse, but that *state* does not have that property; for a state is not a substance. But in order for the objection to stand, the principle to which it appeals must apply, not to the case of events, but to that of substances.

If this is right, then certain ways of developing the PE account of events are actually at odds with the point of a theory of events as described in Section 1 of this chapter. In particular, the question of how one conceives the so-called 'generic events', and how they are to be identified and individuated from other properties whose possession by objects do not imply change, is a crucial one. It is here, rather than in the fundamentals of the account, that the view is most vulnerable to attack.

4. Lombard's Version of the PE Account

Lombard endorses the general view of events embodied in the PE account, viz. that events are best understood as exemplifications (more precisely, exemplifyings) of certain sorts of empirical properties (viz. ones that imply that a change has occurred, is occurring, or will occur) by (physical) objects at (or during intervals of) times.[19] However, his version is predicated on the assumption that events are paradigmatically and fundamentally changes, where these are *not* to be understood as states or persisting conditions. This assumption is founded on the intuition that some properties are such that their possession by an object at a time implies change whereas others are not. These two sorts of properties are labelled 'dynamic' and 'static' respectively, and exemplifyings of the former sorts only by (physical) objects at times are held to imply the existence of events.

Static properties are such that their possession by an object at a time implies that that object is in a certain state. Dynamic properties, in contrast, are ones whose possession by an object at a time entails that that object is changing at that time. Because dynamic properties are indicative of change, they can be possessed only during intervals of time. That is to say, change takes time. If an object has a dynamic property during an interval of time, t, then it will be true that that object is changing that interval from having one static property to having another. This will be true because a dynamic property just is the property of first having one, then another, static property. Thus, there are two clear differences between static properties and dynamic ones (instantaneous ones excluded). Whereas the former may be possessed by an object at times which are not intervals and are ones whose possession does not entail the existence of any other property, static or dynamic (other than properties entailed by their possession, as, for example, being blue entails being coloured), the latter sorts of properties may be possessed by an object only during intervals of time and are ones whose possession entails the existence of at least two distinct static properties.

This relation between dynamic and static properties is more precisely expressed by means of the notion of a *quality space* – a set S of simple static properties, $\{P_O, P_1, \ldots, P_n, \ldots\}$ satisfying the following conditions:

(1) if at any time, t, any object, x, has $P_i \in S$, then at t, for every $_j \neq _i$, it is not the case that x has $P_j \in S$

and

(2) if any object, x, which has $P_i \in S$ at any time t, fails to have P_i at a time t' ($t \neq t'$) (and still exists), then x changes in S (or in respect 'S'), that is, by t' x has, for some $_j$ ($_j \neq _i$), $P_j \in S$.[20]

The effect of (1) is to restrict the kinds of static properties that are eligible for membership in set S to mutually exclusive ones.

The point of (2) is to make explicit the fact that quality spaces consist of sorts or kinds of properties (e.g., colour properties, weight properties, etc.), so that if any object changes with respect to one of its static properties, it can only do so by coming to have another property of the same sort. Effectively, events are movements by objects 'through' quality spaces. The greater the number of distinct quality spaces there are, the greater the number of distinct changes an object can undergo at any one time there will be; and similarly, the fewer the number of distinct quality spaces there are, the fewer the number of distinct changes an object can be construed as undergoing simultaneously there will be.

The question of how properties are to be demarcated into kinds – i.e., how quality spaces are to be individuated from one another – is not one that the account takes to be answerable *a priori*. Rather, the classification of properties into such spaces will be dependent upon observations of changes that various objects can undergo. Moreover, as Goodman's grue/bleen example indicates, such observations are likely to be affected by scientific theories which dictate how such changes are to be described.[21] In general, scientific theories affect our ways of describing and conceiving things and phenomena by telling us, among other things, what objects are ultimately composed or made of, what properties these ultimate constituents have in virtue of which objects composed of them have the properties they do, and what changes these ultimate constituents can undergo in virtue of which objects composed of them can undergo the changes they do. In other words, scientific theories are theories about ultimate objects and the quality spaces through which they move when they change. These thoughts prompt the following definitions:

(D1) An object, x, is an *atomic object* for a theory, T, if and only if it is the case, in T, that x exists and there is no object, y, distinct from x, such that y is a part of x;[22]

(D2) A set, S, is an *atomic quality space* for a theory, T, if and only if S is a dense quality space whose members are qualities that objects that are atomic in T can have (according to T);

(D3) An event, e, is an *atomic event* for a theory, T, if and only if e is a movement of some object, x, which is atomic according to T, where e consists in x's moving from having P_i to having P_k, at some interval of time, t, where P_i and P_k belong to a quality of space, S, that is atomic according to T;

where a quality space is dense if and only if, for any two properties, P_i and P_k, which are members of the space, there exists another property, P_j, 'between' them (examples of which are time and spatial location spaces).[23] These definitions allow for the possibility that some events composed entirely of atomic events are themselves also atomic: since there is, strictly speaking, no such thing as an instantaneous event on this version of the PE account, i.e., an event which has no duration and so no temporal parts, atomic events cannot be construed as the 'smallest' events of a given atomic event kind. Rather, they are to be construed as the most *basic* or fundamental sorts of events that atomic objects may undergo. However, there are many cases where an event composed of other events (even of atomic events) ought not to be conceived of as atomic. To rule these out, (D3) is amended to read as follows:

(D3∗) An event, e, is an *atomic event* for a theory, T, if and only if

   (i) e's subject, x, is an object that is atomic according to T,

   (ii) e is x's moving from having P_i to having P_k, at some interval of time, t, where P_i and P_k belong to a dense quality space, S, which is atomic according to T,

   (iii) e is temporally continuous,

   (iv) no event of which e is composed is a change whose minimal subject is distinct from x,

   (v)   no event of which e is composed is a change in a quality space distinct from S, and

   (vi) there is no property, P_j, in S that x has at two or more times during t,

where an event e is temporally continuous if and only if e is a change in some object, x, through a portion of some quality space S during some interval of time, $t - t'$, such that, at each instant in that interval, x has a different property in S.[24] An object, x, is the *minimal subject* of an event e if it is the *minimally involved subject* of e, where the notions of an object's involvement and minimal involvement in an event are defined as follows:

> If x is any object, e is any event, and t is a time, then x is *involved* in e *at* t if and only if it is the case that if e occurs (or is occurring) at t, then o changes (or is changing) at t, and a change in x at t is identical with e at t); and

> If x is any object, e is any event, and t is a time, then x is *the minimally involved subject of* e *at* t if and only if (*a*) x is involved in e at t, and (*b*) x is the *smallest* object which is such that a change in x at t is identical with e at t.[25]

Thus, as well as atomic events, the theory recognizes as events changes (both atomic and non-atomic) which are composed of atomic events, where these latter consist in atomic objects' changings with respect to properties in quality spaces that are atomic according to some scientific theory T.

Finally on the basis of these definitions, the following hypothesis, which serves as a basis for a criterion of event identity and subsquent discussion of its consequences for identity claims about events, is proposed:

(H) Every event is either
    (*a*) an atomic event, or
    (*b*) an event composed of simultaneous atomic events (a synchronic non-atomic event), or
    (c) an event composed of a temporal sequence of events each of which is either an atomic event or a synchronic non-atomic event (a diachronic event).[26]

Definitions (D1) – (D3∗) and (H) (with a qualification to be discussed below) are crucial to the present version of the PE account. For although the assumption that events are changes, as distinct from states, provides the theoretical backing necessary ultimately to distinguish events from other sorts of particulars (a point to which we shall return), it isn't until this assumption is refined by way of (D1) – (D3∗) and (H) that the clear differences between this account and Kim's begin to emerge.

Atomic events, we now see, are exemplifyings of first one, then another, static property in an atomic quality space during an interval of time. Because a dynamic property just is the property of having first one, then another, static property in a quality space, for every pair of static properties whose exemplifying during an interval of time by an atomic object constitutes an atomic event, there will be an atomic dynamic property which that object will have during that interval. In some cases a verb expressing such a property will already be present in the language of the theory (T). An *atomic event verb* is thus one that is synonymous with, or equivalent in the theory (T) to an expression of the form, 'exemplifies the property of first having P_i and then having P_j', where P_i and P_j are static properties in an atomic quality space whose exemplifying by an atomic object at a time (which is an interval) is an atomic event in T. It is verbs like these and the dynamic properties expressed by them that are associated with (indeed, determine) atomic event types.

An atomic event is thus an event having the property of being a φ-ing, where φ-ing is an atomic event type. Only verbs like 'φ' figure in canonical descriptions of atomic events. A description of an atomic event will be canonical if and only if it is a singular term of the form, '$[x,φ,t]$', where 'x' stands proxy for a name or description of the atomic object involved in the event, 'φ' for the atomic event verb expressing the dynamic property involved in that event, and 't' for a name or description of the interval of time during which x exemplifies φ.

Since each atomic event belongs to some atomic event type, the instancing of which by an atomic event during an interval of time is that event, it is of the essence of an atomic event that it be an instance of the atomic event type of which it is in fact an instance. So, although it may be a contingent matter whether an atomic event of a certain type actually occurs, given that it does, it cannot be a contingent matter that it is of the type it is. We can tell what the essences of various sorts of atomic events are from their canonical descriptions alone, since these describe such events in terms of atomic-event verbs that express dynamic properties which it is of the essence of those events to exemplify. Of course, non-atomic events also have essences; and apart from events whose minimal subjects are not partless (see below), we ought to be able to tell what these are from the canonical descriptions of the atomic events which constitute them.

On this conception of a canonical description, not all descriptions of atomic events will be canonical, though for any atomic event there may be more than one such description, as the possibility of sequences of atomic events which are movements by atomic objects through atomic quality spaces which are dense shows. (For instance, an event may be both of the type 'moves from having P_i to P_j to P_k' and of the type 'moves from having P_i to P_k', since the second description does not imply that a movement of the type described involved no other property between P_i and P_k. The distinctness of the types is ensured by the distinctness of their instancings.)[27] To be a canonical description of an atomic event, a singular term must name or describe the dynamic property involved in that event by means of an atomic event verb. In fact, the vast majority of events which serve as 'test cases' for the adequacy of criteria of event identity are picked out by means of descriptions that are not, on this account, canonical.

This last point is of considerable importance, since the criterion of identity associated with this account is formulated in terms of canonical descriptions as follows:

(E) Necessarily, for any entities e and e', if e and e' are events, then $e = e'$ if and only if e and e' have all the same canonical descriptions.[28]

This criterion is intended to apply not only to atomic events, but also to non-atomic events, which fall into at least two sorts. An event of the first sort consists in a sequence of atomic events, all of which are changes in the *same* subject during either the same or distinct intervals of time. Such an event would have a canonical description of the form 'the event composed of $[x, \phi_0, t_0]$, $[x, \phi_1, t_1]$, . . ., and $[x, \phi_n, t_n]$', where each of the terms in brackets is a canonical description of that event's constituents. An event of the second sort consists in a sequence of atomic events all of which are changes in *distinct* subjects during the same interval of time (e.g., water's boiling). Such an event would have a canonical description whose form differs from the first only in the terms which replace '*x*'; for here each term that replaces '*x*' must name a distinct atomic object. Events of the first sort are termed 'simple', whereas ones of the second sort are termed 'complex'. If $t_0 = t_1 = \ldots = t_n$, then the non-atomic event in question is *synchronic*; otherwise it is *diachronic*.

However, there is an important qualification to all this. The above account implies that the identity conditions of *every* non-atomic event can be specified by means of canonical descriptions of their atomic constituents, even assuming that the former are *distinct* from the latter, in a way analogous to the way in which the identity conditions for sets can be specified in terms of their members, assuming the former to be distinct from the latter. But some non-atomic events, such as the sinking of the Ship of Theseus, seem to be such that their identity conditions cannot be specified in this way. The reason has to do with the fact that canonical descriptions of events pick them out in terms of their *minimal* subjects, their *minimal* intervals of time, and the dynamic properties whose exemplifyings by those subjects are those events. And, as Lombard himself argues, it is implausible to suppose that the minimal subjects of such events as a ship's sinking are 'smaller' than the entire ship.[29] Since macroscopic objects such as ships are unlikely to figure in any scientific theory as atomic according to that theory, the identity conditions for events whose minimal subjects are macroscopic objects with parts cannot be viewed as being specifiable in terms of canonical descriptions of those events' (atomic) parts. In short, since not all minimally involved subjects of events are atomic, the identity conditions for every non-atomic event cannot be construed as being specifiable by means of canonical descriptions of the atomic objects, properties and times of that event's atomic constituents.

The reasoning to the conclusion that such macroscopic objects as ships are minimal subjects of events like their sinkings stems from a concern to show that, while it may be true that an event could have been a change in *an* object other than the one that it was in fact a change in (i.e., that not every subject of a given event is essential to it), it is false that the minimally involved subject of an event is inessential to it. To this end, Lombard adopts the following principle, which he calls 'The Principle of Event Enlargement':

(PEE) Any event which is a change in any object is (is identical with) a change in any other object of which the first is a part.[30]

This principle, he argues, implies that an event could have been a change in *an* object other than the one that it was in fact a change in. Suppose that at time t, e is a change in an object, x, which is a proper part of y; and so, by PEE, that e at t is a change in y. Then, since x could have been a proper part of z, distinct from y, e could have been a change in z. ((PEE) is not to be confused with The Principle of Event Contraction (PEC), according to which, if a change occurs in any object that has parts, that change is identical with a change in at least some part or parts of the original object.[31] This principle is rejected on the grounds that it requires viewing changes in objects with parts as identical with the (sums of the) changes in those parts. (See the discussion below.)

However, PEE does not imply that *every* subject of a given event is inessential to it. In particular, it does not imply that the change in x, the minimal subject of the event in the example just given, could have been a change in an object other than x. In fact, Lombard thinks that this latter claim is false; and so he proceeds to address himself to what he sees as the strongest argument in favour of the view that the minimally involved subject of an event is inessential to it. Since his conclusions regarding such macroscopic objects as ships *vis-à-vis* events which are their sinkings, are of particular importance to the question – which must be raised in the next section – of what the minimal subjects of mental events are, it is worth a brief diversion to consider the grounds for those conclusions.

The argument supposes that the Ship of Theseus (which, we are to assume, actually existed from t_1 to t_2 to t_3 with all the same parts, members of S) *might* have undergone a complete replacement of parts between t_2 and t_3 (with the result that at t_3 it had as parts members of S'), while another ship was constructed out of the members of S, in fact sailed the same course, and sank at exactly the same time the actual Ship of Theseus did due to precisely the same causes. Lombard, allowing the assumption that an object's identity can survive complete replacement of the parts that constitute it, contends that the conclusion that the subject of an event is inessential to it only follows from the argument if one assumes that the sinking of the Ship of Theseus is identical with the sum (or aggregate) of the sinkings of its parts. However, he thinks this assumption false. In his opinion, at least some events, such as the sinking of the Ship of Theseus, are related to their 'parts' in a way that parallels the relation (of constitution) that holds between physical objects and their parts. If this is right, then it is a mistake to think that the only minimally involved subjects that events can have are atomic ones, or ones whose parts have subjects that are atomic. There are events whose minimal subjects are (physical) objects with parts, and the changes which these undergo are not identical with the sums of the changes in their parts.

Now, nothing in hypothesis (H) implies that every non-atomic event must be conceived of as a mere aggregate or sum of atomic events; and so nothing in (H) is incompatible with the claim that such events as ships' sinkings are distinct from any sum of sinkings of their parts (where the latter are conceived of as atomic) since their respective minimal subjects are distinct. But the view, implied by Lombard's remarks about non-atomic events, that the identity conditions of every non-atomic event can be specified by means of canonical descriptions of their atomic constituents, must be incompatible with that claim. For a canonical description of an event on this version of the PE account is one that specifies that event in terms of its *minimal* subject, *minimal* time of occurrence, and dynamic property whose exemplifying by that subject is that event. If macroscopic (non-atomic) objects like ships are minimal subjects of events which are their sinkings, then the identity conditions of such events cannot be specified merely by specifying the atomic objects, properties, and times at which those properties are exemplified, of which those events are composed.

Of course, this in itself entails no modification either in (H) or in the criterion of event identity associated with this version of the PE account. But it does represent something of a concession to a Kim-type view of events. It effectively recognizes the existence of a large class of non-atomic events whose canonical descriptions (on the assumption that their subjects are non-atomic objects composed of parts from which they are distinct) cannot be derived from canonical descriptions of events (atomic and/or non-atomic) that constitute them. Such events would appear to be ones whose canonical descriptions are straightforwardly derivable from sentences attributing an empirical property to an object at a time.

On the other hand, it is unclear how much significance to attach to this concession. For one thing, even in cases of events whose canonical descriptions are derivable from sentences attributing an empirical property to an object at a time, there is the distinction between dynamic and static properties of objects. This account therefore succeeds in providing the necessary theoretical backing for the claim that events constitute an irreducible category of particular. Since dynamic properties consist in the havings by objects of first one, then another, of a *pair* of static properties belonging to the same quality space during intervals of time, there is no question of there being clear differences between those properties whose possession or exemplification by objects do not imply change and those which do.

Nor is it as though the claims and hypotheses made on behalf of atomic events in the present account are irrelevant to the identity conditions of events whose minimal subjects are non-atomic objects with parts. It is true that the essences of such events must be viewed as distinct from the essences of the atomic and/or non-atomic events which constitute them, since the former events could have occurred while the latter did not. That fact notwithstanding, the identity conditions for events are addressed to *actual* events with their actual compositional parts. Consequently, if any non-atomic event, e, composed of (but distinct from) atomic and/or non-atomic events, members of S, is identical with event e', then e' must be composed of members of S. This follows from the Principle of the Indiscernibility of Identicals alone; and the fact that a given event might have been composed of changes other than those of which it was in fact composed does not touch the point.

Finally, the distinction between subjects and minimal subjects itself represents a major departure from a Kim-type view of events. Because that view takes any sentence attributing an empirical property to an object at a time to be one from which a canonical description of an event is derivable, it is unable to avoid commitment to type-type identities between the so-called 'constitutive' properties of events in any case where a particular event identity statement is endorsed. This in turn has the result that, in cases where intuitions run counter to the type-type identities, proponents of the account are committed to denying the truth of particular identity statements linking instances of those types (for more on this, see Section 3 above).

However, the distinction between subjects and minimal subjects blocks any straightforward association between sentences attributing empirical properties to objects at times and canonical descriptions of events. Specifically, in cases where the subject of the event described is *not* minimal, it blocks the assumption that the property type of which that event is an instancing is one which it is of the essence of that event to be. Events may be (and often are) of more than one type; and it is only in cases where the subjects of events are minimal that one is entitled to draw any conclusions regarding their essences. For it is only in cases like these that the objects that serve as their subjects are the most basic objects of a kind, changes in which *are* the events in question.

The present version of the PE account clearly satisfies the condition (Condition (1)) that it generate identity conditions for events which suffice to individuate events from particulars of other, distinct kinds (specifically, from physical objects or substances). What about the condition (Condition (2)) that it generate identity conditions for events sufficient to individuate them from one another? In fact, this is not a problem for either version of the PE account in the way that it was seen to be for any account of events which seeks to specify their identity conditions in terms of spatiotemporal coincidence or sameness of cause and effect. One major problem with the PE account as developed by Kim is that it appeared to individuate events too *finely*, not that it failed to discriminate sufficiently between events which intuition would hold are distinct. In general, the PE account is more apt to suffer from objections of this kind than from ones having to do with the failure to satisfy Condition (2), the reason being that event identity requires the identity of properties constitutive of events, where these are typically, if not exclusively, derived from sentences which attribute an empirical property to an object at a time (see Section 3 above).

On the present account, however, canonical descriptions are not simply derivable from any sentence of the form '*x* φed at *t*'. For example, descriptions of events that make use of causal verbs like 'shot', 'killed', etc., when not reflexively construed, such as '*a*'s shooting of *b*', express properties whose exemplification by any event is not logically independent of the existence of any other event (apart, in cases of non-atomic events which are changes in objects with parts, from those involved in the event itself or in any of its compositional or temporal parts). Such properties are ones whose possession by an event is logically contingent upon the existence of some other event (compositional parts excluded), and so are ones whose non-possession by any event would not entail that it did not exist. One consequence of this is that one cannot legitimately claim on the basis of the fact that not all shootings are killings that this particular shooting and killing are distinct. For only in the case of properties which it is of the essence of the events in question to exemplify does it follow that all instancings of one must be instancings of the other. Since being a shooting and being a killing are only contingently properties of events which possess them and so are not indicative of properties (i.e., the property 'kills' and the property 'shoots') that figure in their identity conditions, a particular shooting could be a killing despite the fact that other shootings and killings are distinct.

The consequence is that the present account does not entail that events which intuition might deem identical are distinct. As for the question of whether its criterion of identity suffices to individuate events which intuition would hold *are* distinct, this is an issue concerning the classification of properties into quality spaces – an enterprise that cannot, according to the present account, be undertaken independently of observations of objects and the changes that they can undergo (themselves coloured by current scientific theories). For, what sorts of physical objects exist, what sorts of static properties they can have, and therefore what sorts of dynamic properties they can have, are all questions that fall, at least in part, within the purview of science.

5. Non-Reductive Monism and the PE Account

The present version of the PE account is explicitly developed only for the case of physical events. If it is to work in favour of the identity of mental and physical events, the theory must be extended to the context of mental events consistently with the argument for non-reductive monism. To this end, two issues need to be addressed. The first concerns the minimal subjects of mental events; and the second concerns the status of mental properties themselves – properties whose exemplifyings by persons at times are mental events. We address the former issue in this section and the latter one in the next.

The present version of the PE account assumes spatiotemporal coincidence to be at least a necessary condition of event identity. This means that, whatever else mental events may be, they are *ipso facto* spatially and temporally localizable on this account. Plainly, this rules out the tenability of any variant of Cartesian dualism from the start. However, it causes no serious objections from location for the identity theorist. For one thing, since physical events are, if nothing else, essentially spatiotemporal, there is something to be said for the claim that the question would be begged against the identity theory from the start if mental events were not. For another, it does not automatically rule out all forms of dualism. Because *any* event must, in addition to having positional properties, be an exemplifying of a dynamic property or properties, the question of whether a given event is mental or physical will depend, at least in part, on the nature of the property or properties exemplified.

On the other hand, the distinction between subjects and minimal subjects of events, to which the present account is committed, does cause serious location problems for the identity theorist. For, suppose that we concede that the mere assignment of spatiotemporal properties to mental events begs no questions. Still, one might argue, the physical locus of many mental phenomena would appear to be in the brain rather than the entire body of the person who serves as their subject. That is to say, the minimal location of many of the physical phenomena typically viewed as plausible correlates of mental events, being specifically brain phenomena, seems to differ from the minimal location of most mental phenomena, these latter being typically circumscribed by the entire body of the person who serves as their subject. Since events with distinct minimal subjects cannot be identical, this would seem to show that the identity theory is false.[32]

There are two distinct, though related, responses that the

identity theorist can make to this objection. The first is to insist that the very formulation of a plausible version of the identity theory requires that there be parity with respect to the minimal subjects of mental events and those physical events that can be viewed as *plausible* candidates for identity; and that to assume that the minimal subjects of those physical events typically correlated with mental phenomena, viz. brain events, must be brains, is to come close to begging the question against the identity theorist from the start.[33] It is true, it might be argued, that a good number of physical events are ones whose minimal subjects are smaller than, or are proper parts of, physical objects, whether these are of animal or vegetable kinds. And it is true that if a mental event whose subject is a person is identical with a physical event of that person's body, and that physical event happens to be a brain event (i.e., the change in that person's body occurs because (in a non-causal sense) a certain event occurs in that person's brain), then that mental event is identical with a brain event of that person's body. However, there is a crucial difference between a brain event of a person's body and an event of the brain. Whereas the former has a body as its subject, the latter has a brain as its subject. Moreover, while it may be the case that a person's body is the subject of a certain brain event when and only when that person's brain is the subject of a certain event, it does not follow that these events are the same. Indeed, it is more likely that if these events have distinct subjects, they are themselves distinct. In short, it might be argued, it is events such as a person S's body's being in Brain State α that are the minimal subjects of those physical events which correlate with mental phenomena; and these are never identical with events such as S's brain being in state α.

It is important to see that this view is easily motivated by considerations that are quite independent of the issue of psychophysical identity. In order to suppose that events such as S's body's being in Brain State α are identical with those such as S's brain's being in state α, one must assume the principle (PEC) that any event whose subject is an object with parts is identical with an event whose subject is at least one of those parts (see Section 4 above). But anyone who thinks that no object with parts is ever identical with (the sum of) its parts – i.e., who thinks that the constitution relation is not one of identity – is apt to reject this assumption on the grounds that the identity of an object with parts can survive a (complete) replacement of its parts, and so any event whose subject has parts could occur in the absence of any change in any of its actual parts. But no event whose subject has parts can be identical with one whose subject is one of those parts if the former could exist while the latter did not. Similarly, it might be argued, on the supposition that a human body could survive complete replacement of cells throughout a lifespan while remaining the same body, and thus that human bodies are distinct from (sums of) their atomic constituents, one cannot assume that the changes undergone by the former are identical with any of the changes or sums thereof of the latter.

This strategy may be correct; but it is unlikely to prove effective against opponents of the identity theory. The reason has to do with the fact that it trades heavily on the intuition that, whereas the principle that any change in a part of an object with parts is a change in that object itself (PEE referred to in Section 4) is *true*, the principle that any change in an object with parts is a change in at least one of those parts (PEC) is *false*. Now, opponents of the identity theory will be quick to reply that although the latter principle may not, in general, be true, it is true in certain cases, viz. in ones where a change in a non-atomic object, x, is 'due to' a *single* change in a single part of x. Indeed, it is true in these cases just because the resulting identity is a consequence of PEE. But then, in the case of my body's being in Brain State α and my brain's being in state α, it follows from PEE that if the former event is due to a single event of my brain, then my brain's being in state α just *is* my body's being in Brain State α.

Of course, the charge that one must locate the subjects of those physical events that might be construed as plausible correlates of mental events more minimally than the body of the person now requires taking a view about whether a single event within my body is one whose occurrence, by PEE, just is my body's undergoing that change. And while it seems clear that no identity theorist ought to be forced to take a stand on this, it is equally clear that the identity theory itself is considerably weakened by the fact that the possibility is a viable one, particularly in the light of PEE. For it puts the identity theorist on the defensive: though the theory cannot be proved false, the onus is on its adherent to produce reasons for thinking that it is more *likely* to be true than it is to be false.

Fortunately, there is a second, more promising strategy available to the identity theorist; and that is to attack the assumption that the minimal subjects of *mental* events are persons. Our normal, day-to-day attributions of mental phenomena uncritically suggest that their subjects are neither bodies, nor parts of bodies, nor indeed parts of anything, but are rather individual persons. However, the objection envisaged assumes something even stronger, viz. that persons are *minimal* subjects of mental events. Why should we think that this is true?

One clear line of reasoning designed to show that persons must be minimal subjects trades on the intuition that they are in some sense irreducible units despite the fact that they may have parts (in the sense, say, that part of my body is a part of me); and this is because it simply does not make sense to suppose that when it is true that a person undergoes a change (e.g., Sue suddenly remembers an appointment), it is true because (in a non-causal sense) some part of that person undergoes that change. In other words, in many if not all attributions of mental phenomena, nothing *less* than the entire person would seem to do as an appropriate subject. Now, this reasoning concedes that in cases of objects with parts, if it is true that an object, x, ϕs, it is true because at least one of x's parts (say, y) changes. Thus, for example, if the Ship of Theseus sinks, it does so because at least one of that ship's parts changes. But it goes on to suppose both that, in a case where x ϕs because y changes, y's changing is *identical* with x's ϕing and that y's changing *is* y's ϕing. However, both of these suppositions are suspect.

The first supposition is dubious because it rests on the principle (PEC) that any change in a non-atomic object with parts is identical with a change in at least one of those parts – a principle likely to be rejected by anyone who thinks that objects with parts are distinct from their parts on the grounds that any change in the former will for that reason be distinct from any (sum of) changes in the latter. But suppose that we grant it here on the grounds that it is true in just those cases where the principle PEE is true and that this is one such case. Even granting it and the identity it licenses, there are objections to the further assumption that when such an identity holds, the change in the part(s), y, which makes it true that x ϕs, is itself a ϕing. Suppose, for example, that the desk in my office changes today from being four-legged to being three-legged in virtue of its front left leg's falling off and that the desk's changing in the respect it does just is its leg's falling off. Though it is true that the leg changes in some respect, it does not itself change from being four-legged to being three-legged. Similarly, suppose that on Monday morning at 9 a.m. Sue stammers. She stammers because her tongue catches. Hence it seems reasonable to say that her stammering just is her tongue's catching. But surely, Sue's *tongue* doesn't stammer; only persons do that.

What is notable about such examples is that a good number of them – indeed, arguably the most plausible – have nothing to do with the mental. Nor do they presume that in order for an event which is a change in an object with parts to be identical with one which is a change in at least one of those parts, the object and its parts must be identical. Granting that PEC is true in just those cases where PEE is true, there is still a flaw in the argument that persons must be the minimal subjects of mental events; and that is that the assumption that lies behind it (viz. that it doesn't make sense to attribute mental phenomena to anything less than a person) supposes, falsely, that when an object with parts changes and that change is identical with a change in at least one of its parts, the change in that object is a change of the same *type* as that undergone by the part(s). It is important to see that the objection needs this supposition if it is to be justified in its assumption that persons are minimal subjects. For it is the fact that there is no proper part, y, of a person, x, such that when x ϕs, y ϕs, that is required to back the claim that it is absurd to say of anything less than a person that it is the subject of mental phenomena. It may indeed be absurd to do so; but this fails to show that persons must be minimal subjects. For it need not be the case, for example, that my brain thinks of Vienna in order for it to be true that my thinking of Vienna is identical with some event whose subject is my brain.[34]

There is, however, a residual problem here. The distinction between subjects and minimal subjects of events blocks the assumption that the property type or types of which any event is an instancing is/are one(s) which it is of the essence of that event to be, thereby making it possible that there should be true identity statements linking particular events, where these are expressed by means of descriptions at least one of which is not canonical. However, there is a question as to how events which are exemplifyings of *distinct* dynamic properties in distinct subjects (only one of which may be minimal), as in the examples above, *can* nevertheless be identical. It is true that the criterion of event identity entailed by the present account requires only that identical events have all the same *canonical* descriptions. But by the Principle of the Indiscernibility of Identicals, events which are identical must have all the same properties. How can my desk's changing from being four-legged to being three-legged be identical with its left leg's falling off if it is false both that the former event is (identical with) an exemplifying of the property 'falls off' and that the latter event is (identical with) an exemplifying of the property 'changes from being four-legged to being three-legged'? For this implies that the former event has a property (of being an exemplifying of the property 'changes from being four-legged to being three-legged') that the latter does not and that the latter event has a property (of being an exemplifying of the property 'falls off') that the former does not.

The issue of how events with distinct subjects, only one of which is minimal, might nevertheless be identical (whether or not they are exemplifyings of the same dynamic property or properties) is discussed at length in Chapter Five, Section 5. Still, something can be said here about how, supposing them to be identical, ones which are exemplifyings of *distinct* dynamic properties might satisfy the Indiscernibility of Identicals Principle. Events with distinct subjects may or may not be exemplifyings of the same dynamic properties. Whether they are will depend on what kinds of (static) properties their respective subjects have, since these will determine the dynamic properties whose exemplifyings are those events. Since distinct subjects will differ in at least some of their properties, particularly if they are themselves of distinct kinds, they may well be capable of changes of distinct types. The problem here is not simply in seeing how events whose subjects are distinct can be identical and so have all the same properties. If the changes are of the *same* event type(s), then, despite distinctness of subjects, there is no serious difficulty in seeing how the Indiscernibility Principle can be satisfied. Thus, supposing that my pencil's shrinking is identical with its parts shrinking, there is no special problem in seeing how that principle can be satisfied, since both the pencil and its parts can be said to be exemplifyings of the property 'shrinks'. The problem here is in seeing how changes of *distinct* types in distinct subjects can be identical, since the distinctness of the types themselves implies that changes of those types have, correspondingly, distinct properties.

What must be said in such cases is something like this. Since the principle PEE seems quite clearly to be true, there are cases where a change in one subject (e.g., a house's becoming damaged) just consists in a change in its part (e.g., its window's shattering). Since, however, the subjects of such changes are distinct and so differ in their static properties, we cannot assume that the change in the part and the change in the object of which it is a part are of the same type, even if the change in the latter *is* the change in the former. Nevertheless, the change in the part and the change in the object of which it is a part, if identical, must share all properties. Thus, if my house's becoming damaged is identical with its window's shattering, then my house's becoming damaged has, if not the property of being a shattering, the property of being a *window*-shattering, or of being an exemplifying *by its window* of the property 'shatters'. Similarly, if my window's shattering is identical with my house's becoming damaged, then my window's shattering has the property, if not of being a damaging, of being a house-damaging, or of being an exemplifying *by my house* of the property 'becomes damaged'. Since the types of which events are exemplifyings are determined by the properties of their subjects, and since distinct subjects do not have all the same properties, the dynamic properties of one subject cannot be assumed to be dynamic properties of the other. In these sorts of cases, specification of the dynamic properties whose exemplifyings are the events in question requires specifying the subjects whose dynamic properties they are. It is only in cases where the subjects of events whose identity is in question are the same that specification of the dynamic property or properties of which they are exemplifyings requires no reference to those subjects.

If this is right, then although the present version of the PE account is, by way of the distinction between subjects and minimal subjects, vulnerable to the objection that mental events must differ in location from physical ones because they have distinct minimal subjects, it can effectively counter that charge. For, in order for the objection to succeed, it must be assumed *both* that brains are the minimal subjects of those physical events that serve as correlates of mental ones *and* that persons are the minimal subjects of mental events. It is the latter that is dubious, since the strongest grounds in its favour rest on an assumption that is not, in general, true.

6. Mental Properties and Type-Type Identities

This skirts one main objection to the argument for non-reductive monism based on the present version of the PE account of events. However, there is a second, more serious, objection to contend with. Any version of the PE account has the consequence that token identities expressed by means of canonical descriptions entail type-type identities between properties constitutive of events. In fact, Kim explicitly commits himself to the view that expressions like 'pain' serve to pick out properties constitutive of particular mental events, and so are capable of figuring in their canonical descriptions.[35] However, commitment to type-type identities between mental and physical properties generates a twofold problem for the non-reductive monist. First, it seems to be incompatible with the principle PAM (the Principle of Psychophysical and Psychological Causal Anomalism of the Mental) to which that position is committed, since it strongly suggests that, at the very least, psychophysical correlation laws can be expected to be forthcoming (indeed, it threatens the non-reductive part of the position); and second, it invites objections from phenomenal properties (see Chapter One, Section 3). For both of these reasons, it needs to be shown that type-type identities between mental and physical properties are not entailed by the present version of the PE account.

The present version of the PE account provides no general means of deriving canonical descriptions of events, whether atomic or non-atomic, from sentences attributing an empirical property to an object at a time. This is because the vast majority of such sentences, even if true of the events they describe, will not identify them in terms of properties which it is of the essence of those events to exemplify. As was noted in Section 4 above, this will be the case with sentences containing verbs such as 'kills', 'shot', 'explodes', and the like; since these are indicative of properties whose possession by an event, apart from reflexive cases, implies the existence of an event other than itself (compositional parts excluded). And it will be the case in general for *any* sentence which, though descriptive of an event, describes it by means of a property which is 'relational' in the sense that its attribution to any event entails the existence of either another (distinct) event (compositional parts excluded) or another object distinct from that event's subject (and its compositional parts). Crucial for present purposes is the fact that this envisaged amendment to Kim's version was deemed necessary for reasons that are independent of the issue of mind-body identity.

Given this, there is a real question as to whether the present version of the PE account does entail type-type identities between mental and physical properties (e.g., ones of the form 'Pain = C-fibre stimulation') when extended to cover mental phenomena, and so whether it falls prey to phenomenal-property objections of the sort voiced by Kripke and to inconsistency when combined with the argument for non-reductive monism. It is true that expressions like 'is having (a) pain' or 'is in pain' (predicated of persons) do not appear to be indicative of properties of events that are causal-relational. That is to say, they do not appear to be such that properties derivable from them imply the existence of any event distinct from them and their compositional parts or of any subject apart from those undergoing the phenomena in question (and their compositional parts). But there are other ways in which a description can fail to be canonical. Recall that, for a description, '$[x,P,t]$', of an event to be canonical, x must be a minimal subject. However, the claim that persons must be the minimal subjects of mental phenomena has already been discredited on the grounds that it assumes, falsely, that if any change in a non-atomic object with parts is identical with a change in at least one of those parts, the change in the whole must be of the same *type* as the change in the part. So it cannot be assumed that expressions like 'S's having a pain at t' (or 'S's thinking of Vienna at t') are canonical descriptions of phenomenal (or intentional) mental events. Indeed, for just this reason one cannot assume that expressions like 'having (a) pain' (or 'thinking of Vienna') are indicative of properties that are essences of events that have them. If, for instance, persons *are* non-atomic objects with parts (in the sense that part of my body is a part of me) and they are *not* the minimal subjects of mental phenomena, then a change in a part of a person which *is* a minimal subject, even if identical with some change whose subject is that person, may be a change of a type distinct from that described by 'having (a) pain'. In short, a canonical description of a change which makes it true that a person, *S*, has or undergoes a pain at *t* or has a thought about Vienna at *t* may be of a type other than that described by 'having a pain' or 'thinking of Vienna'. Consequently, one cannot assume that expressions such as 'having a pain' or 'thinking of Vienna' are indicative of properties essential to at least some of the events that have them.

This provides one main source of support for the view that the present version of the PE account of events can be reconciled with the argument for non-reductive monism and avoid phenomenal-property objections based on the identification of mental with physical properties. A second source might be found in the claim that it is question-begging against any token physicalist identity theorist of mind and body simply to assume that mental properties of persons are ones that it is of the essence of mental events to exemplify, and consequently that if any particular mental event is a physical event, mental and physical properties constitutive of those events are identical. This might be thought question-begging on the grounds that it cannot be of the essence of any physical event that it be an exemplification of *any* mental property. A constitutive property of an event is one that an event could not fail to exemplify without failing to exist. But no physical event is essentially an exemplification of any mental property. This is not to say that it is false that, necessarily, all pains are painful, or false that, necessarily, any thinking of Vienna is a thinking of Vienna. These are claims about events that any token identity theorist can accept, since they are read *de dicto*. Nor is it to say that it is false that all pains are necessarily painful or that any thinking of Vienna is necessarily an 'of Vienna' thinking. On at least one clear understanding of this latter claim, it is to acknowledge that mental *types* have their contents (intentional or qualitative) essentially. This is explicitly acknowledged in Chapter Six, Section 3. It is to say that it is question-begging against token identity theorists to insist on the stronger claims that all (necessarily painful) pains are necessarily *pains* and that any thinking which is necessarily an 'of Vienna' thinking is necessarily a *thinking* (of Vienna). For these latter are claims about essences of events; ones that are incompatible with the supposition of token identity.

Both of these considerations provide grounds, though largely negative, for thinking that the present account of events does not entail type-type identities between mental and physical properties of events. They establish at most that it cannot be assumed, simply from the fact that that account entails the existence of at least some type-type identities, viz. identities between properties constitutive of events picked out by canonical descriptions of those events in true sentences identifying them, that type-type identities follow specifically from true statements identifying particular mental and physical events. Is it possible, however, to provide a more positive rationale for the view that mental properties (of persons) – both phenomenal *and* intentional – are not constitutive properties of the events which are the exemplifyings of them and so are not properties which it is of the essence of any event to exemplify?

One thing seems clear, and that is that certain properties of persons, such as that of having (a) pain, are ones whose existence and identity conditions are fixed by the ways in which those properties are felt. Thus, no event which is a person's having of a pain could be such that it isn't felt in a certain way. Any property whose exemplifying by a person felt that way would be of the type 'having pain'. Indeed, the point of the so-called 'adverbial manoeuvre' described in Chapter One (Section 2) was to accommodate this fact about phenomenal mental occurrences without falling prey to traditional objections from phenomenal properties. It is precisely because the property of having pain has associated with it a characteristic felt, or phenomenological, feel that Kripke's attack has the force it does.

However, none of this resolves the question of whether properties like that of having pain are constitutive rather than characterizing properties of phenomenal mental events – i.e., are ones whose exemplifying by a person it is of the essence of any event to be – and so whether properties like that of being a (having of a) pain are kind-determining essences of phenomenal mental events. At most it suggests that the 'properties' of being dull, or being throbbing, are essential to certain mental types or properties (e.g., having pain) themselves. But the crucial question here is whether these types or properties are themselves constitutive of the events that are exemplifyings of them. This is effectively the question of whether a certain view of the nature of pain (or any other type of phenomenal mental occurrence) is correct: one according to which it is of the essence of every event that is in fact a pain that it be of the type 'having pain' – that it have the property of being a (having of a) pain. Intuitive as it may sound, grounds need to be given for thinking it true in the light of the distinction between constitutive and characterizing properties, and so between essences and other properties, of events.

One of the most notable proponents of the view that the property of being a (having of a) pain (henceforth, being a pain) is an essence of those events that possess it is Kripke himself. As is well known, he sees a close parallel between kinds of mental phenomena (such as pain) and other, physical, phenomena (such as heat). Indeed, expressions like 'pain' are in his opinion rigid designators of kinds of mental phenomena, and identity statements involving these and other rigid designators are, if true, necessarily so, principally because the property of being pain is held to be an essence of those mental events which possess it in much the same way as the property of being molecular motion is an essence of the phenomenon which is heat.[36] Kripke clearly believes that the relation that holds between a natural kind of phenomenon and its essence is a necessary one. Thus, heat is held to be a natural kind because and in so far as the phenomena which fall within it share an underlying essence, empirically discoverable, which is definitive of the kind. Because the essences definitive of natural kinds are empirically discoverable, it is his belief that the initial criteria by which we may judge a phenomenon to belong to a certain kind might diverge from those properties that are definitive of that kind. So, for instance, any phenomenon which had all the phenomenological, or felt, qualities of heat but which lacked the underlying properties definitive of that phenomenon (i.e., that of being molecular motion) would not be heat. Similarly, fool's gold is not gold, despite the fact that it looks and feels like gold; water and heavy water are distinct chemical compounds despite being indiscernible with respect to qualitative properties observable with the naked eye. In general, the ways in which ordinary macroscopic things and events present themselves to the naked eyes of a normal human being provide the basis upon which we classify, identify, and individuate such entities. But we can conceive of this basis being systematically replaced by another whose classifications proceed by way of properties other than these ordinary observable ones, where the former provide the identity and individuation conditions for such entities. These conditions can and often do result in judgements that conflict with ones made on the basis of everyday observable behavioural properties.

By this criterion, however, mental properties, both phenomenal and intentional, do not obviously qualify as essences of the events that have them. For here our basis for classifying, identifying, and individuating such phenomena – viz. intentional behaviour or action, and introspection – is one that we cannot similarly conceive of as being systematically replaceable by any other.[37] Indeed, it is at least partly because of this that we are prepared to countenance the possibility of variable realization. This possibility threatens the view that mental properties are essences of the events that have them because, on the view of essences envisaged here, the initial criteria by which we may classify, identify, and individuate objects or phenomena of a given kind can 'come apart' from the properties which provide their identity and individuation conditions.

To suppose that the intentional behavioural and introspective basis upon which attributions of mental phenomena are typically made could be replaced by some other basis is to suppose that we might regard creatures as different psychologically when their behavioural dispositions are indiscernible. As was pointed out in Chapter One, Section 4, however, the introspective and behavioural basis for attributing mental properties is so tied to the physical properties of persons' bodies and their environments that we could have no reason to discern a difference in mental properties where there was no corresponding difference in such physical properties. The reason has at least partly to do with the fact that mental properties are, as the principle PCI asserts, causally efficacious with regard to the physical world. Our conception of causality is such that we expect like causes to have like effects and vice versa; and this, given causal interaction between the mental and the physical, has the consequence that where organisms differ in their mental properties, this difference must make a potential physical difference.[38] Given variable realizability, such physical differences as might occur within the confines of persons' bodies could not ground the belief that they differ psychologically. For one thing, we typically do not have access to these in our day-to-day attributions of mental properties. But even if we did, we would not deem such differences significant if they were not apt to effect corresponding differences in introspection and intentional behaviour or action. Attributions of mental properties, both intentional and phenomenal, are governed by intentional criteria – rationality, consistency and coherence – which apply, not only to mental phenomena themselves, but also to these and the behaviour (verbal as well as other) that they typically cause. (e.g., inductive rationality applies to sensations as well as to intentional mental phenomena. It is inductively rational, for instance, for a person whose proximity to a source of extreme heat is the cause of her experiencing pain to move away from the source of heat.) Ultimately only such differences between persons' mental properties as would make for intentional behavioural differences, not for differences in behaviour, physically described, could, it seems, ground the belief that they differ psychologically. Thus, although mental properties may have identity and individuation conditions distinct from those of any physical property (as non-reductive monism acknowledges), their attribution is answerable to criteria which we cannot suppose to be satisfied without having consequences for how things are in the physical world, ultimately in the (intentional) behaviour of persons. Causal interaction between the mental and the physical, combined with the belief that distinct mental properties, if causally efficacious, must differ in their causes, or their effects, or both, with respect to physical (ultimately intentional behavioural) phenomena, is incompatible with the suggestion that we might regard creatures as different psychologically when they are indiscernible in their intentional behavioural dispositions.

Furthermore, variable realization itself is incompatible, given token identities between mental and physical events construed in terms of the present version of the PE account, with the supposition that mental properties like that of having a pain are ones which it is of the essence of any mental event to exemplify (and hence with the supposition that properties of events such as that of being pain are essences of them). For, suppose that S's having pain at t is identical with S's C-fibres' firing at t; and suppose that the properties of having pain and C-fibres' firing are constitutive of those events. Then, since identical events must share all the same canonical descriptions, any creature that realized its mental states differently, whether physically or non-physically, *could* not exemplify the property of having pain.

These grounds for thinking that mental properties of persons are not constitutive of events which are exemplifyings of them are, of course, open to question. In fact, they are unlikely to convince someone who is not already predisposed to think both that non-reductive monism is plausible and that the present version of the PE account of events is correct. Doubts about the plausibility of non-reductive monism can to some extent be allayed by addressing the most pressing of objections to it; and this we do in the following two chapters. As for the grounds themselves, they do have considerable plausibility given the intuitive appeal of the principle PCI, the thesis that distinct mental properties must differ ultimately in their potential introspective and intentional behavioural effects, and the thesis of variable realizability. Moreover, they can be reinforced by considerations of the sort that the Churchlands adduce in favour of functionalism.[39]

These considerations take the form, in part, of an attack on the view that mental kinds are natural kinds – a view traceable to two assumptions, both of which are questionable. The first is that mental kinds such as pain share a single nature which is intrinsic to them and essential to every event which is an instance of them. In the case of sensations it is natural to suppose that their qualia constitute that nature. The second is that one's sensations are known directly and completely introspectively, i.e., that introspection is not only the most authoritative, but also the most reliable, source of knowledge about the nature of one's sensations.

To the first it is pointed out that the question of whether

mental kinds do have a single underlying essence is not a conceptual matter but rather an empirical one. The empirical evidence (which includes variable realization) against the view that sensation kinds have a single underlying *physical* nature is substantial. As for the view that they might have a single underlying *non-physical* nature, the evolutionary process itself makes any form of dualism extremely implausible.

To the second it is pointed out that the fact that we typically identify and individuate our sensations introspectively is entirely compatible with the claim that introspection identifies sensations by way of features that are contingently possessed by, i.e., are non-essential to, them.

This second point requires qualification in the light of the adverbial manoeuvre (see Chapter One, Section 2), according to which phenomenal properties such as those of being dull and being throbbing are to be construed as part of, or as being 'absorbed into' the mental event types with which they are associated (e.g., having pain). This is both the most natural and the most promising way of avoiding objections from phenomenal properties to event-identity theories of the mental and the physical. But it has the consequence, noted in the previous section, that it is true, not false, that necessarily, all (havings of) pains are painful, *and* that all (havings of) pains are necessarily painful. Thus, any dull, throbbing, pain event is necessarily a dull, throbbing, pain event.

The second point must therefore be construed as stating that even if it is true that all pains are necessarily painful, it does not follow that all pains are necessarily pains, i.e., that it is of the essence of any event which is the exemplifying of the property 'having (a painful) pain', that it be an exemplifying of that property. Just as the question of whether mental events are physical events is at least partly an empirical matter, so too is the question of what properties are constitutive of events; and our introspective and intentional behavioural methods of identifying and individuating mental events cannot be assumed to be either infallible or complete. If individual mental events are physical events, then mental phenomena do have natures which are physical despite the fact that introspective contemplation of their natures do not reveal this. Short of begging the question entirely against the identity theorist, this possibility cannot be dismissed.

In the light of all this, the view that mental properties of persons are constitutive of the events that are exemplifyings of them (hence that mental properties of events are essences of them) is at best dubious and arguably false on the view of essences favoured by many. Independently of that view, there is no clear reason why it should be assumed to be true, given the distinction between subjects and minimal subjects of events invoked by the present version of the PE account and given the faulty reasoning that lies behind the supposition that persons must be the minimal subjects of mental events. This effectively removes the second main obstacle to the claim that the present version of the PE account of events can be reconciled with the argument for non-reductive monism.

However, there is one final issue to address before turning to objections to non-reductive monism construed in this way. The argument for non-reductive monism requires not only that mental types be distinct from physical ones, but also that there can be no causal or correlation laws linking the two types. This second requirement is not met simply by meeting the first one. To meet the second is to defend PAM for mental types in *general*. In Chapter Three, Section 2, the argument for PAM as it applies to intentional mental types was elaborated upon and defended at length. But it was noted there that if non-reductive monism is to apply to all mental phenomena, some analogue of that argument must be constructed for phenomenal mental types.

There seem to be at least two ways in which to generalize PAM so as to cover phenomenal mental types. The first is to argue that laws connect terms for natural kinds (phenomenal as well as intentional), but mental kinds are not natural kinds, so there can be no laws linking any mental type with any physical type.[40] This argument exploits the claim that mental kinds are not natural kinds for reasons of the sort given earlier (pp.148–9). Since these are perfectly general, i.e., they apply to propositional attitudes and sensations alike, the only additional premiss needed in order for non-reductive monism to apply to both sensations and propositional attitudes is that laws connect terms for natural kinds.

Note that this argument is not unconnected with that discussed in Chapter One, which traced the absence of any type-type identities between intentional mental properties and physical ones to an irreconcilable difference in their ascription conditions, mental properties being constrained by principles of rational coherence and consistency which have no place in physical theory. The main difference between the two arguments is that, whereas the former applies such considerations directly to the domain of propositional attitudes without regard to the question of whether intentional mental properties are natural kinds, the latter exploits them directly in an argument for the claim that mental kinds in general are not natural kinds.

However, this argument relies on a certain conception of the relation between laws and natural kinds which some may find objectionable. According to it, a law is an 'intelligible principle of necessitation', i.e., a principle stating a necessary connection between objects or phenomena of one kind and objects or phenomena of another, backed up by an appropriate empirical theory according to which it either requires no further explanation or is capable of further analysis by reference to some other generalization which (relative to the theory) requires no further explanation. The connection between laws and natural kinds is established in this underlying theory, whose concern is to articulate the real essences of natural kinds, since to be a natural kind is to have a (Lockean) real essence or nature which it is the business of empirical science to articulate.

This conception of the relation between natural kinds and laws is apt to be rejected by anyone who thinks that there exist 'foundation laws', i.e., laws *not* backed by a theory. It is also vulnerable to the charge that the identification and individuation of natural kinds within a theory cannot be effected independently of judgements as to whether terms for such kinds can figure in lawlike generalizations. If so, then the notions of a law and a natural kind are interdependent, and the latter cannot be used to provide a reductive explanation of the former.

A second way in which to generalize PAM across phenomenal mental types, that by-passes the claim that laws connect terms for natural kinds, is to argue that the principles of rationality which constrain the ascription of intentional mental properties to persons also constrain the ascription of phenomenal mental properties to them. The argument might go something like this. The thesis of the holism of the mental applies not only to propositional attitudes but also to sensations. Just as it is true that an agent's desires will only dispose him to act in a given way

conditionally on the possession of further beliefs, so too is it true
that a person's sensations – say, of pain – will only dispose him to
act in a given way conditionally on the possession of further
beliefs and desires. This is not surprising given that sensations
and propositional attitudes are causally efficacious both with
regard to one another and with regard to agents' actions. But
then, given that the holism of the mental is a holism characterized by principles of rationality, such principles must constrain
both the ascription of intentional mental types and the ascription
of phenomenal ones. Thus, a person who is experiencing extreme
pain in his hand due to its being in contact with boiling water and
who perceives – and believes – that the water is causally
responsible for that pain ought to withdraw his hand from the
water and is violating a principle of inductive rationality if he
does not. Similarly, a person who prefers the taste of apples to
the taste of pears, the taste of pears to the taste of cherries, and
the taste of cherries to the taste of apples is, at least *prima facie*,
failing to conform to a standard principle of preference
transitivity.

The argument here is not that the essences of sensation types
are not phenomenal, or felt. On the contrary, one of the central
aims of this book is to attempt to accommodate the phenomenal
aspect of sensation types within a physicalist monist theory of the
mental. The point is, rather, that the ascription of sensation
properties to persons, given that the mental domain is in fact
holistic, is constrained by principles of rationality. This means
that the basis upon which attributions of sensation (as well as
intentional mental) properties to persons are typically made must
answer to rationality constraints. Thus, even though it may be
true that no sensation type is such that its possession by a person
must dispose her to act in one way or another, any intentional
behaviour which she is disposed to engage in must answer to
rationality constraints. Such constraints will prohibit the formulation of any lawlike empirical correlation or causal generalizations
between sensation types and physical ones based on intentional
behaviour and introspective reports for just the reasons cited in
Chapter One against type-type identities between intentional
mental and physical properties.

This strategy is appealing because it makes use of resources
already available in the argument for PAM *vis-à-vis* the

propositional attitudes, plus the claim that there is causal interaction between sensations and propositional attitudes as well as between these and agents' actions. But it too has its problems. If the holism of the mental is only contingently true of persons, then we must presume that sensation properties might be possessed by creatures who lacked intentional mental ones entirely. In that case, the attribution of sensation properties would not be constrained by principles of rationality. But this implies that sensation types, unlike intentional ones, are not *intrinsically* rational. And this in turn implies that, in the case of persons, constraints having to do with rational consistency and coherence, if they do apply to the ascription of sensation properties, only do so because it is contingently the case that (*a*) persons have attitudes as well as sensations, (*b*) sensations causally interact with intentional mental phenomena, and (*c*) mental phenomena operate holistically.

This seems right. Sensations do not appear to be intrinsically, let alone essentially, rational. But then this is quite consistent with the view, already endorsed, that sensation properties are essentially phenomenal. What more they may be they are contingently upon the existence of intentional mental and phenomenal properties, causal interaction between intentional and phenomenal mental events, and the holism of the mental. Nevertheless, contingent though these may be, they suffice to prohibit lawlike associations between sensation and physical types.

Chapter Five

Non-reductive monism has suffered from two major objections. First, there is the charge that it leads either to inconsistency or to epiphenomenalism (call this the epiphenomenalist objection). Second, there is the charge that it requires a conception of events which is both false and incompatible with monism (call this the mereology objection). Both focus on the alleged compatibility, given monism, of (i) the Principle of Causal Interaction (PCI) with (ii) the Principle of the Nomological Character of Causality (PNCC) and (iii) the Psychophysical and Psychological Causal Anomalism of the Mental (PAM). Neither takes issue with (i). Our concern in this chapter will be to address these two objections.

The first objection queries the compatibility of (ii) and (iii) with (i). The claim is that not both can be compatible with (i) given monism, for (i) – (iii) together entail epiphenomenalism.[1] Any attempt to avoid epiphenomenalism by giving up (iii), however, purchases monism at the price of psychophysical and psychological causal anomalism. Significantly, proponents of this type of objection typically make no attempt to query whether (ii) might be given up by the non-reductive monist, and with what effect (a question that will be taken up when we consider the mereology objection). Evidently, they endorse both (i) *and* (ii), querying instead the compatibility of (iii) with these and monism taken together.

The second objection, unlike the first, endorses (iii) along with (i). What it queries is the compatibility of monism with (i) and (iii), on the one hand, and with (ii) on the other.[2] Specifically, it queries a certain mereological conception of events which, it is claimed, non-reductive monism requires. This conception is required by the position's commitment to (ii). But, it is argued, the conception is false; and any identity theory based upon it is therefore also false unless a special reason can be given for thinking that that conception holds for just those physical events which are mental events. The upshot of the objection is that the monist part of non-reductive monism is compromised by its commitment to (ii), which is false unless it can be grounded independently of the mereological conception of events it requires. This latter is false for reasons which have their source in (iii). So the truth of (ii) is dubious for reasons which ultimately stem from (iii).

Despite their differences, these two objections have a point of connection which will require extended discussion in the following pages. This has to do with the relationship between causality and nomologicality – specifically, with the PNCC. Both locate the trouble with non-reductive monism here. The first objection endorses the connection between causality and nomologicality (what many refer to as the 'broadly Humean' conception of causality) embodied in the PNCC, and for this reason finds fault with the attempt by the non-reductive monist to endorse both (iii) and monism. The second rejects that connection for reasons which ultimately have their source in (iii), and therefore finds fault with the non-reductive monist's attempt to endorse both (ii) and monism. Since so much seems to hang on (ii), the obvious place to begin discussion of both objections is with it.

1. The PNCC: What Does It Entail?

Baldly stated, the PNCC asserts that any two events related as cause and effect are covered by a (causal) law, where by 'law' is meant a strict, i.e., homonomic, deterministic generalization (see Chapter Three, Section 2). Though there are difficulties associated with this conception of a law, they are not central to issues at hand here and will play no part in the discussion to follow. What is central is that the PNCC itself entails no claim concerning the precise conditions under which events related as cause and effect instantiate laws. It thus requires no more than that such events have at least one description under which they instantiate a law; not that they must instantiate a law under any or all of their descriptions. Laws, even if they aren't linguistic entities, are typically individuated in part at least by the terms which are used in their expression. The PNCC does not require that every description of events related as cause and effect entail a law, for many descriptions will fail to use terms by which the relevant law subsuming them is expressed.

More relevant still is the 'broadly Humean', or regularity, conception of causality presumed to be embodied in the principle. A regularity conception of causality can be taken as involving both the claim that causality is present in the singular case by virtue of being an instance of a lawful generalization governing events of the same types and the claim that laws are mere universal generalizations expressing regularities – i.e., systematic coincidences – in the behaviour of events.[3] The PNCC requires that for any two events to be causally related, they must have descriptions which instantiate a law. Does the PNCC then embody a regularity conception of causality? Certainly it embodies the first claim. It is less clear whether it embodies the second. One might think that, for all it says, laws could be (expressions of) contingent necessitations between pairs of properties.[4] We shall take it that the PNCC embodies a regularity conception of causality to the extent that it embodies the first claim. That conception evidently also entails a generalist conception of causality, which requires that for causality to be present in a single instance is for events thus causally related to be instances of a generalization relating types of events.[5]

Now, the PNCC may embody a regularity conception of causality; but, in the form in which it is put to use by the non-reductive monist, it does not license the claim that pairs of events under any and every description entail laws. If this latter claim were true, *non-reductive* monism would collapse, since any event mentally described would entail a law covering that event under that description. To see this is to see that laws relate pairs of events under certain of their descriptions (or with respect to certain of their properties) only. This caveat is the main source of the first objection to non-reductive monism mentioned earlier.

2. *Mental Causation and the Epiphenomenalist Charge*

Central to the argument for non-reductive monism is the view that whereas the causal relation is extensional, nomologicality is not. Thus, if *a* and *b* are causally related events, they are so no matter how they are described. But the modification required in the reading of the PNCC for it to be compatible with PAM has the consequence that any causal law under which *a* and *b* may be subsumed is a law at least in part because of the terms or descriptions embedded in it. It is this that ensures that not just any descriptions of pairs of events causally related entail laws. According to the epiphenomenalist objection, decomposing events causally related will reveal that some but not all of their properties are causally relevant. Thus, if mental and physical events do interact, they must do so in virtue of certain but not all of their properties. Given the PNCC and its consequence that there are no causal relations where there are no corresponding laws, these properties, the 'causally relevant' ones, are the prime candidates for properties that might figure in laws linking such events. The PNCC ought, in the light of this, to be amended to read 'The Principle of the Nomological Character of Causally Relevant Properties' (PNCCR).[6]

The objection is that the PNCCR is required by any reasonable account of causation, but that this understanding of the relation between causality and laws causes trouble for non-reductive monism. For the question arises – in virtue of which properties does a mental event causally interact with a physical event? If the reply is, 'the mental ones', the denial of psychophysical and psychological causal anomalism (PAM) would appear to follow, as it is expressions referring to these properties which would appear in the laws linking the events causally related. (This is the charge of inconsistency.) If, on the other hand, the reply is, 'the physical ones', then the 'mentality' of any given event would appear to cease being relevant to its interactions with other events, and epiphenomenalism – the view that mental phenomena are causally inefficacious – would seem to follow.

Given the non-reductive monist's clear commitment to PAM and thus to the restricted reading of the PNCC, we can assume here that the first reply is not a serious option for any proponent

of that position. The question is, then, whether the charge of
epiphenomenalism can be countered. The charge is that mental
properties, since they cannot figure in causal laws, cannot be
causally relevant to any mental event's interactions with any
other event. But the phrase 'causally relevant' in fact covers two
quite distinct aspects of the epiphenomenalist objection, corresponding to two quite distinct functions that the PNCCR accords
to causal laws *vis-à-vis* the phenomena they subsume. The first
has to do with the relation between causality and laws, and the
question of whether any pair of events can be causally related
without the backing of a causal law (the emphasis here is on the
'causally' in 'causally relevant'). This is an issue having to do with
the nature of causality. The second has to do with the
explanatory function served by causal laws, i.e., with a supposed
link between causal efficacy and genuine explanatory value. This
is an issue having to do with the nature of causal explanation. To
conflate the two is to obscure the distinction, crucial to non-
reductive monism, between the causal relation, on the one hand,
which holds between events in extension, and causal explanation
and nomologicality, on the other, both of which, if they relate
events at all, relate them under certain of their descriptions only
(i.e., in virtue of certain but not all of their properties). Short of
begging the question against the non-reductive monist, these two
aspects of the epiphenomenalist objection must be kept separate.
We address the issue of the supposed causal inefficacy of the
mental in this section, and the issue of the link between causal
efficacy and the explanatory value of mentalistic explanations in
the next.

Suppose that the relation between causality and laws is as the
PNCCR depicts it, i.e., that events related as cause and effect
have descriptions which instantiate a law – one subsuming those
events in virtue of certain of their properties only. Still,
psychophysical and psychological causal anomalism of the mental
(PAM) leads to the inefficacy of the mental only with further
argument. Moreover, such argument, to be effective, requires
dualist assumptions. What has been overlooked by the proponent
of the epiphenomenalist objection is the crucial distinction
between a property and its instance. The non-reductive monist
construes causality as a relation between particular (token)
events. Thus construed, it is instancings of properties associated

with event types which are causally efficacious, and the PNCCR itself should be amended to read 'The Principle of the Nomological Character of Causally Relevant Instances of Properties'. Read in this way, the PNCCR provides no support for the epiphenomenalist objection. An example here may help to illustrate why.

Associated with any event type, such as 'shooting', is a property, such as that of being a shooting. This property will be instanced by any event which is (i.e., is identical with) a token of that type. Indeed, the sense in which any token event 'has' such a property consists in the fact that it instances that property. Thus, for example, John's shooting of Joe at 12:00 p.m. on Sunday 23 November 1988, is (identical with) a token of the type 'shoots', and that event has the property of being a shooting in virtue of instancing it. (See Chapter Four for the distinction between properties whose instancings are (i.e., are identical with) events and properties instanced *by* events.)

Suppose now that a given mental event – say, Susan's desiring a drink – causes a physical event of Susan's body – say, a moving of her arm. Then it will be true that an event which is an instancing (but is not identical with that instancing; see above) of the property, being a desiring for a drink (perhaps among others) is causally related to an event which is an instancing of the property 'being a moving of Susan's arm'. But surely any event may be an instancing of more than one property. That is, different properties may share a *single* instance. Susan's desiring a drink, for example, may not only be an instancing of the property 'being a desiring for a drink'; it may be an instancing of the *distinct* property 'being a desiring for some water'. John's shooting of Joe is an instancing of the property 'being a shooting'; but it may well also be an instancing of the property 'being a moving of a finger' and of the property 'being a pulling of a trigger'.

The PNCCR requires that events bearing causal relations to one another be instances of the properties referred to by expressions occurring in causal laws. It does not require that *every* property instanced by an event does so: indeed, the amendment of the PNCC to read 'causally relevant properties' is in part intended to bring this point out. The PCI requires that events that are causally related be so because of certain of their properties; and thus, that if any event which is an instancing of the property 'being a desiring for a drink' (in virtue of being identical with a token of the type 'desires a drink'), causes one which is an instancing of the property 'being a moving of an arm', it must do so in virtue of certain of its properties. But 'property' here is ambiguous between properties and their instances. Since any event can have two or more distinct properties by instancing them, it may well be the case that one and the same event instances both the property 'being a desiring for a drink' *and* another, physical, property – say 'being a brain event α' – where instancing the former just is instancing the latter. That is to say, the different properties are co-instantiated; they share, in this particular event, the same instance. Their difference at the property level is ensured by the two properties not being always co-instantiated. Now, the instancing by an event of the (mental) property, 'being a desiring for a drink', will satisfy the PNCCR, amended to read '. . . Causally Relevant Instances of Properties'. The instance is causally relevant because it is covered by a law.

In what sense does the 'mentality' of any such mental event cease to be causally efficacious? In the sense that mental properties, like that of being a desiring for a drink, fail to figure in laws linking the mental with the physical? But this is simply to ignore the point that causality is a relation between individual token events, and thus that it is the instancings of certain properties by events which do or do not link them causally with others. And an event's instancing of a mental property may well be causally efficacious. Indeed, if an instancing of a mental property by an event just *is* an instancing by it of a physical one, then, despite the distinctness of the properties themselves, the non-reductive monist is right to insist that the former can be both causally efficacious and an instancing of a property that is capable of figuring in causal laws. To insist otherwise is tantamount to insisting that no instancing of a mental property can be (i.e., can be identical with) an instancing of a physical one. And it is not clear that this is anything more than a dualist prejudice.

Now this response may fail to convince. One reason, perhaps, might lie in a tendency to suppose that in order for a mental property to be causally efficacious, any instancing of it by an event must be distinct from any instancing by it of a physical property. Thus, if every mental event is a physical event, then the causal efficacy of any event *qua* mental would appear to require that it both instance a mental property *and* instance a physical property, where these instancings are distinct.

But why should we presume that this must be so? Suppose that mental properties of events supervene on physical ones in roughly the sense that if any two objects (organisms) are indiscernible with respect to the latter, they cannot diverge in the former (an issue treated at length in Chapter Six). Then it is reasonable to suppose that although mental properties of events fail to correlate systematically with any single physical property of any event (let alone in any lawlike way), they may correlate with a disjunction (perhaps an infinite one) of such properties. This encourages the following thought. Many physical properties, like that of being coloured, or being an animal, are plainly distinct from the many determinate forms which they may take (such as being red, or being a tiger), since possession of a more determinate property (e.g., that of being red) by an object entails possession of the more determinable one (e.g., being coloured), but not vice versa. No one would suppose, however, that an object's exemplifying of a colour – say, red – requires, first, that it be an instancing of the property of being red, and second, that it be a (distinct) instancing of a second, related property, viz. that of being coloured. To be an exemplifying of the former just is, in this case, to be an exemplifying of the latter, despite the distinctness of the properties themselves. Does this mean that colour is causally inefficacious? Of course not; for any causally efficacious case in which a more determinate form of that property is exemplified is a case in which the exemplifying of colour *itself* is efficacious, by the extensionality of the causal relation (think, e.g., of the property of having weight and that of weighing 2.3 kg).

Similarly, it may be argued, mental properties of events correlate in a one-many way with physical properties of events (though in no systematic way), with the consequence that any instancing of the former is an instancing of one or another of some more determinate physical property. Just as to exemplify redness is to exemplify the property of being coloured, one might say, to instance the property 'being a brain event α', can be to instance the mental property 'being a pain'. Moreover, if an instancing of the former is causally efficacious, then so is the latter. One might be tempted to object that the red/colour case is quite different from the envisaged brain event α/pain case, since in the former but not the latter, possession by an object (organism) of the subvenient (or base) property (red) logically entails possession of the supervenient property (colour). But this, even if true, is beside the present point. Supervenience, as characterized here, is that relation between properties (or between a property and a (distinct) set of properties) such that if any two objects (organisms) are indiscernible with respect to the subvenient ones, they cannot diverge in their possession of the supervenient ones. The reason, or grounds, for the modal 'cannot' may, however, differ from one case to another (again, see Chapter Six for more on this).

To insist in the face of this that an instancing of a mental property by an event must be different from an instancing by it of a physical property is to reveal a dualist prejudice. Short of this, the epiphenomenalist charge misses its intended target even when the PNCC is amended in the required way. What was at stake was the causal efficacy of the mental, where causality is understood as a relation which holds between individual (token) events.[7] However, there is another, slightly different route to the epiphenomenalist conclusion.

3. Causal Relevance and Explanatory Value

The second aspect of the epiphenomenalist objection focuses, not on the question as to the nature of causality, but rather, on the question of whether genuine causal explanations can be given of mental phenomena without invoking mental properties of events ineliminably. Such doubts are expressed by those who claim that denials of epiphenomenalism require 'the intensional explanatory relevance of that feature in virtue of which the objects are supposedly interacting', or 'the conviction that an event as mental is an ineliminable part of any full explanation of action'.[8] Since causal explanations typically invoke properties instanced as well as instancings of properties, the response to the first aspect of the epiphenomenalist objection does not meet this second complaint. The objection here is in fact twofold: first, that mentalistic causal explanations, i.e., explanations which invoke mental properties of events cannot be provided consistently with the argument for non-reductive monism; and second, that even if they could be provided, they would be redundant by the lights of that position and hence ultimately irrelevant. Taken together, these two charges imply that if epiphenomenalism is to be avoided, mental properties of events must figure in an ineliminable way in any genuine explanation of mental phenomena.

Since the second claim effectively queries whether non-reductive monism leads to the reduction of mental to physical properties – an issue considered in connection with supervenience in the next chapter – we will only consider the first claim here. The epiphenomenalist charge is that genuine mentalistic explanation is impossible for the non-reductive monist given PCI, PNCCR, and PAM. Why? Because, it seems, such explanations invoke mental *properties* of events. However, reference to mental properties of events could only conflict with non-reductive monism on the assumption that a certain model of causal explanation alone is correct, viz. one according to which explanations proceed via causal *laws*. On this model (the so-called 'covering law model'), two causally related events – say a and b, will instantiate causal laws under certain (but not all) of their descriptions. These descriptions will typically specify the relevant events in terms of their 'causally relevant' properties. They will also form the antecedent and consequent of a conditional specifying the law under which those events are subsumed. Since the antecedent and consequent of the law covering a and b will contain canonical descriptions of these causally relevant properties – i.e., descriptions of such events in terms of their essences (see Chapter Four for more on this) – explanation is conceived of as proceeding by showing that in any case where the causally relevant property of event a is instanced, one can expect the causally relevant property of b to be instanced.[9]

It would be unreasonable to suppose that the descriptions of a and b which form the antecedent and consequent of a lawlike statement must pick those events out in exactly the same terminology as that which figures in the finished law subsuming them. (No one supposes, for example, that there are laws subsuming such events as brick-throwings and window-shatterings under these descriptions, despite the fact that brick-throwings cause window-shatterings.) On the other hand, the considerations adduced by the non-reductive monist for PAM prohibits supposing that generalizations containing mental terminology could be refined enough even to *approximate* descriptions that might instantiate causal laws governing mental and physical events. If causal explanation could only proceed by way of causal laws, then PAM evidently would prohibit the possibility of giving genuine mentalistic causal explanations.

However, there is, on the face of it, another type of causal explanation, viz. singular causal explanation, which might serve the purposes of the non-reductive monist here. According to this type of explanation, descriptions of the form '*a* caused *b*', where *a* and *b* are singular terms referring to events, are genuine explanations inasmuch as they warrant the conclusion that event *a* explains why event *b* occurred.[10] Obviously, this type of explanation is much weaker than that envisaged by the proponent of the epiphenomenalist objection, since it has no consequences for events other than *a* and *b*. Thus, it could have no predictive power. But it is not obvious why the fact that it is restricted in its generality should show that it is not genuinely explanatory. For singular causal explanation does seem to meet other desiderata of a genuine causal explanation. Specifically, given the effect event described in the explanandum, it does specify its cause. More importantly, it licenses singular counter-factual claims – ones to the effect that if the event referred to in the explanans had not occurred, that referred to in the explanandum would not have occurred. It meets these desiderata because the instancing of the property picked out in the explanans by an event *is* causally efficacious.[11] It is precisely because of this that the counterfactual – that if the event referred to in the explanans had not occurred, then (barring cases of overdetermination) things would not have turned out as they did – is warranted. Any causal explanation – apart, perhaps, from certain probabilistic ones – whether singular or nomological, shares this feature of showing how the actual outcome was to be expected rather than other possible ones.[12] Nomological causal explanation may have ramifications for pairs of events other than those mentioned in the explanans and explanandum; but this in itself is not a decisive reason for refusing to regard singular causal explanation as a genuine form of explanation given that it meets other crucial requirements for something to be a causal explanation.

Perhaps the worry here is not with the lack of predictive power of singular causal explanations but rather with the fact that explanations of this type seem to require justification. It might be thought that this can only be provided *via* regularities concerning other events of the 'causally relevant' types of which *a* and *b* are instances. But in singular causal explanation the only thing that requires justification is the claim that the event mentioned in the explanans caused that mentioned in the explanandum. Such a claim can be justified because it can be tested (here we need only assume that causal relations between individual token events can be perceived); and it can be tested in cases where the explanans contains mental terminology as well as in cases where it does not. If the worry amounts to more than this, it would seem to consist in the doubt as to whether singular causal explanations can be adequate unless one can justify the claim that the event referred to in the explanans really was the *cause* of that mentioned in the explanandum, where this requires reference to causal laws. But this is either to return to the issue of causality, which has already been covered, or to insist that the only legitimate model of causal explanation that there is is nomological. And this is to beg the question against those who think that singular causal explanation is a genuine type of causal explanation.

A worry may nevertheless persist that singular mentalistic causal explanations cannot be genuinely explanatory unless restrictions are placed on the sorts of descriptions that can figure in the explanans and explanandum. This is, of course, quite correct: such descriptions must pick out the events related as cause and effect in terms of properties of events, instancings of which are causally efficacious. Entirely relational or extrinsic descriptions of mental events, such as 'the first thing I thought about this morning' or 'the most unpleasant experience of Susan's life', are thus unlikely to serve any genuine explanatory purpose unless there are other descriptions of such events available in virtue of which we might obtain some insight into the nature of those events. But this is true quite generally: the cause of the explosion in the cellar last night might have been the leak in the boiler; and the leak in the boiler may happen to have been the only leak that the boiler has ever had. But the fact that that leak was the only leak the boiler has ever had does not causally explain the fact that the explosion occurred. This is just to say that the explanation relation, like nomologicality, is non-extensional; and non-extensional whether the explanation concerned is singular or nomological. Just as certain properties but not others are causally relevant to a pair of events' being subsumed under a law, certain descriptions but not others are relevant to a given event's occurrence explaining the occurrence of another. Fortunately, in the case of mental as well as physical phenomena, we typically do have independent access to descriptions which do pick out such events in terms which can serve a genuine explanatory purpose. Given that we do, we can at least sometimes be warranted in the claim that event *a*, mentally described, explains why event *b*, physically described, occurs.

4. The Mereology Objection

The mereology objection, we earlier noted, takes exception to the PNCC for reasons which ultimately have their source in PAM. As stated by Jennifer Hornsby, the charge is that monism (physicalism) in general assumes a mereological conception of events – one which is required by the PNCC but which is false in general and undermined, in the specific case of non-reductive monism, by considerations which favour PAM. If the PNCC could be grounded independently, then we would have a reason for thinking that the mereological conception is true at least for those physical events which are mental events. In the absence of such grounding, however, considerations which favour PAM actually undermine the truth of the mereological conception and hence of the PNCC. And without the PNCC, there is no non-reductive *monism*.[13]

A number of issues are raised by this challenge. First, and perhaps most obviously, there is the question of whether physicalism in general does presume the mereological conception to be true. We shall assume here that certain physicalist doctrines at least do work with that conception (shortly to be specified).[14] Physicalism is sometimes construed as the doctrine that all of the phenomena (event types as well as tokens) described by the various sciences and common sense are physical (fall ultimately within the domain of physics). Thus construed, it is an ontological thesis; but it is often combined with a claim about the explanatory supremacy of physics.[15] A weaker version of this, which is stronger than the (mere) ontological physicalist thesis, asserts the explanatory supremacy of physics without assuming reducibility. This thesis asserts only that all events under their physical descriptions are capable of complete explanations within the terms and vocabulary of physics.[16] It is this third conception of physicalism that is at stake in the mereology objection.

A second issue raised by the objection is whether the conception of events it supposes the physicalist to be committed to *is* false. Hornsby takes any mereological conception, whether of objects or events, to be committed at the very least to the following principle:

(A) $(x)(y)(\exists!z)(z$ is a fusion of x and $y)$

which has two components:

(E) $(x)(y)(\exists z)(z$ is a fusion of x and $y)$
(U) $(x)(y)(z)(w)[(z$ is a fusion of x and $y)$ & w is a fusion of x and $y \rightarrow (w = z)]$.

Whereas (E) asserts the existence of fusions, i.e., it asserts that, for any two (or more) events, there is an event that is the mereological sum of them, (U) asserts their uniqueness.[17] The objection to (A) as it applies to events focuses on (E). The claim is that (E) is false because it is in the nature of events to cause and be caused, and this cannot be accounted for by a barely spatiotemporal ideology. A mereological conception of events would need to invoke some principle by means of which the causal properties of event fusions can be fixed or determined by the causal properties of their parts, such as

(C) IF {event c causes event e AND $f = c + d$ AND [NEITHER d occurs later than e NOR d and e have common parts NOR part of e causes part of d]}

THEN f causes e.[18]

But (C) seems absurd, both on a counterfactual account of

causation and on a regularity account. Its consequences for the regularity account are of particular importance for non-reductive monism.

Any regularity theorist (hence anyone committed to the truth of the PNCC) will be committed to the view that what distinguishes causally related pairs of events from others is that they instantiate a law (or lawlike generalization). But (C) will license absurdly *ad hoc* generalizations as lawlike. Suppose, for instance, that under some descriptions, this brick-throwing and this window-shattering instantiate a lawlike regularity. Then (C) will license a regularity governing, say, the fusion of this brick-throwing and Kennedy's assassination, on the one hand, and this window-shattering, on the other. (A), which licenses the introduction of such fusions, thus seems incompatible with any regularity account of causation, since no regularity theorist is likely to think that there is any lawlike regularity holding between fusions of events like brick-throwings and assassinations, on the one hand, and window-shatterings, on the other.

Even if we restrict our attention to cases of physical events, then, it seems clear that no reasonable account of causation will count every event fusion as itself an event. Evidently, the mereological conception of events is false in general. But now any physicalist wishing to make use of that conception must ground it independently. Non-reductive monism would seem to provide a reason, independent of the mereological conception, for thinking that token mental events are physical events, based on the PCI, the PNCC, and PAM. So one might think that it could provide the independent motivation for the mereological conception. Notice, however, that PAM is grounded in the belief that there is an irreconcilable ideological difference between physical and mental event ontologies. Indeed, all but the most extreme versions of physicalism suppose a single ontology to underlie rival ideologies. The ideologies – conceptual frameworks – associated with the mental and physical domains are notoriously different. Given these differences, there is a real question as to whether the entities associated with the one ideology are the same as those associated with the other. Crucially, it is questionable whether the identity conditions for mental phenomena can be fixed in terms of purely physical and topic-neutral vocabulary, as the mereological conception requires. If the argument for non-reductive monism is to work *for* identity rather than against it, then it would seem that the PNCC must do the work that the mereological conception of events was thought to do.

The trouble is that the kinds of physical events concerning which the PNCC is most plausible quite apart from the issue of physicalism are not macrophysical ones like avalanches and car crashes, but microphysical ones. If it is true that this avalanche caused the death of the mayor of the town, for instance, then one can suppose a lawlike generalization to subsume these events only in so far as *other* lawlike generalizations subsume events of which avalanches and deaths are comprised. If this is to be countenanced along with token identities, fusions evidently must be countenanced. And if that is so, then non-reductive monism is in no better a position *vis-à-vis* the mereological conception than any other physicalist view – unless, that is, the PNCC can be independently grounded.

The case is evidently worse; for if non-reductive monism does require the mereological conception, the position is actually inconsistent. This is because the PNCC presumes an account of causality that is incompatible with principle (A). No regularity theorist is likely to license nomological generalizations covering any event fusion whatsoever. But (A) fails to discriminate between those event fusions which we might wish to countenance as genuine events and concerning which we may wish to countenance laws and those that we do not consider to be genuine events (e.g., the fusion of this brick-throwing and Kennedy's assassination). Anyone committed, as the non-reductive monist is, to the PNCC, is thus forced to reject (A) on pain of recognising absurdly *ad hoc* generalizations as nomological. (This issue is independent of the truth of physicalism.)

Assuming that physicalism in general does presume a mereological conception of events and that that conception is false, the mereology objection raises a number of important issues to which the non-reductive monist must respond. First, there is the issue of whether the PNCC does require the mereological conception of events. Second, there is the issue of whether, supposing that it does, it can be independently grounded. Finally, supposing that it cannot, there is the issue of whether non-reductive monism might survive the loss of the PNCC. We deal with these issues in turn.

5. *The PNCC: Does It Require the Mereological Conception?*

From the point of view of the mereology objection, this is really the crucial issue. In fact, there is a more general issue at stake here, viz. whether *any* physicalist view requires the mereological conception of events. The reasoning behind the mereology objection appears to be that because the events with which scientists deal are typically conceived of as microphysical, it is these that causal laws are most plausibly viewed as covering. Inasmuch as mental phenomena are conceived of as macroscopic, they cannot be identified with such microphysical events but must rather be identified with fusions of microphysical events with which the macrophysical ones are to be identified. If *identity* is to be countenanced, such fusions must themselves be single events. However, if it can be shown that the PNCC at least does not require a mereological conception of events, then non-reductive monism will provide one counterexample to the general claim that any physicalism requires a mereological conception of events.

The PNCC says that where events are related as cause and effect, there are causal laws subsuming those events under some of their descriptions. If we think of such events as avalanches and brick-throwings, it is natural to assume that the PNCC could only be true for them if we suppose that they are identical with fusions of events which are themselves instances of properties covered by laws. But must we assume this? Is it not possible to take a more neutral stand here, maintaining that events like brick-throwings and avalanches are related in some way to microphysical events which are themselves subsumed by causal laws and from which macrophysical events may or may *not* be distinct? Can we not, in short, do *away* with fusions, yet insist on the *bona fide* existence of both events such as brick-throwings and avalanches *and* the microphysical events to which they are related? Nothing in the PNCC seems to require fusions in addition to events of these other two sorts.

If we do, we must find some other way of explaining how it is that events like avalanches and brick-throwings can have descriptions under which they instantiate laws. One suggestion is that events like avalanches are related to their microphysical parts by some kind of composition relation distinct from identity, in which case such descriptions would seem to be available in the form 'the event composed of $[x_1,\phi_1,t_1]$, $[x_2,\phi_2,t_2]$, . . ., $[x_n,\phi_n,t_v]$', or 'the event composed of $[x,\phi,t_1]$, $[x,\psi,t_2]$, . . .,$[x,\chi,t_n]$', where expressions of the form '$[x,\phi,t]$' are canonical descriptions of the those events' microscopic parts. Any case in which a complex event with parts (e.g., an avalanche) causes another (e.g., a death) will be a case where a description of the cause in terms of its so-called 'compositional parts' exists (see Chapter Four). There is no obvious reason to suppose that the 'parts' of complex events mentioned in such descriptions do not themselves have descriptions under which they instantiate laws (indeed, canonical descriptions seem to be the prime candidates for such descriptions).

Opponents are likely to object to this by saying that if macrophysical events like avalanches are viewed as *distinct* from those microphysical events which are their parts and there are no fusions, then though their *parts* will be covered by laws, *they* won't be. But this depends on how one views the relation between macrophysical and microphysical events. One major reason for holding that the former are distinct from the latter is that they instance causally efficacious properties that are distinct from the properties that the latter instance. Indeed, it is this more than anything else that causes trouble for the mereological conception of events. However, laws relate events in terms of their properties. In particular, they relate events of certain *types* in virtue of those events instancing properties of certain types. We may have good reasons for thinking that event *types* like the type 'being an avalanche' have associated with them certain properties distinct from any of the properties associated with event types which their so-called 'parts' instance, i.e., that the properties associated with macrophysical and microphysical event types are distinct. But this only leads to the conclusion that *tokens* of macrophysical event types are not covered by laws if one assumes that the *instancings* by events of those very properties which make for the distinctness of avalanches from their 'parts' (e.g., the property of being an avalanche) are *themselves* distinct from instancings of the properties associated with such events' parts which do figure in laws. And there is no obvious reason why we should assume this, particularly if we suppose that macrophysical properties of events supervene on microphysical ones.

This response might seem to require commitment to the view that macrophysical and microphysical events are not distinct from one another (and so, by implication, to the mereological conception of events), since events just are instancings of event properties at times in objects. But it does not. For one thing, events are not (identical with) instancings of event properties. They are identical with instancings of dynamic properties of physical *objects*; and they have event properties by instancing them. Even if we consider those properties of events which are their essences (where these are determined by their canonical descriptions), it is not obvious that the response requires commitment to the view that macrophysical and microphysical events are not distinct, since events can have more than one canonical description and so more than one such essence. A macrophysical event's co-instancing of *one* such essence with a microphysical event (thereby ensuring that it is subsumed by a law), for example, seems to be compatible with its instancing other properties which are also its essences, where these latter are *not* shared by any microphysical event. Thus, even when the properties involved are essences, the fact that any event may have more than one essence prohibits assuming without argument that event identity follows from the fact that a macrophysical and a microphysical property may have a single instance. The case is especially clear if one considers Kim's version of the property-exemplification account of events. Since event identity requires the identity of properties constitutive of events and macro-physical and microphysical properties of objects *are* (we presume) distinct, even if one assumes that events have only *one* essence, event identity does not follow from the fact that a macrophysical event may co-instance a macrophysical and a microphysical property (just as, for example, the identity between the event of my pen's changing colour at time *t* and the event of my pen's changing from red to blue at time *t* does not follow from the fact that the property of being a changing of colour and the property of being a changing from red to blue may be co-instanced by the former event, i.e., instancing the latter property just *is* instancing the former).

Hence, it is not the distinction between macrophysical and microphysical events that is of crucial importance to the issue of whether the PNCC might be independent of a mereological conception of events. Rather, it is the distinction between macrophysical and microphysical event *types* and the properties whose instancings by events ensure that they are of those types, on the one hand, and macrophysical and microphysical token events which instance the properties by virtue of which those events fall into the types they do, on the other. Failure to appreciate this distinction is the source of many misguided attacks on event-identity theories in general and on psycho-physical event-identity theories in particular. It is, as we have seen, at least one main source of the epiphenomenalist objection. But it is this distinction that contains the resources by which to defend the claim that the PNCC is independent of a mereological conception of events.

In short, the PNCC requires the mereological conception only if it requires, in addition to macroscopic events (tokens), mental or physical, and microscopic events, fusions of microscopic events with which the macroscopic ones can be identified. This it does not appear to do. One might think that it must because otherwise events would be countenanced which, while having 'parts' covered by laws, would not *themselves* be covered by law. But this is so only if we assume that the properties in virtue of which macroscopic event types are distinct from microphysical event types are ones whose instancings by events (*a*) are causally efficacious, *and* (*b*) are *not* of properties that figure in laws. But to assume (*b*) is to assume that every case where properties are distinct is a case where all *instancings* of those properties must also be distinct. As discussion of the epiphenomenalist objection showed, this claim is unfounded. Moreover, it seems false in general: the relation between at least some determinate proper-ties, like that of being red or that of being a thinking of Vienna, and determinables under which they fall, like that of being coloured or that of being a thinking, is such that an object's or an event's instancing the latter type of property just is its instancing the former type of property.

The presumption that the PNCC requires a mereological conception of events seems to be based on the thoughts that (*i*) in order for it to be true it must cover all events, and (*ii*) the only conception of the relation between macrophysical and micro-physical events which will ensure this is a part-whole one. However, (*ii*) is suspect: given the conception of events at work here, the foregoing discussion suggests that it is much more plausible to construe the relation between such events and their associated types as a property-instantiation one. On this conception, distinct event types may be related in virtue of their associated properties being co-instanced. This much the PNCC evidently does require. But because the relation between properties and their instancings is not, or not obviously, a part-whole one, a property-instantiation conception of the relation between macrophysical and microphysical events is silent on the issue of how *many* microphysical events may constitute a given macrophysical event. If we view macrophysical events as related to microphysical ones by way of co-instancing certain (though perhaps not all) of their properties, then the temptation to 'add up' events by 'adding up' instancings of properties does not exist. Nor, for that reason, does the temptation to think that one must generate causal descriptions, hence explanations, of macrophysical events from causal descriptions of microphysical ones.

So, even if we assume that macrophysical events are distinct from, but bear some kind of composition relation to, microphysical ones, still it would not follow without further argument that macrophysical events cannot be subsumed by causal laws governing microphysical events. In fact, it is questionable whether the notion of event composition, if at work at all here, is anything like the notion of composition at work *vis-à-vis* continuants and their parts. In the case of continuants, we know that there cannot be two parts in exactly the same spatiotemporal region, for the parts of a continuant exclude one another. But on a property-instantiation conception of the relation between macrophysical and microphysical events, events of distinct event types may or may not co-instance distinct event properties: nothing in the notion of an event requires that the occurrence of an event of one type at a given time and place precludes the occurrence of another event of a distinct type occurring in exactly the same spatiotemporal region. The case is further complicated by the fact that, since events themselves may have more than one canonical description and, correspondingly, more than one essence, nothing in the property-instantiation conception itself can determine, in general, what counts as a single event. Cases where an event instances a more determinate form of a determinable property (e.g., being a desiring for a drink of water, and being a desiring for a drink) will presumably be ones where distinct properties may be co-instanced by a single event. But there are clear cases where distinct properties make for distinct instancings by distinct events (think of the property of being a shrinking and that of being an expanding). The property-instantiation conception of the relation between macrophysical and microphysical events is silent on the question of what counts as a single event precisely because distinct properties *can* be co-instanced. Thus, while we may have an idea in the case of continuants of how we can 'add up' parts (though this too is arguable), we have no such idea of how we are to 'add up' property instances in the case of events. Inasmuch as we do not, we have no better *a priori* idea in the case of microphysical events as to what counts as a single event than we do in the case of macrophysical ones. Our grip on event individuation in both cases is thrown back on the ideologies (and the properties invoked by them) by which we describe and explain such events. But ideological differences alone are not decisive in the case for *or* against event identity when this is seen to concern, not properties, but their instancings.

Nevertheless, there is a residual worry lurking here. One might doubt whether grounds can be given for thinking that, in cases *other* than ones where properties either logically entail one another or are necessarily coextensive, distinct properties *can* be co-instanced, i.e., have a single instance. Such doubt may be grounded in the belief that the mereological conception of *continuants* is false, i.e., in the belief that macrophysical objects, e.g., biological organisms, though constituted by parts which are microphysical, are distinct from such parts because their continued identity can survive complete replacement of parts. If the PNCC requires that macrophysical events be covered by law in virtue of the fact that microphysical events, in instancing microphysical event properties, instance macrophysical ones, then does it not require, if not a mereological conception of *events*, at least a mereological conception of continuants? For if macrophysical and microphysical events are ones whose subjects are, respectively, macrophysical and microphysical objects, and if these subjects are distinct, does it not follow that events which are (identical with) instancings of macrophysical and microphysical properties of such objects are also distinct? And if this is so, then does it not also follow that any instancing by a macro-physical event of a macrophysical event property must itself be distinct from any instancing by a microphysical event of a micro-physical event property?

This depends on whether distinct subjects must make for distinct events – a question that was discussed at length (in Chapter Four, Sections 4 and 5) both in connection with the supposition that persons must be the minimal subjects of mental events and in connection with the supposition that continuants like ships must be the minimal subjects of events like their sinkings. In both cases it was pointed out that distinctness of events only follows from distinctness of subjects when such subjects are minimal ones. In the case of persons, it was argued that the relevant supposition is unfounded in so far as it requires assuming, in cases where an object, x, ϕs, and does so because another object, y, changes, both that x's ϕing is y's changing and that y's changing is y's ϕing (for both of these assumptions are false). In the case of macrophysical objects like the Ship of Theseus, it was maintained that the relevant supposition is correct in so far as (*a*) ships are the minimal subjects of events which are their sinkings, and (*b*) objects like ships are distinct from their compositional parts.

One might think that because the conclusion in this latter case was that the event which is the sinking of the Ship of Theseus is distinct from the sinkings of its parts (because the ship is distinct from its parts), the PNCC's requirement that macrophysical events be covered by law in virtue of the fact that microphysical events, in instancing microphysical event properties, instance macrophysical ones, can only be met if a mereological conception of continuants is presumed to be true. However, the conclusion that the sinking of the ship is an event distinct from the sinkings of its parts was not derived from the conjunction of (*a*) and (*b*) alone. What prompted it was, rather, that given both (*a*) and (*b*), it is difficult to see that there could be another *single* subject at *all* apart from the ship which could serve as a subject (let alone a minimal one) of the single event which is that sinking. The temptation to think that the sinking of the ship has more than one subject has its source in the thought that, since the sinking of the ship just is the sinkings of its parts, the sinkings of the parts must themselves constitute a single sinking (i.e., that fusions of events like sinkings must themselves be single events of the same type). And the subject of this, given (*b*), would have to be distinct from the ship. But of course there is no motivation here for the mereological conception of events. Nor, as a result, is there any motivation for the mereological conception of objects which are their subjects. On the assumption that the parts are distinct from one another, the sinkings of the several parts of the ship are not a single sinking.

Several remarks about this rationale for distinguishing events like the sinking of the Ship of Theseus from the sinkings of its parts are in order. First, the difficulty it seeks to resolve, viz. how a single event can have more than one minimal subject, is *not* a case where distinct properties are envisaged as being co-instanced, and so is not a case of the kind that might support the worry here being considered. Indeed, it is the fact that the property instanced in the case of the ship's sinking and its parts sinking is the *same* that gives rise to the supposition that there is a single event of the sort that might require distinct minimal subjects (viz. the sinking of the ship = the fusion of the sinkings of its parts). It is because the temptation to say that the sinking of the ship just is the sinkings of its parts is so great that the question of whether a single event can have more than one minimal subject arises in the first place. In cases where the properties whose instancings by events are distinct, there is no such similar temptation to identify the events themselves. The difficulty of seeing how distinct properties can be co-instanced in a single event (or indeed, in distinct events) remains; but this is not the problem of how the same event can have distinct minimal subjects.

One point that is not at issue either here or in the earlier discussion of events like the sinking of the Ship of Theseus is that a single event can have more than one subject. A second remark worth making about the above rationale, therefore, is that it takes an extreme line in response to the question of the relation between events like the sinking of the Ship of Theseus and the sinkings of its parts. In distinguishing such events from one another, it in fact eliminates the problem (in this case at least) of how macrophysical and microphysical properties can be co-instanced. The rationale effectively rejects the mereological conception of events embodied in the suggestion that the sinking of the ship is identical with the sinkings of its parts. In rejecting it, however, it undermines the only clear reason one might have for thinking that a single event might have more than one subject. Macrophysical and microphysical properties cannot be co-instanced in the case of the sinking of the Ship of Theseus because, in so far as the parts of that ship are distinct from one another, their sinkings are not a sinking. In short, the rationale rejects both the mereological conception of events *and* the mereological conception of continuants. On this basis it distinguishes between sinkings of ships and sinkings of their parts.

However, a less radical line might be taken. This would be to say that although the ship and its parts are indeed distinct from one another (i.e., the mereological conception of continuants is false) and though the sinkings of the parts are not a single sinking (i.e., the mereological conception of events is also false), since the actual parts (as well as any possible ones) involved in the actual sinking must occupy the same spatiotemporal region as the ship, the ship's instancing the property 'sinks' just is its parts instancing the property 'sinks'. This only leads to conflict if we also suppose that the parts of the ship are also minimal subjects of that event. Any event can have more than one subject; what it cannot have is more than one minimal subject. In the case of the ship's sinking and its parts' sinking, the parts only qualify as subjects at all because they are parts of that ship. It is the ship, therefore, that is the minimal subject of the event which is the *ship's* sinking.

This strategy clearly does not require a mereological conception of continuants. It is less clear, however, whether it requires a mereological conception of events. The suggestion is that, though the ship and its parts are distinct from one another, and though the ship is the minimal subject of the event which is its sinking, the sinking of the ship just is the sinking of its parts, where this latter event is not an event fusion. Now, this cannot mean that the sinkings of the ship's parts *is* a *single* instancing by multiple subjects of the property 'sinks'. Since the ship's parts are distinct from one another, any instancing of the property 'sinks' by one part must be distinct from any instancing of that property by any other part (distinct minimal subjects make for distinct events). What it must mean, rather, is that the instancings by each of the ship's parts of the property 'sinks' just is the instancing of the property 'sinks' by the ship (in a sense to be elaborated upon shortly).

Is it possible to hold this without endorsing a mereological conception of events? Arguably so, for reasons connected with the fact that a single event may have more than one subject. It was pointed out above that the parts of the ship are only thought to qualify as subjects at all of the event which is the sinking of the ship because they are parts of that ship. Since the ship is distinct from its parts, no fusion of sinkings of that ship's *parts* can be an event whose subject is the ship if the minimal subjects of those sinkings are the ship's *parts*. Viewed in this way, it is indeed difficult to see how the sinkings of the parts could be the sinking of the ship. On the other hand, it seems clear that nothing further has to happen for the ship to sink than that all of its parts sink. It is also clear that the sinking of the ship occupies all and only the portions of space and takes exactly the same amount of time as the sinkings of all of its parts.

This encourages the thought that the ship's instancing the property 'sinks' just is its parts instancing the property 'sinks', i.e., that each of the ship's parts, in instancing the property 'sinks' (a property possessed by each part), instances the property 'sinks' (a property possessed by the ship). One way of justifying the claim that the parts' sinking is a single event without recourse to the mereological conception of events is to maintain that the issue of how many events there are in a given spatiotemporal region depends on the issue of what their *minimal* subjects are. Given that the ship is the minimal subject of the event which is its sinking, we have reasons other than the mereological conception of events for thinking that, despite the fact that the ship is composed of parts distinct from one another and from it, the sinking of the ship just is the sinking of its parts (an event not to be confused with the several sinkings of those parts). We might put this by saying that each event which is a sinking of one of the ship's parts is a single instancing of two, distinct properties: first, an instancing of the property of being a sinking of a part of the ship (where the minimal subject of this event is that part), and, second, along with all the events which are the individual sinkings of the remaining parts of the ship, an instancing of the property 'being a sinking of the ship' (where the ship is the minimal subject of this single, but complex, event). That is to say, just as no event which is a sinking of a part of the ship is a sinking of the ship (these having distinct minimal subjects), no event which is a fusion of sinkings of parts of the ship is a sinking of the ship. Despite this, however, the sinkings of the ship's parts might nevertheless count as a single event because the ship whose parts are the subjects of the sinkings of the *parts* is the minimal subject of the event which is the sinking of the *ship* (cf. Chapter Four, Section 5).

Irrespective of whether this last point is correct, it is clear that the supposition that macrophysical and microphysical properties of events might be co-instanced does not obviously require a mereological conception of continuants – a doubt which discussion of the case of the sinking of the Ship of Theseus was concerned to dispel. Moreover, the discussion suggests two further points. The first is that there is no *a priori* way of telling, given a description of a macrophysical event and its macrophysical subject, and a description of that event's so-called microphysical parts and their subjects, whether a single event is being described. The second is that, even supposing that two such descriptions *are* of the same event, there is no *a priori* way of telling which of its subjects is its minimal one. In the case of events like the sinking of the Ship of Theseus, where the property instanced is the same for the ship and its parts, the grounds for thinking that the ship is the minimal subject may be strongest. On the other hand, in cases of events like a pot of water's boiling, or my stammering, where the properties whose instancings are macroscopic and microscopic events are *distinct*, the grounds for thinking that the subjects of the microscopic events are the minimal ones may be the stronger ones.

6. The PNCC: Can It be Independently Motivated? Does Non-Reductive Monism Need It?

The arguments in the preceding section may fail to convince either because of stubborn resistance to the idea that there can be a single instance of a property in distinct subjects, even when such subjects are contiguous in space and time, or because of a more general resistance to the idea that distinct properties which are neither logically connected nor necessarily coextensive might nevertheless have a single instance. This latter idea might receive some support from the suggestion that certain properties may be such that one supervenes on the other, an issue that is taken up in the next chapter. However, it is worth briefly exploring other avenues of defence open to the non-reductive monist on the supposition that the PNCC does require a mereological conception of events. We here consider two.

First, one might enquire whether the PNCC can itself be independently grounded, in which case it might be seen to provide the additional reason for thinking that, in the case of those physical events that are mental events at least, fusions of events are themselves single events. To ground the PNCC independently is to offer reasons for thinking that, quite apart from the mereological conception, events causally related must be backed by law. This is effectively to offer reasons for thinking that the relation between causality and laws is as the PNCC depicts it.

Now, the PNCC was earlier said to embody a 'broadly Humean', i.e., a regularity, conception of causality to the extent that it involves the claim that events causally related have descriptions under which they are subsumed by causal laws. (Recall that a regularity conception of causality is committed to two quite distinct theses: the first concerns the nature of the causal relation, and the second concerns the nature of causal laws.) This claim, crudely put, is that the causal relation, though holding between particular events and so itself particular, involves an element of generality as well. This is not necessarily to say that when two events are causally related, they are so in part because of facts about other events (so that the causal relation, when it holds between two particular events, holds in part because of properties of events other than those said to be causally related). To say that any two events are causally related is at least to say that they are instances of certain types of (monadic) properties, whose instancing by any other pair of events would, in relevantly similar circumstances, be both necessary and sufficient for those events to be causally related.[19] (The qualification is needed to ensure the satisfaction of relevant 'background' conditions, e.g., the presence of oxygen in a match striking/match lighting sequence, as well as to cover cases of interference where the presence of an additional factor, e.g., the match's being wet, prevents the 'effect' property being instanced. It is thus intended to cover cases where event pairs differ in either other relational or other non-relational properties from the two said to be causally related, despite instancing the 'cause-relevant' and 'effect-relevant' properties. Obviously, not every relational property of a given event will figure in circumstances which we might regard as relevant to its being causally efficacious. But the purpose here is not to develop a theory of causality so much as it is to explore what connections there might be between the generality of the causal relation on a regularity account of causality, on the one hand, and the nomologicality of that relation on such an account, on the other.)

A regularity conception of causality is thus able to construe the causal relation as one which holds between particular events in virtue of their instancing certain types of non-relational event properties, i.e., ones whose instancing by any event does not presuppose the existence of any other event. It involves generality because it requires commitment at least to the claim that, were any two events to instance these properties in relevantly similar circumstances in this world, they would be causally related. The generality is therefore due to the fact that the properties whose instancing in the relevant circumstances makes for a particular causal relation are ones that can be (though need not be) instanced by other pairs of events.

Thus construed, the first thesis is one, not about the nature of causal laws, but rather about the generality of the causal relation (a view earlier referred to as generalist). It stands in contrast to a singularist conception of causality, where this is typically understood as the view that causality can be present in a single instance only.[20] In the context of the present discussion, this must be understood as involving a denial of the claim that to say that two events are causally related requires commitment to a counterfactual claim regarding other possible pairs of events that are instancings of certain types of properties (or a denial of the claim that true singular causal statements entail at the very least true counterfactual claims involving other events of certain types). A singularist evidently must take exception to the idea, embodied in the generalist conception, that causality involves relations between instancings of properties of certain *types*, i.e., that not only the instancings, but the types of properties instanced, are relevant to a particular causal relation's obtaining. For if it were thought that the properties instanced *were* relevant to whether a causal relation obtains in a particular case, it would be difficult to see how a singularist could avoid commitment to a counterfactual claim about other instances of those types.

Now, causality, on a regularity theory, involves generality; but it also involves nomologicality. Generalizations linking pairs of events by way of their instancing certain types of event properties may express regularities in the behaviour of events which are of those types. But there is nothing in this (generalist thesis) alone that entails nomologicality. Such generalizations may be expected to have the form, 'Whenever events of types A and B occur, they will be causally related' or something similar. What they do not license is any conditional of the form, 'Whenever an event of type A occurs, an event of type B will occur'. That is to say, a generalist conception of causality is committed to no more than the claim that any *pair* of events that instance certain types of event properties will be causally related. But that conception is itself silent on whether it is in virtue of those events' instancing just those types that they are causally related. That is to say, it is silent on the issue of whether it is the fact that a pair of events are of the types A and B whenever they are causally related *that* they are causally related. Conditional generalizations of the form 'Whenever an event of type A occurs, an event of type B will occur', on the other hand, assert the causal efficacy of instancings of properties of type A *vis-à-vis* instancings of properties of type B, and not merely that any two events co-instancing these properties will be causally related. We might put the point by saying that whereas the conditionals licensed by the generalist conception assert that whenever events of certain types co-occur in this world, we can expect that they will be causally connected, they do not assert that it is because such events are of just these types that they are causally connected (i.e., they do not say why or in virtue of what they are causally related). Conditionals of the form, 'Whenever an event of type A occurs, an event of type B occurs' are in this respect stronger; they go beyond the generalist conception in licensing the claim that whenever an event of the former type occurs, we can expect an event of the latter type to follow.[21]

Now, the nomological conception of causality is committed to the view that events causally related are backed by laws. Clearly, what are required for such a conception are not merely conditionals of the form licensed by the generalist conception, but the stronger conditionals; ones that would entitle us to make counterfactual claims about what would or would not occur if the cause event were or were not to occur. So a question that anyone committed to the PNCC needs to answer is why we need the nomological conception of causality.

The answer can be traced to the generalist conception it clearly requires. Anyone committed to the generalist conception of causality will be apt to find the singularist conception implausible precisely because it implies that there can be 'brute' instances of causation. The issue between the generalist and the singularist cannot simply be that whereas the singularist insists that the causal relation is 'wholly and completely' in each instance, the generalist insists that other facts or phenomena beyond those involved in that instance are at least partly involved. For the generalist can agree with the singularist that the causal relation is a particular one which holds between particular events in virtue of their particular properties. What are wholly and completely present are *instancings* of properties of certain types. Where the generalist and singularist must part company is in their view of the relation between such instancings and the properties instanced. The generalist will hold that whenever pairs of events are causally related, this entails that any similar instancings will be causally related.

Whether the generalist is ultimately in the right in this claim is not at issue here. What is of concern is why that theorist might not rest content with a generalist view of causality. What discussion of the debate between the singularist and the generalist shows clearly is that the types of properties of which related pairs of events are instancings are, for the generalist but not for the singularist, relevant to whether those pairs are causally related. This shows up in the kinds of generalizations to which the generalist is committed. But it is difficult to see how the *types* of properties of which a pair of events are instancings could make a difference to *whether* such events are causally related if those types are not themselves ones whose instancings are causally efficacious. That is to say, it is hard to see how a generalist could be committed to conditionals of the form

'Whenever events of types *A* and *B* co-occur, those events are causally related' if she were not also prepared to say that it is *because* an event is an instancing of type *A* that an event of type *B* occurs. Indeed, conditionals of this form may be seen to be explained by the view that whenever an event of type *A* occurs, an event of type *B* will occur. But conditionals of this latter form are just what is involved in the nomological conception of causality.

One can see, then, how anyone committed to a generalist conception of causality, as one who endorses the PNCC is, might wish to endorse the nomological conception of causality and hence the PNCC itself in order to ground the conditionals to which the generalist conception is committed. Without the nomological conception, the conditionals to which the generalist is committed express brute facts which themselves require explanation, perhaps no less so than the so-called brute facts of singular causal instances to which the singularist is committed. Indeed, the need can be seen to be more pressing in the case of the generalist in the light of the fact that any event can instance any number of properties, many of which are not ones whose instancings are causally efficacious *vis-à-vis* other events to which it may be causally related.

But again, this attempt to ground the PNCC may fail to convince, perhaps because of doubts concerning the distinction between a generalist conception of causality and a nomological conception. There is one further avenue of defence that the non-reductive monist might appeal to in the face of this, and that is to deny that a full-blooded version of the PNCC is actually required by the position. To opt for this strategy is to deny that non-reductive monism *requires* the thesis that where any two events are related as cause and effect, they must have descriptions which instantiate laws. How might one proceed to reconcile this denial with the PCI, PAM, and token event identity?

One way of doing this is to defend a minimal physicalism. To say that each mental event is a physical event is at least to say that each event that is an instancing of a mental property (of a person) is (identical with) an instancing of a physical property (of that person's body). There are at least two ways in which one might proceed to defend this claim without recourse to the PNCC. Both focus on the nature and scope of physical theory.

The first focuses on the explanatory powers of physical theory *vis-à-vis* physical events (for more on this, see Chapter Three, Section 2).[22] The second focuses on the scope of physical theory *vis-à-vis* events which causally interact. These two ways of proceeding are in fact linked to a common source: the PCI. Whereas the first is concerned with causal explanation of events linked as cause and effect, the second focuses on the open-or-closed nature of the domain of causally linked events with which physical theory deals.

Earlier, when the thesis of physicalism was briefly described, it was noted that any minimal physicalism is committed, if not to the reduction of all theories to physical theory (where this involves both ontological and explanatory reduction), at least to the reduction of all ontologies to that of physical theory, i.e., to the claim that all of the entities that fall within the domain of, e.g., the special sciences, fall within the domain of physical theory. This is to say no more nor less than that all events are physical events, even if not all of the descriptions and explanations of such events are physical (i.e., are couched in the terms and vocabulary of physical theory). Non-reductive monism is one such physicalist position. One way of defending it independently of the PNCC, then, is by way of defending the minimal physicalism that it embodies.

Let's begin with the PCI and PAM. Suppose that physical events interact causally both with one another and with at least some mental events. (This, of course, is the one principle that is left unchallenged by both the epiphenomenalist and the mereology objection.) Since to be a physical event is to be an instancing of a physical property, those physical events that interact with each other will fall within the domain of physical theory by virtue of being instancings of physical properties. So too will those physical events that interact with mental events. What of the mental events? Given PAM, we cannot assume that such events have physical descriptions, for we cannot assume reduction of psychological theory, either folk or theoretical, to physical theory. Nor can we assume that mental events are instancings of physical properties, since mental descriptions pick out events in terms of properties that are irreducibly distinct from physical ones. What reason could we have, independently of the PNCC, then, for thinking that those mental events which interact causally with physical events are themselves physical?

One reason that we might have concerns the difficulty of reconciling the denial of that claim with (*a*) the claim that physical events can have mental causes (one component of the PCI), and either of (*b*) the claim that every physical event that has a cause has a physical cause, or (*c*) the claim that every physical event that has a causal explanation has a physical causal explanation. Consider (*b*). It implies that the presence or absence of a mental event, if *distinct* from a physical event, would make no (causal) difference to whether or not a given physical event occurs, since that event already has an efficacious physical cause. This effectively renders mental phenomena causally redundant, thus undermining (*a*).[23] We have no reason, in the face of this and (*b*), for thinking that if the efficacious physical cause did not occur, the effect event would nevertheless have occurred (indeed, this latter would itself imply that the physical cause event is not the (whole) cause). If (*b*) is to be compatible with (*a*), then, identity of mental with physical events would seem to be required.

A similar line of reasoning applies to the attempt to reconcile distinctness of mental with physical events and (*c*) with (*a*). (*c*) implies that all causes of physical events can themselves be explained using only the terminology and associated properties of physical theory. This is just to say that all causes of physical events are instancings of physical properties and so are physical events. But then the attempt to reconcile distinctness of mental and physical events with (*c*) as well as with (*a*) faces essentially the same difficulties as the attempt above to reconcile distinctness of mental and physical events with (*b*) and (*a*).

The reasoning here is admittedly sketchy; but the point was only to indicate how one might go about providing a defence of non-reductive monism which is independent of the PNCC. One might, of course, wish to challenge the truth of (*b*) and (*c*). Indeed, one might insist that unless these can be grounded independently of the PNCC, the claim that non-reductive monism does not require that principle is unfounded. That both (*b*) and (*c*) *need* not require the truth of the PNCC should be clear enough from the arguments in the preceding pages of this chapter. (*b*) asserts only that physical events have physical causes. It entails no claim about what is required for pairs of events to stand in causal relations. It is therefore compatible even with a singularist conception of causality. As for (c), it is only if one assumes that the only legitimate model of causal explanation is a nomological one that one is justified in supposing that (c) requires the truth of the PNCC. It was argued earlier that that assumption itself requires defence; singular causal explanation shares with nomological explanation features required of any causal explanation, crucially that of licensing counterfactuals.

The issue of the truth of (b) and (c) is another matter. One cannot simply assume their truth, since (b) in particular (and (c) in so far as it entails (b)) asserts what anyone taking issue with non-reductive monism may find exceptionable in the position, viz. that all physical events have physical causes. Many dualists will take this to be false and so will find objectionable any attempt to defend non-reductive monism by way of appeal to such a principle. This reaction seems natural in the light of the fact that it is the monist part of non-reductive monism that may be felt to be compromised by the loss of the PNCC. On the other hand, both (b) and (c) have a great deal of intuitive appeal. For one thing, there is a strong presumption that part, at least, of what makes an event physical is that it occupies a place in a causal nexus with other events of the same kind. This presumption, while seeming to be compatible with the idea that a physical event may lack a cause, seems incompatible with the idea that it should have a cause which lies *outside* the physical causal nexus. Perhaps the source of this presumption can be traced to the ideological differences between physical and psychological theory and the jarring thought that if certain physical events were conceived of as having causes that fall into a domain outside physical theory, we could not give an adequate (let alone complete) physical explanation of those events. But since events are posited by theories to serve the explanatory purposes by which the theories are themselves constrained, to conceive of certain physical events as having mental causes where these latter are distinct from physical events is to conceive of them as having causes whose descriptions serve entirely different explanatory purposes from those couched in physical terminology. This raises doubts as to why we should think that events described in mental terms, if they are indeed distinct from physical ones, *should* causally explain events described in purely physical terms.

Connected with this is the belief that it is reasonable to expect that any physical effect event *should* have a physical causal explanation. After all, it may be thought, one clear purpose of a theory is to explain the phenomena that fall within its domain. Given this aim, there is no clear reason whatever for thinking that the thought expressed by (*c*) is either unfounded or otherwise implausible. Indeed, its plausibility increases when one considers the less plausible alternative of supposing that such events are both causally explicable and have no physical causal explanation and the vastly less plausible one of supposing that such events have explanations whose explanans events fall outside the domain of physical theory altogether.

These musings are not intended to constitute a defence of (*b*) and (*c*); at best they may be seen to provide a rationale for a kind of unthinking presumption of their plausibility, if not of their truth. A thoroughgoing defence of the claim that non-reductive monism can survive the loss of the PNCC would require a proper defence of both (*b*) and (*c*). Here only a gesture has been made toward the direction that such a defence might take.

Chapter Six

The aim of the preceding two chapters has been to defend a token event-identity thesis of the mental and the physical. The defence proceeded by way of argument for a version of the property-exemplification account of events, which was then shown to be capable of consistent combination with non-reductive monism. The resulting position was further defended against two major objections. One of these, the epiphenom-enalist charge, specifically concerned the position's failure to entail type-type identities between the mental and the physical. Although that charge was effectively countered, the fact remains that the existence of irreducible mental properties itself demands explanation. Without it, non-reductive monism is open to the charge that it is irredeemably dualist, since it acknowledges the presence in the natural world, if not of non-physical events, of non-physical properties. Many will think that such a position does not deserve the name 'physicalist'. It is commonly assumed by proponents and opponents of the position alike that the notion of *supervenience* best captures the relation which holds between mental and physical properties.[1] The aim of the present chapter is to examine and defend that assumption.

One major problem with any psychophysical supervenience thesis has to do with the number and kinds of physical properties to be included in the supervenience base. In particular, the problem of the 'context dependence' of many properties, i.e., the fact that the possession or exemplification of certain properties by an object or event requires the existence of some object(s) or event(s) distinct from it (and its parts), may generate doubts as to whether certain (intentional) mental phenomena can plausibly be said to occur within the confines of an individual person's body.[2]

Such doubts, if correct, present a formidable challenge to any event-identity thesis that asserts that particular mental events are physical events of a person's body. While the complexity of the issues involved in this challenge makes it impossible to deal with them here with the completeness they deserve, some attempt must be made to allay the doubts that give rise to it.

Bearing this in mind, the discussion will proceed as follows. First, various attempts to define a relation of strong supervenience for the mental and the physical will be examined, and their compatibility with non-reductive monism will be considered. Some, at least, of the ramifications of the problem of context dependence for such definitions will then be considered. Finally, the possibility that some weaker notion of supervenience might be compatible with non-reductive monism will be explored. No attempt will be made here to consider supervenience in general: what follows is confined specifically to psychophysical supervenience.

1. Conceptions of Supervenience

Supervenience between the mental and the physical has been characterized as that relation which holds between a mental property (or set of properties), M, and another, physical, one, P, such that any two objects (events) indiscernible with respect to P cannot diverge with respect to M. Alternatively, it has been characterized as that relation between M and P which is such that no object (event) can change with regard to the former without changing with regard to the latter.[3]

These two ways of characterizing psychophysical supervenience are thought by Kim and others to be logically distinct, the first corresponding to what they call *weak* supervenience, and the second corresponding to a stronger notion, that of strong supervenience.[4] Kim suggests that the two characterizations be formulated respectively in the following ways:

(1) M weakly supervenes on P just in case necessarily for any x and y if x and y share all properties in P then x and y share all properties in M

or

(1′) M weakly supervenes on P just in case necessarily for any property F in M if an object x has F then there exists a property G in P such that x has G and if any y has G it has F.

(2) M strongly supervenes on P just in case necessarily for each x and each property F in M if x has F then there exists a property G in P such that x has G and necessarily if any y has G it has F.

where M and P are two non-empty families of monadic properties closed under Boolean operations of conjunction and disjunction (perhaps infinite), and complementation.[5] (Here we take x and y to range over events.) M is called the supervenient (or supervening) family and P the supervenience (or subvenient) base. The crucial difference between (1′) and (2) lies in the presence in (2) of a second modal operator, 'necessarily', in the final clause of its definiens. This difference has the consequence that, whereas (1′) ensures that a general G/F connection holds *within* each possible world only, (2) ensures that that general connection holds *across* possible worlds.

Certain features of these definitions are worth briefly remarking upon. First, the force of 'necessarily' in both (1′) and (2) is unspecified; and there are grounds for thinking this desirable.[6] Different readings of (1′) and (2) will yield different supervenience theses, and different cases of supervenience may require different theses. In the case of moral/natural property supervenience, for instance, it may be plausible to read both occurrences of 'necessarily' in (2) as expressing metaphysical or logical necessity. In cases of determinable/determinate property supervenience (being coloured on being red, for example, or being four-sided on being square), it seems plausible to read both occurrences as expressing logical necessity. In the case of psychophysical supervenience, neither occurrence is plausibly read as expressing logical necessity. Here either or both occurrences are better construed as expressing metaphysical or nomic necessity. (Which of these is preferable is not of direct concern here, though the issue will surface briefly again later.) In so far as all three cases count as ones of supervenience, it is desirable that all three should be shown to be instances of a single common type of relation.

Second, Kim restricts both (1') and (2) to cases of monadic properties. His reasons for doing so may not be obvious; but without some restrictions on the number and kinds of properties allowed to figure in both the supervening family and the subvenient base, any supervenience thesis runs the risk of being either trivial or false. Suppose that any relational property (or n-adic property of degree greater than 1) is allowed to figure in the subvenient base family by which a psychophysical supervenience relation is defined. Then, assuming the Principle of the Identity of Indiscernibles, any such definition would appear to be trivially true, since there cannot be two events with exactly the same physical properties.[7] Intuitively, the fact that two events of the same physical type may occur in distinct bodies should not prohibit a supervenience thesis being true of them. It would, however, if the spatiotemporal properties of such events were allowed to figure in any supervenience base. Restricting base properties to monadic ones allows for differences in properties of events indiscernible in ways relevant to their possessing mental properties. By the same token, the base properties must not be restricted to just those properties that events have in virtue of having the consititutive properties, objects, and times they do; for events with all the same canonical descriptions are identical, and this would again result in the triviality of any supervenience thesis.

Suppose, on the other hand, that relational properties are allowed to figure in the supervening family or set by which a psychophysical supervenience relation is defined. Then any such definition runs the risk of being false. Consider such properties of mental events as those of being my favourite thought, or being my most unpleasant experience, or being the most bizarre thought I ever had. Two events indiscernible with regard to their (relevant) physical base properties cannot both possess these mental properties, since such properties cannot be shared. However, if mental properties supervene on physical ones, then these properties presumably do. Relational properties like that of being a perceiving of a building in the distance pose different problems. Though they can be possessed by more than one event, they do not seem to supervene on the physical properties of persons' bodies alone. Any psychophysical supervenience thesis that allows such properties to figure in the supervening family thus runs the risk of being false if some form of the identity theory is true. (This second problem concerns the issue of context dependence and will be taken up again later.) Evidently, some restriction on both the base and supervening properties is required if either of (1') or (2) is to be non-trivially true.

Finally, both (1') and (2) require the assumption that it is possible that some event should be both G and F. Without it, they are trivially true, since both are conditionals whose antecedents contain existential clauses. Similarly, we must assume that all properties F in M are contingent ones (since if any F in M is non-contingent, its possession by any event x is entailed by x's possession of any property whatever).[8]

These issues aside, most, if not all, of the existing formulations of psychophysical supervenience appear to be versions of either weak or strong supervenience. This is important from the point of view of non-reductive monism. For it is commonly thought that, whereas weak supervenience is too weak, strong supervenience is too strong for that position's purposes. If critics of non-reductive monism are correct, and strong and weak supervenience exhaust the possibilities, proponents of that position cannot turn to supervenience to provide an explanation of the relation between mental and physical properties.

Exactly why is weak supervenience thought to be insufficient for non-reductive monism? Critics seem to think that the position is compromised by the fact that (1') ensures a general F/G relation only intra-worldly.[9] This, they say, does not do justice to the notion of determination or dependence that is embodied in the concept of supervenience and which non-reductive monism needs to discharge its physicalist commitments. If all the physical properties in this world fix the mental ones in the sense that events indiscernible with regard to the former *cannot* diverge with respect to the latter, the implication is that what there is to physical reality *exhausts* what there is to mental reality. How, then, can it be possible *either* that there should be another world physically indiscernible from this one but differing in its distribution of mental properties (either by lacking them altogether, or by systematically relating different ones from those in this world with the same physical properties) *or* that there should be a world indiscernible from this one in its distribution of mental properties while differing from it to the extent that it lacks physical ones entirely? The fact that both of these possibilities are compatible with (1′) undermines the supposition that all mental properties are exhaustively determined by physical ones; and this supposition is required by non-reductive monism if it is to be faithful to its physicalist principles.

What, then, of strong supervenience? This, it is said, is too strong for the purposes of the non-reductive monist since it ultimately leads to the necessary coextension of mental and physical properties; and this, even if insufficient for reduction, is sufficient for psychophysical correlation laws.[10] But then strong supervenience cannot be appealed to by the non-reductive monist to explain the relation between mental and physical properties. Since it has the consequence that there are psychophysical correlation laws, it is incompatible with non-reductive monism.

The consensus of opinion amongst critics seems to be that strong supervenience is what is required by non-reductive monism, but that it cannot be accommodated consistently with the autonomy of the mental also required by that position. Let us assume that strong and weak supervenience exhaust the types of supervenience relations that there are. Then two main issues need to be addressed by the non-reductive monist. The first is whether strong supervenience *is* too strong for the purposes of that position. The second is whether non-reductive monism *needs* strong supervenience (i.e., whether weak supervenience might not suffice for that position's purposes).

2. Strong Supervenience: Too Strong?

Consider (2). It says that a family of properties, M, supervenes on another, P, just in case, for any (event) x and each property F in M, if x has F, then there exists a property G in P such that x has G *and* necessarily if any y has G it has F. This last clause evidently accomplishes what (1′) does not, viz. it captures the idea of determination or dependence embodied in the concept of supervenience. It follows from this definition that there is no possible world in which the totality of physical monadic properties is indiscernible from this one but where the distribution of mental properties differs. Inasmuch as the idea of determination is meant to capture the intuition that if the mental supervenes on the physical, then the totality of physical properties exhausts the mental ones, (2) appears to do justice to that idea (but see Section 4). This notion of supervenience is a strong one indeed: it has the consequence that the totality of physical properties completely determines, in every detail, the mental ones.[11] Given all the physical properties of this world, no world with just these properties can vary one whit in the number, kinds, and distribution of mental properties from the actual world.

Kim thinks (2) so strong a conception of supervenience as to lead to the necessary coextension of mental and physical properties. This is a surprising result, since although both weak and strong supervenience express dependency relations between mental and physical properties, it is commonly assumed that the dependency holds in one direction only, viz. of mental on physical properties. That is to say, supervenience is thought to be an asymmetrical (as well as reflexive and transitive) relation, despite the fact that both (1') and (2) are themselves neither symmetrical nor asymmetrical. There are two main reasons why this is thought to be so. The first has to do with the possibility of variable realization. This would seem to have the consequence that physical properties determine or fix mental ones, but not vice versa. The second has to do with the supposed autonomy of the mental – effectively, for non-reductive monism, the independence of mental from physical properties (where this would seem to require at least the absence of psychophysical correlation laws). Both require that, while there may be some property or other in the supervenience base family which suffices for the existence of a mental property, there is no single base property that is both necessary and sufficient for the existence of that mental property.

Kim, however, argues to the contrary. Adapting an example of Hare's, he supposes a set (or family) of monadic properties, A, containing the property of being a good person (G), to supervene upon a distinct set, B, containing as members the properties of being courageous (C), being benevolent (V), and being honest (H).[12] Since both sets are closed under Boolean operations, B consists of all the properties constructible by means of Boolean operations from properties C, V, and H in B. In this case there are eight: $C\&V\&H$, $C\&V\&-H$, $C\&-V\&-H$, . . ., $-C\&-V\&-H$. These are called 'B-maximal properties', since they are the strongest consistent properties able to be constructed by means of Boolean operations in B. A similarly consists of the properties $-G$, $Gv-G$, and $G\&-G$ as well as G. Now each object that has a property in A must have a B-maximal property. This has the consequence, given strong supervenience, that the following biconditionals hold not only within each world but across all worlds:

(2a) $(x)(B*(x) \leftrightarrow G(x))$
    $(x)(B\#(x) \leftrightarrow -G(x))$

where both $B*$ and $B\#$ are disjunctions of B-maximal properties.[13] It follows that both G and $-G$ have not only coextensive B-maximal base properties, but necessarily coextensive ones.

Turn now to (2). If M strongly supervenes on P, then, for every F in M, there is a property G in P such that necessarily $(y)(G(y) \rightarrow F(y))$. Of course, this alone is not enough to establish necessary coextension of M and P properties. To establish this, we need P-maximal properties, constructed by means of Boolean operations of complementation and infinite conjunction and disjunction (operations we did not need for the previous case since the bases of both A and B were assumed to be finite). Given this, the argument for the necessary coextensivity of mental and physical properties is as follows.

Suppose that there is a contingent monadic property F in M, i.e., that some event x has F in some world w. Then (2) says that there is a G in P such that x has G in P and necessarily $(y)(G(y) \rightarrow F(y))$. We know that if x has F in M in w, then there is a P-maximal property which x has in w. Let Pxw be that property. Then the following conditionals hold:

(2b) Necessarily $(y)[Pxw(y) \rightarrow G(y)]$
(2c) Necessarily $(y)[Pxw(y) \rightarrow F(y)]$
(2d) Necessarily $(y)[Pvu(y) \rightarrow F(y)]$ for each v in a world u that has F.

Let $P*$ be the infinite disjunction of P-maximal properties. Then we know that any y that has some F in M has some P-maximal property. It follows not only that

(2e) Necessarily $(y)[P_*(y) \rightarrow F(y)]$ (given (2d))

but also that

(2f) Necessarily $(y)[F(y) \rightarrow P_*(y)]$.

If this were not so, then there would be some world $w\#$ where some event x had F in M but not P_*. But then by (2) there would be *some* property, say H, in P such that x had H and necessarily $(y)[H(y) \rightarrow F(y)]$. We know that x must have some P-maximal property in $w\#$. Suppose $P\#$ is that property. Then again it follows from (2) that $(y)[P\#(y) \rightarrow F(y)]$. So $P\#$ must be one of the disjuncts in P_*. But if this is so, then x must, contrary to the supposition, have P_*. Evidently, strong supervenience leads to biconditionals of the form

(2g) Necessarily $(y)[P_*(y) \leftrightarrow F(y)]$.

While Kim claims that necessary coextension of mental and physical properties follows from strong supervenience as formulated by (2), Hellman and Thompson claim that psychophysical bridge laws are entailed by their (hereafter, H/T supervenience) characterization.[14] This is specifically geared toward the concept of *determination* – in particular, toward the determination of all psychological truths by all physical truths. Two kinds of determination are defined for structures, where these are specified by specifying a domain D of entities and an n-place relation amongst entities in D for each n-place predicate of a language L.[15] Working with the notion of a restriction of a structure m to a vocabulary v (symbolized m/v), where this is the structure that is obtained when the interpretation of all terms not in v are omitted, determination both for P-truths and S-truths (which can for our purposes be taken to correspond to physical truths and psychological truths respectively), where truths are taken to be sentences, and for P-reference and S-reference, is defined. Both definitions are relativized to a class α of structures, where this includes some but not all of the structures by which L

is interpreted. Since the totality of structures by which L is interpreted effectively constitutes a definition of logical necessity and possibility, the restriction of both definitions of determination to a class of structures α ensures that the relation of determination is not a logically necessary one.

Consider any two structures, m and m', restricted first to the P vocabulary and then to the S vocabulary. S-truth determination by P-truth is defined as follows:

(3a) In α structures, P-truth determines S-truth if and only if $(m)(m')[m,m' \in \alpha$ & m/P eleq $m'/P \rightarrow m/S$ eleq $m'/S]$

where the term 'eleq' is to be read as 'm is elementarily equivalent to m'' and means that the same sentences are true in m and m'. Since truth does not fix reference, a second notion of determination for P and S predicates is defined. Since identical structures will be ones in which predicates have the same interpretation, S-reference determination by P-reference is defined thus:

(3b) In α structures, P-reference determines S-reference if and only if $(m)(m')[m,m' \in \alpha$ & $m/P = m'/P \rightarrow m/S = m'/S]$.

Neither of (3a) or (3b) entails the other, i.e., both are model-theoretically independent of one another. That (3b) does not entail (3a) can be seen by supposing that two structures, m and m' (a) agree in P-truths but differ in S-truths, and (b) differ in P-reference. (3b) is then vacuously true, but (3a) is not. ((3b) will imply (3a), however, in just those cases where α is restricted to all and only models of some theory T.)

Hellman and Thompson think that (3a) at least entails the existence of psychophysical laws (it is unclear, however, whether they consider all or most of these to be biconditional, or merely conditional, in form).[16] This, they maintain, is not to say that determination involves reduction, since reducibility requires definability of the *terms* of the reduced vocabulary by the terms in the reducing vocabulary. If reducibility of S-terms to P-terms holds, then every law formulated by means of S-terms (bridge laws included) is reducible to one in which only P-terms occur.

But the claim that reference-determination entails reducibility requires the assumption that α contains structures that are all and only models of some theory T (where T is taken to be the whole of scientific theory). In general, α will include non-standard models that do not represent scientific possibilities. To avoid reducibility, α is restricted to a subset of models of T in which predicates receive only standard interpretations (i.e., α is restricted to standard models alone).[17]

H/T supervenience differs noticeably from (2) (*a*) in being formulated in terms of predicates (and truths, where these are sentences) rather than in terms of properties; and (*b*) in being model-theoretic. Both of these features have been subjected to criticism.

Take (*b*). On a model-theoretic formulation of supervenience, any assignment of an extension to a predicate is acceptable as an interpretation of that predicate. Since there is no single fixed interpretation of the predicates and/or sentences in any language L, model theory cannot discriminate between changes in extension due to differences in interpretation of terms or sentences in L (purely conventional ones), and changes in extension due to changes in the entities or relations in a domain D by which L is interpreted. This, it has been claimed, gives rise to counterexamples to (3*a*) of the following kind.

Consider any two biological theories – an outdated one, according to which whales are fish, and a recent one, according to which whales are mammals.[18] William the whale will be described by the first theory as a fish but by the second theory as a mammal. The result will be two structures that are indiscernible with respect to all physical truths but which differ in biological truths. This problem can be generalized, since any model-theoretic account of supervenience will allow for conventional changes in the interpretation of certain terms of L while the interpretation of others is held constant, and so cannot prohibit cases where changes occur only in the interpretation of S-truths or terms while the interpretation of terms/truths in the P vocabulary is held constant. (Requiring that the terms/sentences of a given language L receive only standard interpretations will not avoid this difficulty. Since standard interpretations are ones that represent scientific possibilities, both the outdated and the current biological theory meet this requirement.)

The difficulty seems to be that supervenience theses are intuitively geared toward matters of ontology, assuming the interpretation of supervenience base terms/sentences to be fixed across comparisons of extensions; but model-theoretic formulations of supervenience work with no fixed interpretation of any of the terms or sentences in a given language L across all models. If counterexamples due to conventional changes in the interpretation of vocabulary of a given language L are to be avoided, there must be some requirement that the terms/sentences in L be given the same interpretation across comparisons of extensions.

However, this criticism, though correct, ignores a distinction crucial to H/T supervenience, viz. the distinction between a structure (for a language of a theory) and a model (for that theory).[19] Structures are formulated without regard to the issue of which sentences in them are true. Models, however, require that the theorems of the theory of which they are models be true. Models, in short, are structures whose sentences *are* interpreted (how this interpretation is effected is another matter).

H/T supervenience is formulated with regard to models, not structures, with the result that the above counterexample does not arise. Determination requires the consideration of all (standard) models of *all* laws of the complete (determining plus determined) theory (ϕ and ψ). Only if that theory is incomplete on the biological nature of whales is there a difficulty concerning whales. Otherwise, there are two theories, not one: in the first (outdated) one, 'Whales are fish' is a law, whereas in the second, 'Whales are mammals' is a law. The question is which one subsumes whales.

H/T supervenience requires the kinds of detailed correlations between mental and physical *predicates* (if not between properties) that leads to commitment to psychophysical correlation laws. The reasoning appears to be that the only way in which the interpretation of P-terms or P-truths could fix or determine the interpretation of S-terms or S-truths, given that the P and S vocabularies are distinct, is if there are correlation or bridge laws in the theory T whose vocabulary includes both P-truths and S-truths. This consequence alone suffices to make H/T supervenience unacceptable for the purposes of the non-reductive monist. However, there is another issue to be considered here, and that is whether it is plausible to suppose that psychophysical bridge laws are entailed by any conception of strong supervenience formulated, not in terms of properties, but rather, in terms of predicates. That is to say, there is an issue here as to whether H/T supervenience sets a requirement which it is implausible to suppose any conception of supervenience formulated in terms of predicates can meet. If so, then this version of strong supervenience is inherently inadequate.

Recall that, in both (1′) and (2), the base (P) set or family of physical properties is taken to be closed under Boolean operations of complementation, conjunction, and disjunction. Since, in the case of psychophysical supervenience, we cannot assume any such base to be finite, the relevant Boolean operations will be those of infinite conjunction and disjunction. Consequently, any physical property with which a given mental one might be held to be necessarily coextensive is apt to be infinitely complex (consisting of infinitely long disjunctions of properties, each disjunct of which may itself be an infinitely long conjunction, given that it is a B-maximal property and so will be infinitely complex if the initial base properties are infinite in number).

Although Kim himself thinks that any physical base property with which a given mental one may be necessarily coextensive is very likely to be *equivalent* to one that is infinitely complex in the above way, he sees no reason to assume that such a property cannot be a single, simple, *bona fide* one (we return to this below). As he sees it, there is no guarantee, from the fact that a property is formed by means of the Boolean operations of infinite conjunction and infinite disjunction on others, that it is either complex or artificial. The property of being less than 1 metre long, for instance, can be construed as an infinite disjunction of properties of the form 'being less than n/n+1 metres long' for any natural number n.[20] Whether a *predicate* can be assumed to exist for the expression of each and every such property is another matter. A Boolean disjunction of predicates presumably *will* be a complex predicate; and such operations as infinite conjunction and infinite disjunction will be highly dubious for predicates.

The claim here is that, whereas necessary coextensivity of M and P properties follows from a conception of strong supervenience formulated in terms of properties, psychophysical bridge laws cannot be assumed to follow from one formulated in terms of predicates. Since any physical supervenience base is apt to be infinitely large due to the possibility of variable realization, coextensive mental and physical predicates can only be constructed if one assumes that operations such as infinite conjunction and infinite disjunction are admissible for physical predicates. But such operations are highly questionable for predicates. If this is right, then neither biconditional nor conditional bridge laws follow from a definition of supervenience couched in terms of predicates.

Even if it is not, there would be a residual worry due to the artificial nature of any predicate by which we might define an infinite Boolean combination of predicates. Because any such predicate will be defined as equivalent to an infinite combination of others, it will have associated with it no clear satisfaction condition. In particular, due to the possibility of the variable realization of any given mental state (type), there can be no principle forthcoming from the physical domain by which to *exclude* any physical predicate from any conjunction or disjunction by which the newly introduced predicate is defined. Nor can there be any such principle of exclusion forthcoming from the mental domain. Any and every physical predicate whose satisfaction by an entity *might* suffice for the satisfaction of a mental one will have a claim to be included. But then, since there is no principle here by which to ground the possible in the actual, *any* physical predicate which can be satisfied by any event (we here exclude individual properties, properties peculiar to a given event) will be a candidate for membership in such a disjunction (see Chapters One and Two). By anyone's criterion of terms or predicates admissible in laws, it is wildly implausible to suppose that any predicate defined in terms of Boolean operations of infinite disjunction and infinite conjunction on others will count as admissible. Any such predicate, even if short and simple, will inherit the complexity of the disjunctions and conjunctions by means of which it is introduced. So too will it inherit the heterogeneity (as well as the artificiality) associated with such disjunctions – a feature which makes it highly implausible to suppose that the entities (events) that might satisfy that predicate should *all* behave in a single, regular way.

In the face of all this, it is highly unlikely that any conception of supervenience formulated in terms of predicates will entail psychophysical correlation laws. On the other hand, it is doubtful whether the Boolean operations of infinite conjunction and disjunction are any less questionable for properties than they are for predicates. Reasons for finding such operations questionable were brought to bear both on the type-type identity theorist in Chapter One and on the functionalist in Chapter Two. First, there is the doubt as to whether infinite disjunctions and/or conjunctions of properties are themselves properties, other than in an extended sense. Then there is the doubt whether, even if they are properties, every Boolean combination of physical properties is itself a physical property (i.e., whether the set of physical properties is closed under Boolean operations of infinite conjunction and disjunction). Finally, there is the doubt, analogous to the one just voiced in connection with H/T supervenience, as to whether, even if there is a single property equivalent to one constructed by Boolean operations on others, it is the kind of property that could figure in any psychophysical bridge law (hence be necessarily coextensive with any mental property). Both the size and the heterogeneity of the envisaged disjunctions count against this supposition; and this seems ultimately to be due to the fact that their construction is answerable to no fixed constraints either from the domain of the physical or from that of the mental. For all of these reasons, the claim that strong supervenience leads to the necessary coextension of mental and physical *properties* is also suspect.

Evidently, neither H/T supervenience nor (2) seriously threatens the autonomy of the mental. Since it is unclear whether the former can survive the loss of psychophysical correlation laws, we shall hereafter restrict discussion to property formulations of supervenience, as in (1′) and (2). If there is a threat to nonreductive monism forthcoming from strong supervenience, it is unlikely to be due to any envisaged commitment to the existence of psychophysical bridge laws or the necessary coextension of mental and physical properties. There is, however, another possible source of threat. This has to do with the issue of the context dependence of intentional mental properties.

3. Context Dependence and Token Identity

If H/T supervenience faces certain difficulties due to being formulated in terms of truths and predicates rather than properties, (1′) and (2) face difficulties of another kind. These are formulated specifically for monadic properties of individuals; and the relation of supervenience is defined as holding between macrophysical and microphysical properties of one and the same individual. However, many properties of individuals seem to be both supervenient and *relational*; their attribution to an individual seems to require the existence of some other individual distinct from it (and its parts). Such properties depend (in a broadly logical sense of 'depend') for their attribution to an individual, not merely on the non-relational microphysical properties of that individual, but on the existence of other individuals and their properties. This gives rise to the problem of context dependence – the problem that some, at least, of an individual's macroscopic properties supervene if at all on properties additional to the microphysical ones of that same individual. This problem extends to the relation between mental and physical properties.

Consider such properties of persons as those of believing that Mozart wrote *The Magic Flute* or of perceiving that the building in the distance is the Eiffel Tower. The correct attribution of these to a person depends (in a non-causal sense) on the existence of other individuals and properties distinct from that person and on the occurrence of certain events involving those individuals. In a number of works, both Hilary Putnam and Tyler Burge have urged that not only the physical environment but also the social environment of a person is at least partly constitutive of that person's psychological attitudes.[21] If they are right, then any conception of intentional mental properties which construes them as attributable to persons independently of the existence of other individuals and their properties (and possibly events involving them) is wrong.

Now nothing in (2) specifically requires that properties in the supervening family be restricted to monadic ones. It is thus tempting to suggest that we allow F properties to include not only intrinsic or non-relational properties of individuals, but also relational ones of arbitrary complexity. But then supervenience threatens to become too weak to capture the idea that the microphysical properties of individuals determine their macrophysical, let alone their (intentional) mental, properties. Let ϕ be a specification of the universe's microphysical history. Then every individual has the property of being such that ϕ.[22] Evidently, what is needed is some formulation which captures the idea of *localized* determination in cases of context dependence.

One such formulation is Horgan's. His is a version of *global* or world supervenience consisting of two general schemata – one (*R*) for regions and the other (*I*) for individuals:

> (*R*) There do not exist any two world-regions which are exactly alike in all qualitative intrinsic features of kind *J*, and which differ in some qualitative intrinsic feature of kind *K*, and which belong respectively to two possible worlds each satisfying accessibility condiion *C*

and

> (*I*) There do not exist any two world-regions, belonging respectively to two possible worlds, each satisfying accessibility condition *C*, containing two individuals which are exactly alike in all qualitative intrinsic properties of kind *J* but different in some qualitative intrinsic property of kind *K*[23].

where any instance of (*R*) entails an instance of (*I*) but not *vice versa*. Restrictions to qualitative properties are intended to rule out counterexamples to supervenience due to such individual properties as being identical with Terence Horgan. This property, though holding of Horgan in this world, won't hold of his counterpart in any world other than this one. Such properties are excluded by (*R*) and (*I*), but the notion of a qualitative property is left unanalysed. One suggestion would be to restrict qualitative properties to the 'perfectly natural' properties of things, where these latter determine or fix objective resemblances and causal powers of individuals.[24] Intrinsic features are features now of world regions, whose presence does not require the existence of any individual or event outside the relevant region. And accessibility condition *C* is intended to restrict the range of possible worlds to which (*R*) and (*I*) apply. For example, worlds in which Cartesian souls exist but do not infringe the microphysical laws of those worlds will be indiscernible microphysically yet differ in some spirit-related respect. These are ruled out by restricting the worlds to which (*R*) and (*I*) apply in cases of microphysical determination (though not for cases of aesthetic or moral supervenience) to ones which contain (*a*) only the (natural) kinds of entities that exist in the actual world, and (*b*) only the kinds of properties that figure in the microphysical laws of this world.

It is doubtful whether this formulation of strong supervenience is an improvement on (2). Its restrictions on supervenient and subvenient properties to those *intrinsic* to a world region seem no less problematic than restricting the number and kinds of relational properties to which a definition like (2) can apply. We know that for (2) to cope with cases of context dependence, relational properties, but not ones of arbitrary complexity, must be allowed to figure in the supervening family. Reference to world regions might appear to handle problems with context dependence in a way that reference to properties of individuals alone does not. But this is so only to the extent that we can restrict the world regions to portions 'smaller' than whole worlds. And it isn't clear that we can do this other than by restricting the number and kinds of relational properties that are allowed to figure as supervenient in a given case. (*R*) and (*I*) thus appear to set limits on the number and kinds of features that can figure in a supervening family only in so far as we have an intuitive grasp of the number and kinds of relational properties that can figure in such a family.

Formulated *without* restriction to world regions, global supervenience does not appear to capture the idea of determination of mental by physical properties necessary for non-reductive monism to discharge its physicalist commitments. Construed in this way, it is roughly the thesis that, for any two families or sets of properties, M and P, any two worlds w_1 and w_2 that are indiscernible with respect to P-properties are indiscernible with respect to M ones.[25] It has the consequence that there could be two worlds, w_1 and w_2, in each of which there exist two individuals, a and b, where in w_1 a has G in P and F in M and b has G in P, and where in w_2 a has G in P but not F in M and b lacks G. Since this consequence is incompatible with (2), global supervenience is not equivalent to (2). But the consequence itself exposes a weakness in global supervenience which, Kim argues, makes it unsuitable for the purposes of any materialist.

To the extent that it permits worlds like w_1 and w_2, it is difficult to see how supervenience of M properties on P ones could ground counterfactuals or subjunctive conditionals and so express a relation of determination of M by P properties. The only explanation that can be given in w_2 of the fact that, in that world, a has G in P but not F in M is that a distinct individual b in that world lacks G in P (even though it has G in w_1). This conception therefore fails to do justice to the intuition that, in the case of psychophysical property supervenience at least, the possession by a person of a mental property at a time is fixed, not by the entire physical state of the world she may inhabit at that time, but only by the physical properties of her body and her (local) environment. It has the consequence that, so long as there is *some* physical difference between worlds w_1 and w_2, no matter how small or insignificant, these worlds can be as different as one cares to imagine in the number and distribution of mental properties that they possess. But then it evidently is too weak a relation to suffice for the purposes of the non-reductive monist.

It is unlikely that any definition of psychophysical property supervenience formulated in terms more restrictive than those used to formulate global supervenience will itself be capable of setting limits on the number and kinds of properties that may figure in any supervenient or subvenient family. On the other hand, it is not clear whether it should: after all, (2) seek to specify a certain kind of *relation* (of covariance) that holds between properties or families of properties. Since different cases of supervenience may well differ as between the kinds of properties that figure in the supervenient and subvenient families, there is no obvious reason why one should place any specific *a priori* restrictions on the types of properties that can figure in either family in the definition itself.

Context dependence seems to create a serious problem for mental/physical property supervenience. If certain (i.e., intentional) mental properties require for their attribution to a given person the existence of some individual distinct from them and their subjects (and parts), then the having of such properties cannot depend, in a non-causal sense, only on the properties of that person's body and/or events occurring within its confines. This seems to pose a threat to the supposition, upon which any token-identity theory of the mental and the physical depends, that mental phenomena occur within the confines of an individual person's body alone. For it implies that objects and events other than those that exist or occur within the confines of a person's body are *constitutive* of intentional mental properties. The reasoning to this conclusion has its origins in Putnam's Twin Earth thought experiments, originally designed to show that meanings 'ain't in the head'.[26] Putnam argues that inasmuch as the meanings of a person's words depend on their extensions, and these can vary independently of the physical properties of a person's body, two persons could be physically indiscernible yet mean different things by their use of the same words. The conclusion for meaning evidently carries over to intentional mental properties or states (types), since these are individuated at least in part by their contents. If the Twin Earth examples show that meanings aren't in the head, equally they would seem to show that intentional mental phenomena aren't in the head.

Tyler Burge further develops this line of thought in several influential papers.[27] Though there are differences between the arguments presented in these papers, all are designed to show that intentional mental phenomena are not 'inner' in the sense that they do not depend for their existence on individuals and events occurring outside the confines of a person's body. If he is right, Putnam's conclusions can be generalized beyond attitudes whose contents are specified by means of natural kind terms and demonstratives. They extend to attitudes whose individuation depends in part on the social as well as the physical environment of the subjects of such attitudes. Now token-identity theorists are committed to the view that mental events occur within the confines of an individual person's body. How is this to be reconciled with the conclusion that mental state (types) or properties are individuated at least in part by their relations to individuals and events other than the bodies of the persons that have them?

There seem to be two ways in which to reconcile the intuition that mental phenomena occur within the confines of an individual person's body with the conclusions of the Putnam and Burge thought experiments. The first, familiar, strategy is to argue that mental states or properties have two components – a 'narrow' component and a 'wide' component.[28] According to it, context dependence does not pose a threat to individualism, conceived of as the view that persons are in the same psychological states when their bodies are in indiscernible microphysical (or neuro-physiological) states. The reason is that intentional mental states narrowly conceived respect individualism even though broadly conceived they do not. The supposed threat to token identity between the mental and the physical may here be countered by insisting that it is intentional mental states or properties narrowly construed whose tokens are identical with tokens of microphysical states or properties of an individual person's body upon which the narrow states supervene.

This strategy might be backed up by pointing out that intentional mental states (types) appear to have two distinct features associated with them, one of which is referential, and the other of which is cognitive. The referential aspect of any such type is typically fixed by objects which exist outside the confines of an individual person's body; it is that feature of such states which enables them to be semantically evaluated (i.e., able to be assigned truth conditions). On the supposition that the content of a thought is essential to it, thoughts are type-distinct in this broad or wide sense of content if and only if they have distinct truth conditions. Thus, for example, my water thoughts and my Twin Earthling's *XYZ* thoughts are type-distinct and have distinct truth conditions given that water ≠ *XYZ*. The cognitive aspect of an intentional mental state, on the other hand, is independent of its referential aspect. It has to do, not with *what* is represented by a thought's content, but rather, with *how* it is represented. It is that feature of content that plays a causal-explanatory role *vis-à-vis* the behaviour of an individual. This is content narrowly construed. Fodor's view is that narrow content plus context yields truth conditions. Narrow content is, strictly speaking, inexpressible: since any English sentence used to express a person's thought will have a determinate semantic value, the content of the thought expressed by means of it will be broad rather than narrow. But it is arguable that the inexpressibility of narrow content should present no real obstacle to a dual component view.[29]

A number of doubts have been voiced about the distinction between wide and narrow content. Two in particular raise serious questions about its viability as a way of reconciling the context dependence of intentional mental properties or state types with the view that mental phenomena occur within the confines of an individual person's body. The first is that the two components of content are apt to come into conflict with one another. If one supposes that total content supervenes both on the referential (wide) aspect and on the cognitive (narrow) aspect, then distinct standards of individuation may lead to attributions of belief components that are incompatible with one another. This possibility comes out clearly in cases like the Twin Earth water/*XYZ* examples. In such cases, individuation by way of the referential component yields distinct beliefs for neurophysiological twins, whereas individuation by way of the cognitive component yields beliefs which are type-identical. One response might be to say that the beliefs are partly type-identical and partly type-distinct. But this is unlikely to satisfy someone who thinks that our concepts of belief and the like are, if not unitary ones, then concepts of states or properties whose cognitive components cannot be seen to function totally independently of their referential components. The following considerations might be seen to recommend such a view. First, it is plausible to hold that thoughts in general, and states such as believing and knowing in particular, are parasitic on perceptual states. However, perceiving is not a psychological state whose referential component can plausibly be seen to function independently of its cognitive component. Second, it is difficult to see how misrepresentation can be adequately accounted for if the cognitive component of psychological states does not at least sometimes function in a way that is dependent on the referential component of such states. For misrepresentation requires that *how* an object is represented bears a systematic relation to *what* is represented. Finally and more generally, there are doubts about the viability of 'splitting' the explanatory role that intentional psychological states play in an overall theory of a person's psychology into (*a*) the causal-explanatory role that the cognitive component of such states narrowly construed are supposed to play, on the one hand, and (*b*) the rationalistic-explanatory role that the semantically evaluable component of such states widely construed are meant to play, on the other.[30] Resistance to this bifurcation of the explanatory role played by intentional mental phenomena has its source in the belief that commonsensical attributions of propositional attitudes are answerable to normative constraints – of what it is rational for an agent to believe, think, or desire, given other attitudes. Such connections as there are between the contents of those attitudes, it is held, are not (or not merely) causal but logical. To say this is not to say that reasons are not causes; it is to say that reasons explanations are not merely causal explanations.

These, and other, objections to the dual component view cast doubt, not on the wide construal of psychological types or properties, but on the narrow one. Since the problem for mind-body identity theorists arises on the wide construal, a second strategy for effecting a reconciliation might begin by questioning *why* the broad construal of intentional mental types should be taken to imply that mental phenomena occur outside the confines of persons' bodies.[31] The answer, it seems, has to do with the fact that (*de re*) intentional mental types, such as the type 'believes that *p*' (for some propositional content *p*), bear (not merely causal but) logical relations to the objects that they are 'about', and so both the existence and the identity and individuation conditions of such types are not independent of the existence and identity and individuation conditions of their corresponding objects. My belief that water is thirst-quenching is on this account type distinct from my Twin Earthling's belief that $water_1$ is thirst-quenching given that water (H_2O) is distinct from $water_1$ (XYZ). Suppose that this is correct for at least some intentional mental properties or types. Still, it is not obvious why we should think that this shows either (*a*) that certain intentional mental *types* are not 'wholly in the head' (in some sense yet to be made clear) or (*b*) that *tokens* of such types occur at least in part beyond the confines of a person's body.

Consider first intentional mental types. Context dependence appears to have the consequence that certain of these are essentially relational: believing that Mozart wrote *The Magic Flute*, for instance, seems to require both that Mozart existed and that certain acts of which he was the agent occurred. Given that logical relations hold, not between things or events, but rather, between certain of their descriptions, to say that certain intentional mental types are essentially relational is to say that their identity conditions are provided, in part at least, by descriptions that entail existential claims about objects distinct from them and their subjects.

Suppose that this is true. One consequence evidently is that no type-type identity theory of mind and body can be true. For it seems plausible to suppose that neurophysiological types are not essentially relational, i.e., that they, and physical types in general, are such that their identity conditions can be specified in terms that do not entail existential claims about objects other than themselves and their subjects.[32] However, none of this shows that intentional mental types are to be located in part at least beyond the confines of an individual person's body, whatever this may mean. To assume so would be to conflate the claim that mental types are such that they require the existence of objects other than themselves and their subjects, with the claim that those objects in part *constitute* the types. This conflation may seem to be justified by the claim that such objects are partly *constitutive* of intentional mental types, combined with the (Humean) view that objects that are not independently identifiable are not truly distinct. But it is not. For one thing, even if mental types are not identifiable independently of objects they are 'about', the objects themselves evidently are capable of independent identification. But more importantly, the conflation requires assuming, falsely, that objects or events referred to by structured expressions must themselves be 'structured' in a way that is analogous to the semantic structure of expressions used to pick them out. One clear example where this fails to be so was mentioned earlier (Chapter Four, Section 2): that of functional expressions like 'the father of *x*', which, when combined with singular terms, serve to map offspring onto their fathers. Despite the fact that such expressions are literally composed of expressions referring to offspring, no one would suppose that fathers are in any sense constituted in part by their offspring. Nor is this the only example. Think of the description of an event as 'the cause of *e*' (where '*e*' is a singular term referring to an event), or of descriptions of conditions as 'colour blindness' or 'heat exhaustion'. Each of these descriptions entails that objects or phenomena other than the event or conditions described exist. But it would be wrong to conclude from this that such objects or phenomena are part of or partly constitute the event or conditions described.

Even if we agree, then, that certain mental types are essentially relational (i.e., that their canonical descriptions are relational), still it would not follow that they are to be located (in some sense of 'located') beyond the confines of persons' bodies. For the move from the claim that objects external to the bodies of persons are partly constitutive of mental types to the claim that the types themselves are not wholly within those bodies (because constituted in part by such objects) is illicit. This removes one obstacle to the attempt to reconcile context dependence with token identity between the mental and the physical. Turn now to individual (token) mental events. Does the relational nature of certain mental types present obstacles to the view that individual tokens of those types are to be located in part beyond the confines of persons' bodies?

To see that it does not, recall the reason why the relational nature of mental types seemed incompatible with type-type identity between the mental and the physical. For mental types to *be* physical is for them to have identity and individuation conditions which do not entail existential claims about objects other than themselves or their subjects. However, this could only be thought to prohibit token identity if we suppose that *instancings* of mental types have no other descriptions in terms of types whose natures are not essentially relational. And we have no *a priori* reason to suppose this. On the contrary, to do so would be to beg the question against token-identity theorists of mind and body. In short, the fact that mental *types* are such that they are determined in part by objects other than themselves and their subjects in no way shows that such objects are constitutive of tokens of those types even if it does show that they are constitutive of the types themselves. If token identity is the case, instancings of mental properties are instancings of physical ones whose identity and individuation conditions do not entail existential claims about objects other than themselves and their subjects. That mental types have no such conditions does not mitigate against the possibility that tokens of those types are also of physical types which do have such conditions (cf. the discussion of the question of whether it is of the essence of any token of any intentional (or phenomenal) mental type that it be of that type in Chapter Four, Section 6).

Thus, the relational nature of intentional mental types fails to establish that they are not wholly in the head; still less does it do so for tokens of such types. Although it evidently does have the consequence that intentional mental types are not identical with neurophysiological types (on the plausible assumption that the latter are not essentially relational), it in no way compromises the supposition of token identity between the mental and the physical.

4. Weak Supervenience: Too Weak?

Recall that the main objection to (1′) as a characterization of the relation between mental and physical properties was that it ensures that a determination relation holds between mental and physical properties only intra-worldly. This, it was said, does not do justice to non-reductive monism's physicalist commitments, since it leaves open the possibility that another world should be physically indiscernible from this one, yet differ in its distribution of mental properties. This seems to contradict the intuition that if the physical properties of things (events) determine mental ones, then once the physical ones are fixed it is not possible to vary the mental ones. To suggest that the mental ones might vary while the physical ones do not is to suggest that the mental is not, after all, determined or exhausted by the physical; and this would seem to compromise non-reductive monism's physicalist commitments.

In fact, there are two sorts of puzzles associated with weak supervenience, both of which require explanation if the thesis is to be accommodated along with non-reductive *monism*. The first concerns the compatibility with weak supervenience, (*a*) of worlds in which mental properties are altogether absent (mindless worlds), (*b*) of worlds in which physical properties are entirely absent (spiritual worlds), and (*c*) of worlds in which different mental properties from those in this world are systematically related to physical properties indiscernible from those in this world. With respect to (*a*) and (*b*) at least, this seems to be an issue having to do with the notion of physical *exhaustion*. The second concerns the *incompatibility* with weak supervenience of worlds in which some objects or events indiscernible with respect to relevant subvenient (P) properties are indiscernible with respect to supervenient (M) properties whereas others are not. Worlds like these are ones in which, in the terminology of definition (1′), some objects or events which have G have F, whereas others do not. The puzzle here is why, given worlds in which a *G/F* relation uniformly holds and worlds in which no object/event which is *G* is *F*, such 'mixed' worlds should be ruled out. This seems, along with (*c*), to be an issue having to do with the notion of physical *determination*.[33]

Let's begin with the first puzzle. The difficulty that weak supervenience appears to present here is that in worlds where objects or events are both *F* and *G* and (1′) is true, it is implied that being *F* is not only fixed but exhausted by being *G*. In the case of psychophysical supervenience, (1′) implies that being of a mental type is exhausted (in a sense to be specified shortly; see below) by being of some physical type or other. Compare this with the case of colour. Being coloured, one wants to say, is not only fixed but exhausted by being blue or being green or being red or . . . or etc. Given that something has the property of being red (or etc.), it is guaranteed to have the property of being coloured. There couldn't be a world in which things had such properties as those of being red or being blue but *didn't* have the property of being coloured. Conversely, there couldn't be a world in which things had the property of being coloured without having either the property of being red or the property of being blue or . . . or etc. (1′) fails to do justice to this notion of exhaustion.

What is it for a property or a family of properties to be exhausted by another? Take Hellman and Thompson's Principle of Physical Exhaustion.[34] According to this principle, our ontology consists of all the referents of basic physical theory predicates plus every sum or part of such entities plus set-theoretical constructs of such entities, and no more. The Principle of Physical Exhaustion ensures that every property or attribute is a mathematical-physical *entity*.[35] Mental properties are physical entities because of the ontological status of the objects or events that possess or exemplify them. This, is compatible with mental and physical properties having different *ideological* status, this difference being responsible for the failure of psychophysical reductionism. The ideological status of a property or entity depends on and is due to the vocabulary by means of which it is specified. Mental and physical properties have different ideological status because the vocabularies by means of which they are specified are distinct.

The Principle of Physical Exhaustion is independent of

Hellman and Thompson's other two principles of determination and of reductionism. Given that these latter characterize a version of strong supervenience, it follows that not even strong supervenience entails that mental as well as physical properties are physical entities.[36] Both strong and weak supervenience allow for the possibility of worlds inhabited by non-physical angels, for instance. This seems to present a serious worry for those who are committed to the contingent truth of materialism *and* who think that materialism is best interpreted in terms of a possible worlds formulation of strong supervenience. The independence of strong supervenience thus formulated from physical exhaustion threatens the truth of materialism, since worlds which are physically possible may nevertheless contain Cartesian souls and the like.[37]

However, reconciling the contingent truth of materialism with either strong or weak supervenience is not a worry for the non-reductive monist. That theorist can interpret materialism, not in terms of the supervenience of mental properties on physical ones, but rather, directly, in terms of tokens of mental types being tokens of physical types. Materialism is held to be true and contingent because token identity is true and contingent: an instancing of a given mental property need not have been an instancing of a physical one, and vice versa. This seems, on the face of it, to be compatible with there being worlds inhabited by non-physical angels. Similarly, the possibility of there being worlds physically indiscernible from this one in which there are no mental properties at all is consistent not only with weak supervenience but also with strong. Neither (1′) nor (2) requires that any object or event that has physical properties must have mental properties also. What (1′) entails is that if any two objects/events, a and b, do or were to have the same G-properties within a given world, then they do or would both have the same F-properties in that world. What (2) entails is that, if b were to have the same G-properties in this or in another world that a does have in this world, then b would also have the same F-properties that a does have. Neither of these definitions entails that any object that has G-properties must also have F-properties. Nor would this be desirable. Both strong and weak supervenience construe that relation as one holding between *distinct* (families of) properties. In the case of psychophysical supervenience, where the relation between subvenient and supervenient properties is not a logically necessary one, it must be possible not only for mental properties to exist in worlds where physical ones do not, but also for physical ones to exist in worlds where mental ones do not.

Evidently, the real worry associated with the first puzzle is not that weak supervenience should be compatible with the existence of mindless worlds, nor is it that it should be consistent with the existence of spiritual worlds. The possibility that causes trouble for weak supervenience is that *different* mental properties from ones that exist in this world should supervene on physical properties indiscernible from those in this world. This is ruled out by (2). For (2) says that if any two objects/events in this world that are indiscernible with regard to their G-properties are indiscernible with regard to their F-properties, any objects/events in any other world with G-properties must be F.

In defence of (1') it might be said that, just as the distinctness of mental from physical properties, combined with the fact that the relation between them is weaker than that of logical necessity, ensures that both mindless worlds and spiritual worlds should be compatible with supervenience, weak or strong, so too should it ensure that, in worlds other than this, different mental properties might exist from those that exist in this world, even given physical indiscernibility. The trouble is that if we are prepared to say that this might be so in worlds other than this, there is no obvious reason why we should not be prepared to say that it might be so in this world too. But this gives rise to the second puzzle. For weak supervenience prohibits the existence of mixed worlds. Any attempt to explain why different mental properties should supervene on properties in worlds which are physically indiscernible from this one should also, it seems, come at least some way toward providing an explanation as to why mixed worlds are not possible.

This problem seems to rest, not on the issue of physical exhaustion, but rather, on the issue of determination. One response that will not work is to suggest that non-reductive monism might alone afford an explanation. What needs explaining is how the physical properties of things could fix the mental ones in this world without, as it were, determining them. So what needs to be accounted for is why an F/G relation should in *this* world be necessary. It may be true that non-reductive monism is a contingent thesis and so does not ensure the existence in another world of any mental properties, let alone ensure that every instancing of a mental property should be an instancing of a physical one. And it may well be that in this world it so happens that non-reductive monism is true. But neither of these claims shows, even with regard to this world, that mental properties supervene on physical ones. Token identity between the mental and the physical establishes no more than that the entities which are instancings of mental properties are instancings of physical ones. It is compatible with this that two instancings of the same physical property or properties should be instancings of *distinct* mental ones, even in this world. In short, non-reductive monism is weaker than weak supervenience. This being so, it cannot afford an explanation of that relation.

A clue to a more promising strategy is nevertheless to be found in that position's commitment to the autonomy of the mental. This would seem to require at the very least that mental and physical properties are logically distinct and so have distinct identity and individuation conditions. An explanation of weak supervenience might be afforded by showing how the distinctness of such conditions is compatible with both (*a*) the supposition that in this world things with the same (types of) physical properties must have the same mental properties *and* (*b*) the supposition that in another world two things might be physically indiscernible from one another and from things in this world yet possess mental properties discernible from ones had by things in this world.

Why should we think that (*a*) is true? One suggestion, discussed at length in Chapter Four, Section 6, is that our evidence or grounds for attributing mental properties, viz. introspection and intentional behaviour, is so tied to the physical properties of persons' bodies and their environments that we could have no reason to discern a difference in mental properties where there was no corresponding potential difference in such physical properties. Discerning differences in mental properties requires discerning some difference in either intentional behaviour (for intentional mental properties) or introspection (for phenomenal mental properties; but see the discussion below). And it does not seem possible that such differences could exist where there were no potential physical differences. The reason, it was said, is that mental properties are causally efficacious with regard to the physical world. Our conception of causality is such that we expect like causes to have like effects and vice versa; and this, given causal interaction between the mental and the physical, has the consequence that where organisms differ in their mental properties, this difference must make a potential physical difference. In the light of variable realizability, such physical differences as might occur within the confines of persons' bodies could not alone ground the belief that they differ psychologically. For neither do we have access to these in our everyday attributions, nor, if we did, would we consider them significant if they did not effect corresponding differences in intentional behaviour and introspection – ultimately in intentional behaviour or action. The consequence is that although mental properties have identity and individuation conditions distinct from those of any physical property (indeed they must if variable realization is possible), their attribution is answerable to criteria which we cannot suppose to be met without having consequences for how things are in the physical world. Causal interaction between the mental and the physical, combined with the belief that distinct properties must make a potential difference in their causes, or effects, or both, is what explains, in this world, the phenomenon of supervenience of mental on physical properties.

If this is so for this world, is it not similarly so for any other physically indiscernible world for which (1') is true? Barring spiritual worlds and mindless ones, the answer is probably yes, since we have no reason to expect that in such worlds, mental properties would not be causally efficacious with regard to physical ones. However, it does not follow from this that, in a world physically indiscernible from this one, the *same* mental properties must exist. For the principle that like effects have like causes and vice versa is one which operates *within* each possible world, not necessarily across worlds. To reach the latter conclusion (i.e., the truth of supposition (*b*) above), one needs to establish the claim that worlds like ours with regard to physical effects and causes *must* be like ours with regard to mental causes and effects. (The difference is that between (*a*) necessarily, like effects have like causes, and vice versa, and (*b*) necessarily, like effects necessarily have like causes, and vice versa.)

To see whether this claim is viable, a good deal more needs to be said than has been said thus far about the identity and individuation conditions of mental properties. In the case of intentional mental properties, such conditions are given, at least in part, by specifying objects, reference to which is involved in attributions of those properties. Though it is possible that differences in such objects may not make for differences in behaviour narrowly construed, we would expect them to make for differences in behaviour widely construed and so in intentional mental properties themselves. In the case of phenomenal mental properties, such conditions are determined partly if not wholly by their (subjective) qualia or feel; and we would expect differences in qualia to make for differences in a subject's introspective awareness. One might think that we cannot consistently suppose that another world should be physically indiscernible from this one yet vary in the types of intentional and/or phenomenal mental properties that there are. But this is only so if we suppose that sameness of causal potentialities of mental properties *vis-à-vis* physical properties is both necessary *and* sufficient for identity of such properties. It is only on this assumption that one is entitled to move from the claim that certain mental properties have the causal potentialities they do in this world with regard to physical properties to the claim that different mental properties from those in this world cannot in another world have causal potentialities identical with mental properties in this world *vis-à-vis* properties physically indiscernible from those in this world.

However, we have no clear reason to endorse the view that sameness of causal potentialities with regard to physical properties is sufficient for the identity of mental properties. Even in the case of intentional mental properties, the most that has been acknowledged is that *part* of their nature is fixed by (physical) objects or events, reference to which is typically involved in their attribution. Moreover, this is not individuation by *causal* potentialities, since intentional mental properties are logically and not merely causally related to objects involved in their attribution. Even if identity of causal potentialities *vis-à-vis* such physical objects and/or events were to be considered necessary, it could not suffice for the identity of intentional mental properties, since it fails to discriminate between such properties as those of believing that Mozart wrote *The Magic Flute* and doubting that

Mozart wrote *The Magic Flute*. If this is clear for intentional mental properties, it is clearer still for phenomenal mental ones. Here there seems to be no reason whatever to claim that it is not possible for the quale of a phenomenal mental property to vary while its causal powers with regard to physical properties remain invariant. This is because the quale of a phenomenal mental property appears to be only contingently associated with any causal potential it may have with regard to intentional behaviour. (This, we have seen, is why phenomenal mental properties present such difficulties for CR/FS identity theorists.)

These considerations suggest that, in the case of phenomenal mental properties at least, part of their nature is fixed by their associated qualia, where these are not in turn fixed either by physical objects and/or events that exist or occur beyond the confines of persons' bodies or by the causal potentialities qualia may have with regard to such objects and/or events (*via* intentional behaviour). Thus, for example, it seems possible that some phenomenal mental property other than that of having pain should, in a world other than this, possess the causal potentialities with regard to physical objects and phenomena possessed by that property in this world. (This is not, of course, to say that weak supervenience would be violated in that world any more than it would be in this one.) Because phenomenal mental properties have natures that are fixed, at least in part, by their associated qualia; and since these latter are not fixed by their causal potentialities with regard to the physical world (specifically, intentional behaviour or action), the relation which phenomenal mental properties bear to physical ones seems adequately captured by weak supervenience.

The case appears to be different for intentional mental properties. Here it is more difficult to see how the causal potentialities of these properties *vis-à-vis* physical properties might remain invariant across worlds while the properties themselves differ. This in turn seems to be due to a difficulty in seeing what more could be involved in the identity and individuation conditions of such properties *besides* physical objects and/or events, reference to which is typically involved in their attribution. Even if such properties aren't fixed by their causal potentialities, they surely serve to fix those potentialities. But if this is so, then how can it be that two worlds might be physically indiscernible and indiscernible with respect to the causal potentialities of intentional mental properties *vis-à-vis* physical ones, yet *differ* in the number, kinds, or distribution of intentional mental properties themselves?

One suggestion might be that *how* objects are represented is as important to the identity and individuation conditions of intentional mental properties as *what* objects are represented; and that the former can vary while the latter does not (cf. Section 3 above). However, it does not seem possible that intentional mental properties might differ as between worlds in *how* they represent an object while remaining invariant in their causal potentialities, any more than it is possible that they can differ in *what* they represent while remaining invariant in such potentialities *vis-à-vis* intentional behaviour or action. Consider, for instance, the property of believing that Hesperus is the star seen in the sky in the morning and the property of believing that Phosphorus is the star seen in the sky in the evening. These seem to be type-distinct, despite the fact that Hesperus = Phosphorus, since they represent that star in distinct ways. Some put this by saying that the 'modes of presentation' of that star are different; and one good reason for thinking that this is so is that the attribution of one of these properties to a person may issue in actions which differ from those of a person to which the other is attributed.[38] Thus, for example, on the supposition that I am ignorant of the fact that Hesperus is Phosphorus, I am apt to point to that star one morning and say, 'There's Hesperus' but not 'There's Phosphorus'. Whatever objections there may be to the dual component view of intentional mental properties, the intuition that lies behind it, viz. that how objects are represented is as important to the identity and individuation conditions of intentional mental properties as what objects are represented, seems to be correct. But then the present suggestion cannot resolve the difficulty of seeing how intentional mental properties can differ across worlds while remaining invariant in their causal potentialities with regard to action. For it is highly implausible to suppose that such properties might differ in *how* they represent objects while remaining invariant in their causal potentialities *vis-à-vis* intentional behaviour.

Nor is it likely that that difficulty can be resolved by turning to the other obvious feature of intentional mental properties yet to be accounted for in their identity and individuation conditions, viz. that feature which determines the attitude types – belief, desire, hope, doubt, etc. – into which they fall. It is also implausible to suppose that the type into which an intentional mental property falls might differ while its causal potentialities with regard to action remains invariant. Think, for example, of desire: its very essence seems to be to dispose a subject to engage in behaviour which seeks to satisfy it. Or think of what distinguishes doubt, at least in part, from belief – that its subject is apt to behave in an uncertain manner toward its object. Indeed, a major strength of the CR/FS identity theory lies in its recognition of the fact that the type identity of intentional mental properties does not appear to be independent of the causal potentialities of such properties *vis-à-vis* intentional behaviour. This may not be all there is to the nature of intentional mental properties, but it is enough to ensure that weak supervenience cannot be accommodated along either of the above lines.

Evidently, weak supervenience is too weak to account for the relation between intentional mental properties and physical ones. For these properties, if not for phenomenal mental ones, considerations about how they relate to physical objects and/or events require the non-reductive monist to go for a stronger conception than that expressed by (1′).

5. A Residual Question

There is, however, a final question worth raising here, and that is whether non-reductive monism requires supplementation by a supervenience thesis at all. The worry expressed at the outset of this chapter was that, in the absence of some explanation of the relation between mental and physical properties, the non-reductive monist is threatened with the charge of dualism. This threat would seem to require some kind of account of how mental properties, even if distinct from physical ones, are somehow fixed or determined by them. Supervenience seemed to be the best explanation of that relation.

One might wonder, however, whether non-reductive monism needs even this. What needs explaining is how mental properties can be fixed by physical ones. But this might be accounted for simply by reference to Hellman and Thompson's Principle of Physical Exhaustion. Recall that this principle has the consequence that mental properties are physical entities inasmuch as they are possessed or instanced by physical things. Now non-reductive monism ensures that, in this world at least, the Principle of Physical Exhaustion is true. By one reasonable standard of what counts as a physical property, properties are physical if they are had by physical things. Need the relation between mental and physical properties be any more systematic than this in order to reconcile non-reductive monism's commitment to the distinctness of mental and physical properties with its equal commitment to physicalism?

Considered from the point of view of token physicalism alone, perhaps this is all that is necessary. However, the type of physicalism to which non-reductive monism is committed is stronger than the mere ontological thesis that all the entities that exist fall within the domain of physical theory. That position is committed to the causal-explanatory supremacy of physical theory – to the view that each mental event has a physical description by which it is subsumed under physical causal laws. It is this that puts pressure on the non-reductive monist to endorse some kind of supervenience thesis (though it is arguable that the position might survive the loss of the PNCC; see Chapter Five). The token identities between mental and physical events entailed by the theory are compatible with the supposition that events which are indiscernible with regard to their physical properties are discernible with regard to their mental ones. But events with indiscernible physical properties will have the same causal potentialities *vis-à-vis* other physical events. To maintain that such events may yet differ with regard to their mental properties is to suppose that mental properties can vary while making no discernible physical difference. Given that distinct properties differ in their causal potentialities, this threatens causal interaction between the mental and the physical. Whatever grounds the non-reductive monist may have for thinking that events are type-distinct physically when they differ in their causal potentialities *vis-à-vis* other physical events, that theorist has them also for thinking that events are type-distinct mentally when they differ in their causal potentialities *vis-à-vis* other physical events. This suggests that there is a more systematic relation between mental and physical properties than non-reductive monism itself entails but which that theory ought to endorse if it is to retain allegiance to its physicalist commitments.

Notes

Preface and Acknowledgements

1. See J. J. C. Smart, 'Sensations and Brain Processes', reprinted in John O'Connor (ed.), *Modern Materialism: Readings on Mind-Body Identity* (New York: Harcourt, Brace, & World, Inc., 1969), pp. 32–47; U.T. Place, 'Is Consciousness a Brain Process?', reprinted in ibid., pp. 21–31; D.M. Armstrong, *A Materialist Theory of Mind* (London: Routledge & Kegan Paul, 1968), and R.J. Bogdan (ed.), *D.M. Armstrong* (Dordrecht: D. Reidel, 1984); David Lewis, 'An Argument for the Identity Theory', reprinted in *Philosophical Papers,* vol. I (Oxford: Oxford University Press, 1983), pp. 99–107, and 'Psychophysical and Theoretical Identifications', *Australasian Journal of Philosophy,* 50, 2 (December 1972), pp. 249–58; Jaegwon Kim, 'On the Psycho-Physical Identity Theory', reprinted in O'Connor, *Modern Materialism*, pp. 195–211, and 'Phenomenal Properties, Psychophysical Laws, and the Identity Theory', *Monist* 56 (April 1972), pp. 177–92; and Donald Davidson, 'Mental Events', reprinted in *Essays on Actions and Events* (Oxford: Clarendon Press, 1980), pp. 207–25.
2. See Donald Davidson, 'Psychology as Philosophy' (along with his 'Comments and Replies'), reprinted in *Essays on Actions and Events* pp. 229–39 and 239–44; Jaegwon Kim, 'Psychophysical Laws', in E. LePore and B. McLaughlin (eds), *Actions and Events* (Oxford: Basil Blackwell, 1985), pp. 369–86; and John McDowell, 'Functionalism and Anomalous Monism', ibid., pp. 387–98.
3. See *Events: A Metaphysical Study* (London: Routledge & Kegan Paul, 1986).

Chapter One

1. See, for example, Smart, 'Sensations and Brain Processes', Michael Levin, 'Phenomenal Properties', *Philosophy and Phenomenological Research,* 42 (1981–2), pp. 42–58; and Richard Double, 'Phenomenal

Properties', *Philosophy and Phenomenological Research,* 45, 3 (March 1985), pp. 383–92.

2. See Smart, 'Sensations and Brain Processes'; Place, 'Is Consciousness a Brain Process?'; Armstrong, *A Materialist Theory of Mind;* Lewis, 'An Argument for the Identity Theory' and 'Psychophysical and Theoretical Identifications'; Davidson, 'Mental Events'; Saul Kripke, 'Naming and Necessity', in D. Davidson and G. Harman (eds), *Semantics of Natural Language* (Dordrecht: D. Reidel, 1972), pp. 253–355; Frank Jackson, 'What Mary Didn't Know', in *The Journal of Philosophy*, LXXXIII, (5 May 1986), pp. 291–5; and Thomas Nagel, 'What Is It Like to Be a Bat?', reprinted in *Mortal Questions* (Cambridge: Cambridge University Press, 1979), pp. 165–80.

3. Or merely temporally related to every event, as Davidson suggests in 'Mental Events'. This version is due to Mark Johnston; see 'Why Having a Mind Matters', in LePore and McLaughlin, *Actions and Events* pp. 408–26.

4. See Davidson, ibid., and 'Psychology as Philosophy', Kim, 'Psychophysical Laws', and Colin McGinn, 'Mental States, Natural Kinds, and Psychophysical Laws', *Proceedings of the Aristotelian Society,* supp. vol. LII (1978), pp. 195–221.

5. See Kim, 'Materialism and the Criteria of the Mental', *Synthese* 22 (1971), pp. 323–45.

6. See D. Kraus, ed., *Psychology From an Empirical Standpoint* (English ed. by Linda L. McAlister, 2nd edn), trans. by A.C. Rancurello, D.B. Terrell, and L.L. McAlister (London: Routledge & Kegan Paul, 1973).

7. See *Perceiving: A Philosophical Study* (Ithaca, NY: Cornell University Press, 1957).

8. See Davidson, 'Mental Events'.

9. See, for instance Kim, 'Pychophysical Laws'. Davidson explicitly points out (in 'Mental Events') that the criterion is too wide rather than too narrow. See also Johnston, 'Why Having a Mind Matters', Brian McLaughlin, 'Anomalous Monism and the Irreducibility of the Mental', in LePore and McLaughlin, *Actions and Events,* pp. 331–68, and Arnold Levison, 'An Epistemic Criterion of the Mental', *Canadian Journal of Philosophy,* XIII, 3. (September 1983), pp. 389–407.

10. See Kim, 'Materialism and the Criteria of the Mental'. The need for the alternative formulation is due to the fact that events may have spatial location without having spatial extent.

11. See Johnston, 'Why Having a Mind Matters'.

12. See Kim, 'Materialism and the Criteria of the Mental'.

13. See Levison, 'An Epistemic Criterion of the Mental'.

14. In Kim, 'Materialism and the Criteria of the Mental', p. 340.

15. Levison, 'An Epistemic Criterion of the Mental', p. 399.

16. ibid. p. 399.

17. See Smart, 'Sensations and Brain Processes', p. 42.

18. See Double, 'Phenomenal Properties', p. 385.
19. See Nagel, 'What Is It Like to Be a Bat?'.
20. See Paul Churchland, 'Reduction, Qualia, and the Direct Introspection of Brain States', *The Journal of Philosophy*, LXXXII, 1 (January 1985), pp. 8–28.
21. ibid. This is Churchland's argument.
22. See Colin McGinn's Critical Notice of *The View From Nowhere, Mind*, XCVI, 382 (April 1987), pp. 263–72.
23. See Frank Jackson, 'What Mary Didn't Know' (but note also Terence Horgan, 'Jackson on Physical Information and Qualia', *Philosophical Quarterly*, XXXIV, 135 (April 1984), pp. 147–52).
24. In 'Epiphenomenal Qualia', *Philosophical Quarterly*, XXXII, 127 (April 1982), pp. 127–36.
25. See Jackson, 'What Mary Didn't Know'.
26. See 'Epiphenomenal Qualia'.
27. See Horgan, 'Jackson on Physical Information and Qualia'.
28. The term is Horgan's (ibid).
29. See, for example, Churchland, 'Reduction, Qualia, and the Direct Introspection of Brain States'; Horgan, 'Jackson on Physical Information and Qualia'; and Paul Churchland and Patricia Churchland, 'Functionalism, Qualia, and Intentionality', in J. I. Biro and Robert W. Shahan (eds), *Mind, Brain, and Function* (Sussex: Harvester Press, 1982), pp. 121–45.
30. Kim, 'Phenomenal Properties, Psychophysical Laws, and the Identity Theory', 180.
31. See 'Naming and Necessity'.
32. See 'Identity and Necessity', in M. Munitz (ed.), *Identity and Individuation* (New York: New York University Press, 1971), pp. 135–64. See also Fred Feldman, 'Kripke on the Identity Theory', *The Journal of Philosophy*, LXXI, 18 (24 October 1974), pp. 665–76, and Graeme Forbes, *The Metaphysics of Modality* (especially Section 5, Chapter 3) (Oxford: Clarendon Press, 1985).
33. See Christopher Peacocke, *Holistic Explanation* (Oxford: Clarendon Press, 1979).
34. See, for example, Hilary Putnam, 'Psychological Predicates', in W. H. Capitan and D. D. Merrill (eds), *Art, Mind and Religion* (Pittsburgh, Pa: University of Pittsburgh Press, 1967), pp. 44–5; Kim, 'Phenomenal Properties, Psychophysical Laws, and the Identity Theory'; and Colin McGinn, 'Mental States, Natural Kinds, and Psychophysical Laws'.
35. See McGinn, ibid.
36. This suggestion is encouraged by Kim's argument to the effect that psychophysical supervenience leads to the necessary coextension of mental and physical properties; see 'Supervenience and Supervenient Causation', in *The Southern Journal of Philosophy*, XXII, Supplement (Spindel Conference: The Concept of Supervenience in Contemporary Philosophy) (1984), pp. 45–56; also, see Paul Teller's 'Comments on Kim's Paper', ibid. pp. 57–61.

37. Teller, ibid., makes this point.
38. See John Post, 'Comment on Teller', *The Southern Journal of Philosophy*, XXII, Supplement (Spindel Conference: The Concept of Supervenience in Contemporary Philosophy) (1984), pp. 163–7.
39. The example is Post's. (ibid., p. 165).

Chapter Two

1. For the early position, see Armstrong, *A Materialist Theory of Mind*, and for the later view, see Bogdan, *D.M. Armstrong*, and D.M. Armstrong and N. Malcolm, *Consciousness and Causality* (Oxford: Basil Blackwell, 1984).
2. Steven White makes this point in 'Curse of the Qualia', *Synthese* 68 (1986), pp. 333–68. See Smart, 'Sensations and Brain Processes', and Armstrong, *A Materialist Theory of Mind*.
3. See, for example, Colin McGinn, 'Functionalism and Phenomenalism: A Critical Note', *Australasian Journal of Philosophy*, 58, 1 (March 1980), pp. 35–46, and Lewis, 'An Argument For the Identity Theory'.
4. See Lewis, 'Psychophysical and Theoretical Identifications'.
5. In 'Mad Pain and Martian Pain', reprinted in *Philosophical Papers*, vol. I, pp. 122–30.
6. D.M. Armstrong and N. Malcolm, *Consciousness and Casualty*.
7. See Lewis, 'Psychophysical and Theoretical Identifications'.
8. $T(t_1. . .tn)$ thus claims that there exists a unique n-tuple which satisfies the open sentence $T(x_1. . .x_n)$. The terms $t_1. . .t_n$ designate members of this *n*-tuple (provided there exists one) and are defined as follows:
$$T_1 = df \, \iota y_1 \exists y_2 . . . \exists y_n(x_1) . . . (x_n)(T(x_1. . .x_n) \equiv y_1 = x_1 \, \& y_2 = x_2 \, \& \, y_n = x_n)$$
(see Lewis, 'How To Define Theoretical Terms', reprinted in *Philosophical Papers*, vol. I, pp. 78–95).
9. This is sometimes understood as the functional-state identity theory. See Ned Block's 'What is Functionalism?', Introduction to Part Three of *Readings in the Philosophy of Psychology*, vol. I, (Cambridge: Cambridge University Press, 1980), pp. 171–84.
10. Armstrong himself suggests both of these. See D.M. Armstrong and N. Malcolm, *Consciousness and Causality*.
11. See Armstrong in ibid., and Lewis, 'Psychophysical and Theoretical Identifications', and 'Mad Pain and Martian Pain'.
12. See Jennifer Hornsby, 'On Functionalism, and On Jackson, Pargetter, and Prior on Functionalism', *Philosophical Studies*, 46 (1984), pp. 75–95.
13. See, for example, Kripke, 'Naming and Necessity'; Lewis, 'Mad Pain and Martian Pain'; and Frank Jackson, Robert Pargetter, and Elizabeth Prior, 'Functionalism and Type-Type Identity Theories', *Philosophical Studies* 42 (1982), pp. 209–25.

14. See, for example, Kripke, 'Naming and Necessity'; Colin McGinn, 'Rigid Designation and Semantic Value', *The Philosophical Quarterly*, 32 (April 1982), pp. 97–115; and Michael Dummett, *Frege: Philosophy of Language* (London: Duckworth, 1973).

15. Hornsby, in 'On Functionalism, and On Jackson, Pargetter, and Prior on Functionalism', makes this point.

16. See Armstrong and Malcolm, *Consciousness and Causality*.

17. This construal of the nature of the type-type identities to which the CR/FS identity theory is committed likens it to the functional-state identity theory discussed in Section 4.

18. There is one notable difference which will emerge as important when we consider the absent qualia objection, and that is that the causal-role identity theorist believes that the roles by which mental types are defined are specifically *causal*, whereas a functionalist may believe that the roles by which mental types are defined are not merely causal but functional in some other way (I am indebted to Lawrence Lombard for bringing this to my attention). This difference will not play a prominent role in the discussion to follow, however; and so, for the purposes of discussion, the causal-role identity and the functional specification theory will be treated as indistinguishable (the exception being in the treatment of the absent qualia objection).

19. See Jackson, Pargetter, and Prior, 'Functionalism and Type-Type Identity Theories'. Also, see Block, 'What is Functionalism?'.

20. See McGinn, 'Functionalism and Phenomenalism: A Critical Note'.

21. See, for instance, Block, 'What Is Functionalism?'. See also Jackson, Pargetter, and Prior, 'Functionalism and Type-Type Identity Theories' for a useful discussion of the various sorts of type-type identities to which functionalists might be construed as being committed.

22. See Lewis, 'An Argument For the Identity Theory', no. 6.

23. See Block, 'What is Functionalism?'.

24. See 'Naming and Necessity'.

25. See, for example, Sydney Shoemaker, 'Functionalism and Qualia', reprinted in *Identity, Cause, and Mind* (Cambridge: Cambridge University Press, 1984), pp. 184–205; 'Absent Qualia Are Impossible', reprinted in ibid., pp. 309–26; and 'The Inverted Spectrum', reprinted in ibid. pp. 327–57; Ned Block and Jerry Fodor, 'What Psychological States are Not', reprinted in Block, *Readings in the Philosophy of Psychology*, vol. I, pp. 237–50; Ned Block, 'Troubles with Functionalism', reprinted in ibid., pp. 268–305; and 'Are Absent Qualia Impossible?', *The Philosophical Review*, 89, 2 (April 1980), pp. 257–74; and Terence Horgan, 'Functionalism, Qualia, and the Inverted Spectrum', *Philosophy and Phenomenological Research*, XLIV, 4. (June 1984), pp. 453–69.

26. See, for example, McDowell, 'Functionalism and Anomalous Monism'.

27. See, for example, Shoemaker, 'Absent Qualia are Impossible'; and

Churchland and Churchland, 'Functionalism, Qualia, and Intentionality'.

28. See Churchland and Churchland, ibid.; and Shoemaker, 'Functionalism and Qualia'.
29. ibid., p. 201.
30. See Horgan, 'Functionalism, Qualia, and the Inverted Spectrum'.
31. See Churchland and Churchland, 'Functionalism, Qualia, and Intentionality'. Also, see McGinn, 'Mental States, Natural Kinds, and Psychophysical Laws'.
32. See, for example, Block, 'Are Absent Qualia Impossible?'.
33. ibid. The term 'ersatz' is due to Lawrence Davis.
34. See 'Functionalism and Qualia'.
35. In 'Are Absent Qualia Impossible?'.
36. 'Absent Qualia are Impossible'.
37. ibid.
38. This objection is voiced by Christopher Peacocke. See *Holistic Explanation*.
39. This objection is voiced by Joseph Owens. See 'The Failure of Lewis's Functionalism', *The Philosophical Quarterly*, 36, 143 (April 1986), pp. 159–73.
40. See Jennifer Hornsby, 'Which Physical Events are Mental Events?', *Proceedings of the Aristotelian Society*, LXXI (1980-1), pp. 73–92.

Chapter Three

1. See 'Mental Events'.
2. Davidson actually says 'events are mental only as described' (ibid., p. 215). This has been noticed and criticized by Mark Johnston, 'Why Having a Mind Matters', p. 420, and by Brian McLaughlin, 'Anomalous Monism and the Irreducibility of the Mental'. As the latter points out (p. 336), the position occupied by '*e*' in '*e* satisfies the open mental sentence '*x* is *M*'' is extensional. So we should read Davidson as saying that *e* is mental only if *e* is describ*able* as mental.
3. See 'Psychology as Philosophy', pp. 231–3.
4. McLaughlin, in 'Anomalous Monism and the Irreducibility of the Mental', p. 335, also makes this point.
5. See Johnston, 'Why Having a Mind Matters'.
6. See 'Mental Events', p. 219.
7. See 'The Material Mind', reprinted in *Essays on Actions and Events*, pp. 245–59. Also, see McLaughlin's discussion in 'Anomalous Monism and the Irreducibility of the Mental', (pp. 353–4).
8. 'Mental Events', p. 222.
9. See, for example, Ted Honderich, 'Psychophysical Lawlike Connections and Their Problem', *Inquiry* 24 (1981), pp. 277-304, and Brian Loar, *Mind and Meaning* (Cambridge: Cambridge University Press, 1981), Chapter 1. This point is explicitly addressed by Jaegwon Kim in 'Psychophysical Laws', and by Colin McGinn in 'Philosophical

Materialism', *Synthese* 44 (1980), pp. 173–206.

10. See McLaughlin, 'Anomalous Monism and the Irreducibility of the Mental', p. 345. A law is explicit (*a*) when it states all boundary conditions, and (*b*) when it is devoid of dispositional or functional predicates. (It may be inherently probabilistic, in which case it will not be exceptionless. But it will be as exceptionless as possible given that the system is inherently probabilistic.)
11. 'Mental Events', p. 224.
12. McLaughlin, in 'Anomalous Monism and the Irreducibility of the Mental', also makes this point.
13. ibid., p. 343.
14. See 'Mental Events', p. 222, and 'Comments and Replies', p. 241, respectively.
15. See Davidson, 'Mental Events', and Kim, 'Psychophysical Laws'.
16. See Kim, ibid., and Davidson, 'Psychology as Philosophy' and 'Comments and Replies'.
17. See Kim, 'Psychophysical Laws'.
18. See Kim, ibid.
19. 'Mental Events', p. 216.
20. See, for instance, 'Psychophysical Laws', and 'Supervenience and Supervenient Causation'.
21. See 'Phenomenal Properties, Psychophysical Laws, and the Identity Theory'.
22. See James Cornman, 'On the Elimination of "Sensations" and Sensations', *The Review of Metaphysics* 22 (1968), pp. 15–35.
23. See Richard Rorty, 'Mind-Body Identity, Privacy, and Categories', *The Review of Metaphysics* 19 (1965), pp. 25–54.
24. See 'Events as Property Exemplifications', in M. Brand and D. Walton (eds), *Action Theory* (Dordrecht: D. Reidel, 1976), pp. 159–77.
25. 'Phenomenal Properties, Psychophysical Laws, and the Identity Theory', p. 183.
26. Richard Brandt and Jaegwon Kim, 'The Logic of the Identity Theory', reprinted in O'Connor, *Modern Materialism*, pp. 212–37.
27. See 'Events as Property Exemplifications'.
28. See 'Phenomenal Properties, Psychophysical Laws, and the Identity Theory'.

Chapter Four

1. See, for example, Lombard, *Events: A Metaphysical Study,* and Myles Brand, 'Particulars, Events, and Actions', in Brand and Walton, *Action Theory*, pp. 133–57.
2. See Brand, ibid., and Lombard, *Events*.
3. This is similar to Lombard's characterization of the form of a criterion in *Events*, Chapter 2.
4. See, for example, Davidson, 'The Individuation of Events',

reprinted in *Essays on Actions and Events*, pp. 163–80. For a comprehensive survey, see Lombard, *Events*, Chapter 3, and Brand, 'Particulars, Events, and Actions', pp. 133–57.

5. The proposal to take *de facto* spatiotemporal coincidence as necessary and sufficient for event identity is E.J. Lemmon's. See 'Comments on D. Davidson's "The Logical Form of Action Sentences"', in N. Rescher (ed.), *The Logic of Decision and Action* (Pittsburgh Pa: University of Pittsburgh Press, 1968), pp. 96–103. The example is Davidson's. See 'The Individuation of Events', (Davidson later retracts his doubts about the spatiotemporal criterion in 'Reply to Quine on Events', in LePore and McLaughlin, *Actions and Events*, pp. 172–6.) One might try to meet condition (1) or (2), or both, by defining the notion of a minimal location of an event (see Davidson, 'The Individuation of Events', and Lombard, 'Events', *The Canadian Journal of Philosophy*, IX, 3 (September 1979), pp. 425–35). But this will not help with the example of the rotating sphere, even if it does help with others, since the changes envisaged encompass the whole of the sphere. The problem with the criterion of *de facto* spatiotemporal coincidence is precisely that it is true of both events and physical objects that they have spatiotemporal properties. Davidson, when reconsidering the spatiotemporal criterion, suggests that the way in which events relate to space and time might suffice to individuate them from particulars (e.g., physical objects) of other distinct kinds. See his 'Reply to Quine on Events'. But this, even if true, is not reflected in standard formulations of the spatiotemporal criterion. Inasmuch as it is not, it requires explanation by way of an underlying theory of events.

6. Lombard, in *Events* (Chapter 3) makes this point. The proposal to take necessary spatiotemporal coincidence as necessary and sufficient for event identity is Brand's. See 'Particulars, Events, and Actions'.

7. The suggestion is Davidson's. See 'The Individuation of Events'. See also 'Causal Relations', reprinted in *Essays on Actions and Events*, pp. 149–62. The fission/fusion example is Brand's. See 'Particulars, Events, and Actions'.

8. See Brand, ibid.; V.W. Quine, 'Events and Reification', in LePore and McLaughlin, *Actions and Events*, pp. 162–71; George Sher, 'On Event-Identity', *Australasian Journal of Philosophy*, 52, 1 (May 1974), pp. 40–7; and Neil Wilson, 'Facts, Events and Their Identity Conditions', *Philosophical Studies* 25 (1974), pp. 303–21. Whereas Wilson concentrates on the logical sort, Sher's interest is in the conceptual sort. The terminology is Brand's.

9. See 'Events as Property Exemplifications'. All references in this section to Kim's version of the PE account, unless otherwise specified, are to this paper.

10. This analogy was suggested to me by Lawrence Lombard.

11. See Alvin Plantinga, *The Nature of Necessity* (Oxford: Clarendon Library, 1974), especially Chapter 5.

12 See *Events*, Chapter 1.

13. See, for example, Davidson, 'The Individuation of Events'; Alvin Goldman, *A Theory of Human Action* (Englewood Cliffs, NJ: Prentice-Hall, Inc., 1970); and R.M. Martin, 'On Events and Event-Descriptions', in J. Margolis (ed.), *Fact and Experience* (Oxford: Basil Blackwell, 1969), pp. 63–73.

14. See Richard Swinburne, 'Are Mental Events Identical with Brain Events?', *American Philosophical Quarterly*, 19, 2 (1982), pp. 173–83.

15. See 'Events as Property Exemplifications'. Judith Jarvis Thompson also suggests this strategy in her paper, 'Individuating Actions', *The Journal of Philosophy* 68 (1971), pp. 774–81.

16. This is akin to Goldman's account of level generation in *A Theory of Human Action*.

17. 'Events as Property Exemplifications', pp. 159–60. See also 'Events and Their Descriptions: Some Considerations', in N. Rescher (ed.), *Essays in Honor of Carl G. Hempel*, pp. 198–215.

18. The term 'substance' is here taken to refer to any particular that falls into a natural kind for which there exists identity and persistence conditions, e.g., animals and vegetables, but not (as the class of material things in general does) artifacts such as clocks, or mereological sums (nor, in general, parts of those particulars which qualify as substances). This is linked to at least one traditional use of the term, stemming from Aristotle (see his *Metaphysics*, trans. by Sir David Ross, 2nd edn (Oxford: Clarendon Press, 1954), especially Book Z)). It accords with the recent use to which it has been put by those such as Wiggins (in *Sameness and Substance* (Oxford: Basil Blackwell, 1980)), Quinton (in *The Nature of Things* (London: Routledge & Kegan Paul, 1973), Brody (in *Identity and Essence* (Princeton NJ: Princeton University Press, 1980)), and Loux (in *Substance and Attribute* (Dordrecht: D. Reidel, 1978)). Loux in particular takes artifacts to be substances along with natural kinds of things. Here, however, we follow Aristotle in restricting its application to natural, i.e., animal and vegetable, kinds.

19. See *Events*. All further references in this section to Lombard's views on events, unless otherwise specified, are to this source.

20. ibid., p. 113.

21. See *Fact, Fiction, and Forecast* (2nd edn) (New York: Bobbs-Merrill Co., 1965). Suppose, to adapt Goodman's example, that an object, x, is grue if and only if it is green before time t, otherwise blue. Then, since x is grue throughout any interval of time during which it changes from being green to being blue, it would seem that the question of whether x has changed if it is green before t and blue thereafter cannot be settled independently of settling the issue of what to count as static properties of objects. As Lombard points out, this latter issue would seem to be incapable of being settled independently of settling the issue of what to count as an object; for only if there were such things as emerires – i.e., objects which were

emeralds before t and sapphires thereafter – would it be true to say that some objects were grue. See *Events*.

22. Atomic objects are, according to this account, ones that have no temporal parts and are extended in time – i.e., are three-dimensional – where having property P at t is a relation between objects and times.

23. See *Events*, pp. 119–20.

24. ibid., p. 171. The definition of a temporally continuous change given here is roughly that given in 'Events'. A slightly different but equivalent version is given in *Events*, p. 116.

25. ibid., pp. 122–3.

26. ibid., p. 172.

27. The example is Lombard's (ibid., p. 173).

28. ibid., p. 180.

29. In 'Events and Their Subjects', *Pacific Philosophical Quarterly*, 62, 2 (April 1981), pp. 138–47, and in *Events*, Chapter 7, Section 3.

30. ibid., *Events*, p. 121.

31. ibid., p. 255, n. 10.

32. It is being assumed here that both persons and their bodies are objects with parts. It may sound odd to speak of parts of a person; but there is a perfectly natural sense in which it is true to say, for example, that parts of my body are parts of me.

33. This kind of strategy is advocated by Kim in 'Materialism and the Criteria of the Mental', p. 334.

34. The ideas in these last few paragraphs had their origins in a conversation with Lawrence Lombard in the summer of 1983. I am indebted to him for discussion on this and related issues.

35. See, for example, 'Phenomenal Properties, Psychophysical Laws, and the Identity Theory', p. 183.

36. See 'Naming and Necessity'.

37. See McGinn, 'Mental States, Natural Kinds, and Psychophysical Laws'.

38. By this is not necessarily meant a neurophysiological difference, or a difference in some physical occurrence that takes place within the confines of a person's body, as the discussion of the problem of context dependence in Chapter 6, Section 3, makes clear. Thus, the main premiss upon which the Twin Earth thought experiments are based is not here being rejected. The claim here is that the relevant difference must ultimately lie in the intentional behaviour or actions of a person; and given that contentful mental types are relationally individuated, differences in intentional behaviour (i.e., physical behaviour described in terms of their mental antecedents) will make for differences in the physical environment of a person (i.e., in objects and/or events that exist or occur beyond the confines of a person's body). To those who say (as does Fodor in *Psychosemantics* (Cambridge, Mass.: MIT Press, 1987), pp. 39-40) that it is absurd to suppose that a mental property or type can make a potential causal difference (in behaviour) *without* making a neurophysiological

difference, the response is that this depends on how 'behaviour' is understood. If it is taken to mean 'behaviour, physically described', then it is highly implausible to suppose that two persons could be indiscernible with regard to their internal physical structure, yet differ in their behaviour. This is because it is difficult to see how creatures that are physiologically indiscernible might nevertheless differ in their causal structure or potential, thereby effecting different bodily movements. But if it is taken to mean 'behaviour, intentionally described' (i.e., action), then the same reasoning does not apply. If mental properties *are* (as is argued in Chapter 6, Section 3) relationally individuated, and not (as Fodor assumes) individuated by their causal powers only, then a difference in mental properties may indeed make for a difference in behaviour, and thus for a difference in the physical environment of a person, without making a neurophysiological difference. This seems to be what lies behind Burge's charge that Fodor confuses causation with individuation in 'Individualism and Psychology', *The Philosophical Review*, XCIV, 1 (January 1986), pp. 3–45.

39. See 'Functionalism, Qualia, and Intentionality'.
40. The argument is McGinn's: see 'Philosophical Materialism'.

Chapter Five

1. See, for instance, Ted Honderich, 'The Argument for Anomalous Monism', *Analysis* 42 (1982), pp. 59–64, and 'Psychophysical Lawlike Connections and Their Problem'; and Howard Robinson, *Matter and Sense* (Cambridge: Cambridge University Press, 1982), especially pp. 8–18. See also Jaegwon Kim, 'Causality, Identity, and Supervenience in the Mind-Body Problem' in *Midwest Studies in Philosophy*, IV (Minneapolis: University of Minnesota Press, 1979), pp. 31–50, especially pp. 46–7.
2. See Jennifer Hornsby, 'Physicalism, Events and Part-Whole Relations', in LePore and McLaughlin, *Actions and Events*, pp. 444–58.
3. See D.M. Armstrong, *What is a Law of Nature?* (Cambridge: Cambridge University Press, 1983), Part I, especially Chapter 1.
4. See Armstrong, *What is a Law of Nature?*.
5. See Graham Macdonald, 'The Possibility of the Disunity of Science', in G. Macdonald and C. Wright (eds), *Fact, Science and Morality* (Oxford: Basil Blackwell, 1986), pp. 219–46. cf. also Armstrong's discussion (pp. 94–6) of singularist conceptions of causality.
6. See Honderich, 'The Argument for Anomalous Monism', p. 62. A slightly different version appears in *A Theory of Determinism* (Oxford: Oxford University Press, 1988), Chapter 1. This version also assumes that events are causally related in virtue of certain but not all of their properties, where these are taken to be 'individual properties', construable as instances of properties (types). However,

it goes further in asserting that nomic connections hold between individual properties or instances of property types, with the consequence that any causally efficacious instance of a mental property must, in accordance with PNCC, have nomic connections with other property instances (see pp. 98–9). This presumes a conception of causality that is likely to be rejected by the non-reductive monist on the grounds that it confuses causality with nomologicality (causality being a relation which holds between instances of property types, laws expressing relations between the types themselves). Specifically, it seems to be incompatible with the generalist conception of causality embodied in the PNCC (see Section 1 above). cf. also Note 19 below.

7. The failure to distinguish between properties and their instancings seem to lie at the heart of the dispute between Honderich and Smith. See Honderich, 'Anomalous Monism: Reply to Smith', *Analysis* 43 (1983), pp. 147–9 and 'Smith and the Champion of Mauve', *Analysis* 44 (1984), pp. 86–9; and Peter Smith, 'Bad News for Anomalous Monism?', *Analysis* 42 (1982), pp. 220–4 and 'Anomalous Monism and Epiphenomenalism: A Reply to Honderich', *Analysis* 44 (1984), pp. 83–6.

8. See Robinson, *Matter and Sense*, p. 12, and Honderich, 'The Argument for Anomalous Monism', p. 64. The ideas in this section owe much to Graham Macdonald.

9. See, for example, Carl G. Hempel, 'Aspects of Scientific Explanation', in *Aspects of Scientific Explanation and Other Essays in the Philosophy of Science* (New York: The Free Press, 1965), pp. 331–496 (pb edn, 1970).

10. See James Woodward, 'Scientific Explanation', *British Journal of the Philosophy of Science* 30 (1979), pp. 41–67, 'A Theory of Singular Causal Explanation', *Erkenntnis* 21 (1984), pp. 231–62, and 'Are Singular Causal Explanations Implicit Covering-Law Explanations?', *Canadian Journal of Philosophy*, 16, 2 (June 1986), pp. 253–80. Here his account of singular causal explanation is accepted, but his account of its extensionality, which depends on the notion of a sentence preserving 'contrastive focus' is rejected.

11. ibid.

12. ibid.

13. See 'Physicalism, Events and Part-Whole Relations'. A similar objection is voiced by Drew Leder in 'Troubles with Token Identity', *Philosophical Studies*, 47 (1985), pp. 79–94. Although he does not explicitly discuss mereological conceptions of events, he argues that ideological differences between the mental and physical domains undermine the assumption of a common ontology.

14. See, for example, J. Fodor, 'Special Sciences (or: The Disunity of Science as a Working Hypothesis)', *Synthese* 28 (1974), pp. 97–115.

15. See, for example, Rudolf Carnap, *The Logical Syntax of Language* (London: Routledge & Kegan Paul, 1954), especially p. 320.

16. See, for example, John McDowell, 'Physicalism and Primitive

Denotation: Field on Tarski', *Erkenntnis*, 13 (1978), pp. 131–52, and G. Macdonald, 'The Possibility of the Disunity of Science'.

17. Hornsby notes that these principles are not intended to constitute a complete theory. Given claims about what there basically is, (*A*) can generate claims about what else there is. Many mereologists will take the basic entities to be either point-sized occupants of space-time or space-time points themselves. And, whereas some mereologists will take (contents of) space-time regions to include continuants and events, others will take them to include continuants only and hold some other view of events. See, for example, W.V. Quine, 'Events and Reification', in LePore and McLaughlin, *Actions and Events*; and David Lewis, 'Events', in *Philosophical Papers*, vol. II (Oxford: Oxford University Press, 1986), pp. 241–69, and 'New Work for a Theory of Universals', *Australasian Journal of Philosophy*, 61, 4 (December 1983), pp. 343–77 (especially n. 3).

18. See Hornsby, 'Physicalism, Events and Part-Whole Relations'. This is an adapted version of a principle endorsed by Judith Jarvis Thompson in *Acts and Other Events* (Ithaca, NY: Cornell University Press, 1977). Note that the claim that it is in the nature of events to cause and be caused is not obvious, since, if the mereological conception of events *is* true, the grand fusion of every event that has occurred, is occurring, and will occur will have no causes or effects (see Thompson, ibid.). I am indebted to Lawrence Lombard for bringing this to my attention.

19. This is not the view that all statements of causality are general. But it does have the consequence that true singular causal statements entail conditionals relating property types of which the events causally related are instances. To this extent, it contrasts with the view of causality expressed by Ted Honderich in *A Theory of Determinism*. His view seems to be that events causally related are so because their individual properties (construable as instances of property types) stand in causal relations and are thereby nomically connected (see Section 1.3). This may not appear to conflict with the first claim embodied in the regularity conception of causality as described by Armstrong (in *What is a Law of Nature?*, p. 11) and to which the PNCC is committed, viz. 'that causal connection is a species of law-like connection'. However, Armstrong assumes, as we do here, that this first claim embodies commitment to a generalist position. Honderich accepts that causality involves nomologicality but denies that nomologicality always involves generality.

20. John McDowell seems to endorse this kind of view in 'Functionalism and Anomalous Monism'.

21. For more on this, see G. Macdonald, 'The Possibility of the Disunity of Science'. I am indebted to him for discussion and advice on the issues addressed in this section.

22. ibid.

23. ibid. Also, see Christopher Peacocke's argument for token psycho-physical identity in *Holistic Explanation*, pp. 134–44.

Chapter Six

1. See, for example, Donald Davidson, 'Mental Events'; and Jaegwon Kim, 'Causality, Identity, and Supervenience in the Mind-Body Problem', 'Supervenience and Nomological Incommensurables', *American Philosophical Quarterly*, 15, 2 (April 1978), pp. 149–56, and 'Supervenience and Supervenient Causation'.
2. See, for example, Terence Horgan, 'Supervenience and Microphysics', *Pacific Philosophical Quarterly* 63 (1982), pp. 29–43; Andrew Woodfield, in the Foreword to A. Woodfield (ed.), *Thought and Object* (Oxford: Clarendon Press, 1982), pp. v–xi; and Donald Davidson, 'Knowing One's Own Mind', in *The Proceedings and Addresses of The American Philosophical Association*, 60, 3 (January 1987), pp. 441–58. The term 'context dependence' is Horgan's.
3. See Davidson, 'Mental Events'.
4. See, for example, Kim, 'Concepts of Supervenience', *Philosophy and Phenomenological Research*, XLV, 2 (December 1984), pp. 153–76, and Harry Lewis, 'Is the Mental Supervenient on the Physical?', in B. Vermazen and M. Hintikka, (eds), *Essays on Davidson: Actions and Events* (Oxford: Clarendon Press, 1985), pp. 159–72.
5. In 'Concepts of Supervenience'.
6. See Kim, ibid., and 'Supervenience and Supervenient Causation'. Also, see Simon Blackburn, 'Supervenience Revisited', in I. Hacking (ed.), *Exercises in Analysis* (Cambridge: Cambridge University Press, 1985), pp. 47–67.
7. Blackburn (ibid.) and Harry Lewis (in 'Is the Mental Supervenient on the Physical?'), also make this point.
8. See, for example, Blackburn, 'Supervenience Revisited'.
9. See Kim, 'Concepts of Supervenience', and Blackburn, 'Supervenience Revisited'. cf. also Paul Teller's discussion of materialism in 'A Poor Man's Guide to Supervenience and Determination', in *The Southern Journal of Philosophy*, pp. 137–62.
10. See Kim, 'Concepts of Supervenience', 'Supervenience and Nomological Incommensurables', and 'Supervenience and Supervenient Causation'; and Howard Robinson, *Matter and Sense*.
11. See Kim, 'Psychophysical Laws', in LePore and McLaughlin, *Actions and Events*.
12. R.M. Hare, *The Language of Morals* (Oxford: Clarendon Press, 1952). Kim's argument appears in 'Concepts of Supervenience'.
13. Kim's example is in fact geared to weak supervenience; but it is clear that the conclusion can be extended to cover strong supervenience. See pp. 169–70 of 'Concepts of Supervenience'.
14. See 'Physicalist Materialism', *Nous*, XI, 4 (November 1977), pp. 309–45.
15. See 'Physicalism: Ontology, Determination, and Reduction' *The Journal of Philosophy*, LXXII, 17 (1975 October 2), pp. 551–64.
16. ibid., pp. 558–9.
17. See Neil Tennant, 'Beth's Theorem and Reductionism', *Pacific*

Philosophical Quarterly 66 (1985), pp. 342–54.

18. The example is Teller's. See 'A Poor Man's Guide to Supervenience and Determination'.

19. See Geoffrey Hellman, 'Determination and Logical Truth', *The Journal of Philosophy*, LXXXII, 11 (November 1985), pp. 607–16.

20. See 'Concepts of Supervenience'.

21. See Hilary Putnam, 'The Meaning of "Meaning"', reprinted in *Mind, Language, and Reality*, vol. II (Cambridge: Cambridge University Press, 1975), pp. 215–71, and 'Is Semantics Possible', reprinted in ibid., pp. 139–52; Tyler Burge, 'Individualism and the Mental', *Midwest Studies in Philosophy*, vol. IV, pp. 73–121, 'Individualism and Psychology', and 'Other Bodies', in A. Woodfield (ed.), *Thought and Object*, pp. 97–120; and J. Fodor, 'Special Sciences', and 'Individualism and Supervenience', *Proceedings of the Aristotelian Society*, supp. vol. LX (1986), pp. 235–62.

22. See Horgan, 'Supervenience and Microphysics', p. 33.

23. ibid., p. 40. John Haugeland, in 'Weak Supervenience', *American Philosophical Quarterly* 19 (1982), pp. 93–103, gives another version of global supervenience.

24. See Lewis, 'New Work for a Theory of Universals'.

25. This is Kim's formulation. See '"Strong" and "Global" Supervenience Revisited', *Philosophy and Phenomenological Research*, 48, 2 (December 1987), pp. 315–26. The example given here is Bradford Petrie's: see 'Global Supervenience and Reduction', *Philosophy and Phenomenological Research* 48 (1987), pp. 119–30.

26. See 'The Meaning of "Meaning"'.

27. See note 21 above. See also Fodor, J., 'Two Thought Experiments Reviewed', *Notre Dame Journal of Formal Logic*, XXIII (1982), pp. 284–93.

28. See, for example, Fodor, 'Individualism and Supervenience', *Psychosemantics*, Chapter 2, and McGinn, 'The Structure of Content', in Woodfield, *Thought and Object*, pp. 207–58.

29. See Martin Davies, 'Externality, Psychological Explanation, and Narrow Content', *Proceedings of the Aristotelian Society*, supp. vol. LX, pp. 263–83, and McGinn, 'The Structure of Content'.

30. See John McDowell, 'Functionalism and Anomalous Monism'.

31. Davidson raises this question in 'Knowing One's Own Mind'.

32. See Fodor, 'Individualism and Supervenience'.

33. See Blackburn, 'Supervenience Revisited'.

34. See 'Physicalism: Ontology, Determination, and Reduction'.

35. See 'Physicalist Materialism', pp. 316–17.

36. ibid. See also Teller, 'A Poor Man's Guide to Supervenience and Determination'.

37. See Haugeland, 'Weak Supervenience', and Horgan, 'Supervenience and Microphysics'.

38. See McGinn, 'The Structure of Content', Christopher Peacocke, 'Demonstrative Reference and Psychological Explanation', *Synthese* 49 (1981), pp. 187–217, and Graeme Forbes, 'A Dichotomy Sustained', *Philosophical Studies* 51 (1987), pp. 187–211.

Bibliography

Aristotle, *Metaphysics*, trans. by Sir David Ross, 2nd edn (Oxford: Clarendon Press, 1954).

Armstrong, D.M., *A Materialist Theory of Mind* (London: Routledge and Kegan Paul, 1968).

Armstrong, D.M., *What is a Law of Nature?* (Cambridge: Cambridge University Press, 1983).

Armstrong, D.M., and Malcolm, N., *Consciousness and Causality* (Oxford: Basil Blackwell, 1984).

Blackburn, Simon, 'Supervenience Revisited', in I. Hacking (ed.), *Exercises in Analysis* (Cambridge: Cambridge University Press, 1985), pp. 47–67.

Block, Ned, 'What is Functionalism?', Introduction to Part 3 of N. Block (ed.), *Readings in the Philosophy of Psychology*, vol. I (Cambridge, Mass.: Harvard University Press, 1980), pp. 171–84.

Block, Ned, 'Troubles with Functionalism', reprinted in N. Block (ed.), *Readings in the Philosophy of Psychology*, vol. I, (Cambridge, Mass.: Harvard University Press, 1980), pp. 268–305.

Block, Ned, 'Are Absent Qualia Impossible?' *The Philosophical Review*, 89, 2 (April 1980), pp. 257–74.

Block, Ned, and Fodor, Jerry, 'What Psychological States are Not', reprinted in N. Block (ed.), *Readings in the Philosophy of Psychology*, vol. I (Cambridge, Mass.: Harvard University Press, 1980), pp. 237–50.

Bogdan, R.J. (ed.), *D.M. Armstrong* (Dordrecht: D. Reidel, 1984).

Brand, Myles, 'Particulars, Events, and Actions', in M. Brand and D. Walton (eds), *Action Theory* (Dordrecht: D. Reidel, 1976), pp. 133–57.

Brandt, Richard, and Kim, Jaegwon, 'The Logic of the Identity Theory', reprinted in John O'Connor (ed.), *Modern Materialism: Readings on Mind-Body Identity* (New York: Harcourt, Brace, World, Inc., 1969), pp. 212–37.

Brentano, F., *Psychology From an Empirical Standpoint* (English ed. by Linda L. McAlister, 2nd edn), ed. by D. Kraus, trans. by A.C. Rancurello, D.B. Terrell, and L.L. McAlister (London: Routledge & Kegan Paul, 1973).

Brody, B., *Identity and Essence* (Princeton NJ: Princeton University Press, 1980).

Burge, Tyler, 'Individualism and the Mental', in *Midwest Studies in Philosophy*, vol. IV (Minneapolis: University of Minnesota Press, 1979), pp. 73–121.

Burge, Tyler, 'Other Bodies', in A. Woodfield (ed.), *Thought and Object* (Oxford: Clarendon Press, 1982), pp. 97–120.

Burge, Tyler, 'Two Thought Experiments Reviewed', *Notre Dame Journal of Formal Logic*, XXIII (1982), pp. 284–93.

Burge, Tyler, 'Individualism and Psychology', *The Philosophical Review*, XCIV, 1 (January 1986), pp.3–45.

Carnap, R., *The Logical Syntax of Language* (London: Routledge & Kegan Paul, 1954).

Chisholm, R. *Perceiving: A Philosophical Study* (Ithaca, NY: Cornell University Press, 1957).

Churchland, Paul, 'Reduction, Qualia, and the Direct Introspection of Brain States', *The Journal of Philosophy*, LXXXII, 1 (January 1985), pp. 8–28.

Churchland, Paul, and Churchland, Patricia, 'Functionalism, Qualia, and Intentionality', in J.I. Biro and Robert W. Shahan (eds), *Mind, Brain, and Function* (Brighton, Sussex: Harvester Press, 1982), pp. 121–45.

Cornman, James, 'On the Elimination of "Sensations" and Sensations', *The Review of Metaphysics*, 22 (1968), pp. 15–35.

Davidson, Donald, 'Causal Relations', reprinted in *Essays on Actions and Events* (Oxford: Clarendon Press, 1980), pp. 149–62.

Davidson, Donald, 'The Individuation of Events', in N. Rescher (ed.), *Essays in Honor of Carl G. Hempel* (Dordrecht: D. Reidel, 1969), pp. 216–34, reprinted in *Essays on Actions and Events*, pp. 163–80.

Davidson, Donald, 'Mental Events', reprinted in *Essays on Actions and Events*, pp. 207–25.

Davidson, Donald, 'Psychology as Philosophy' (along with his 'Comments and Replies'), reprinted in *Essays on Actions and Events*, pp. 229–39 and 239–44.

Davidson, Donald, 'The Material Mind', reprinted in *Essays on Actions and Events*, pp. 245–59.

Davidson, Donald, 'Reply to Quine on Events', in E. LePore and B. McLaughlin (eds), *Actions and Events* (Oxford: Basil Blackwell, 1985), pp. 172–76.

Davidson, Donald, 'Knowing One's Own Mind', in *The Proceedings and Addresses of The American Philosophical Association*, vol. 60, no. 3 (January 1987), pp. 441–58.

Davies, Martin, 'Externality, Psychological Explanation, and Narrow Content', *Proceedings of the Aristotelian Society*, supp. vol. LX (1986), pp. 263–83.

Double, Richard, 'Phenomenal Properties', *Philosophy and Phenomenological Research*, XLV, 3 (March 1985), pp. 383–92.

Dummett, Michael, *Frege: Philosophy of Language* (London:

Duckworth 1973).

Feldman, Fred, 'Kripke on the Identity Theory', *The Journal of Philosophy*, LXXI, 18 (24 October 1974), pp. 665–76.

Fodor, Jerry, 'Special Sciences (or: The Disunity of Science as a Working Hypothesis)', *Synthese* 28 (1974), pp. 97–115.

Fodor, Jerry, 'Individualism and Supervenience', *Proceedings of the Aristotelian Society*, supp. vol. LX (1986), pp. 235–62.

Fodor, Jerry, *Psychosemantics* (Cambridge, Mass.: MIT Press, 1987).

Forbes, Graeme, *The Metaphysics of Modality* (Oxford: Clarendon Press, 1985).

Forbes, Graeme, 'A Dichotomy Sustained', *Philosophical Studies*, 51 (1987), pp. 187–211.

Goldman, Alvin, *A Theory of Human Action* (Englewood Cliffs, NJ: Prentice-Hall, Inc., 1970).

Goodman, Nelson, *Fact, Fiction, and Forecast*, 2nd edn (New York: Bobbs-Merrill Co., Inc., 1965).

Goodman, Nelson, *The Structure of Appearance*, 2nd edn (New York: Bobbs-Merrill Co., Inc., 1966).

Hare, R.M., *The Language of Morals* (Oxford: Clarendon Press, 1952).

Haugeland, John, 'Weak Supervenience', *American Philosophical Quarterly*, 19 (1982), pp. 93–103.

Hellman, Geoffrey, 'Determination and Logical Truth', *The Journal of Philosophy*, LXXXII, 11 (November 1985), pp. 607–16.

Hellman, Geoffrey, and Thompson, Frank, 'Physicalism: Ontology, Determination, and Reduction' *The Journal of Philosophy*, LXXII, 17 (2 October 1975), pp. 551–64.

Hellman, Geoffrey, and Thompson, Frank, 'Physicalist Materialism', *Nous*, XI, 4 (November 1977), pp. 309–45.

Hempel, Carl G., 'Aspects of Scientific Explanation', in *Aspects of Scientific Explanation and Other Essays in the Philosophy of Science* (New York: The Free Press, 1965), pp. 331–496 (pb edn, 1970).

Honderich, Ted, 'Psychophysical Lawlike Connections and Their Problem', *Inquiry*, 24 (1981), pp. 277–304.

Honderich, Ted, 'The Argument for Anomalous Monism', *Analysis*, 42 (1982), pp. 59–64

Honderich, Ted, 'Anomalous Monism: Reply to Smith', *Analysis*, 43 (1983), pp. 147–49.

Honderich, Ted, 'Smith and the Champion of Mauve', *Analysis*, 44 (1984), pp. 86–9.

Honderich, Ted, *A Theory of Determinism* (Oxford: Oxford University Press, 1988).

Horgan, Terence, 'Jackson on Physical Information and Qualia', *Philosophical Quarterly*, XXXIV, 135 (April 1984), pp. 147–52.

Horgan, Terence, 'Supervenience and Microphysics', *Pacific Philosophical Quarterly*, 63 (1982), pp. 29–43.

Horgan, Terence, 'Functionalism, Qualia, and the Inverted Spectrum', *Philosophy and Phenomenological Research*, XLIV, 4. (June 1984), pp. 453–69.

Hornsby, Jennifer, 'Which Physical Events are Mental Events?', *Proceedings of the Aristotelian Society*, vol. LXXI (1980-1), pp. 73–92.

Hornsby, Jennifer, 'On Functionalism, and On Jackson, Pargetter, and Prior on Functionalism', *Philosophical Studies*, 46 (1984), pp. 75–95.

Hornsby, Jennifer, 'Physicalism, Events and Part-Whole Relations', in E. LePore and B. McLaughlin, (eds), *Actions and Events* (Oxford: Basil Blackwell, 1985), pp. 444–58.

Jackson, Frank, 'Ephiphenomenal Qualia', *Philosophical Quarterly*, vol. XXXII, no. 127 (April 1982), pp. 127–36.

Jackson, Frank, 'What Mary Didn't Know', *The Journal of Philosophy*, LXXXIII, 5 (May 1986), pp. 291–5

Jackson, Frank, Pargetter, Robert, and Prior, Elizabeth, 'Functionalism and Type-Type Identity Theories', *Philosophical Studies*, 42 (1982), pp. 209–25.

Johnston, Mark, 'Why Having a Mind Matters', in E. LePore and B. McLaughlin, (eds), *Actions and Events* (Oxford: Basil Blackwell, 1985), pp. 408–26.

Kim, Jaegwon, 'On the Psycho-Physical Identity Theory', reprinted in John O'Connor (ed.), *Modern Materialism: Readings on Mind-Body Identity*, (New York: Harcourt, Brace & World, Inc., 1969), pp. 195–211.

Kim, Jaegwon, 'Events and Their Descriptions: Some Considerations', in N. Rescher (ed.), *Essays in Honor of Carl G. Hempel* (Dordecht: D. Reidel, 1969), pp. 198–215.

Kim, Jaegwon, 'Materialism and the Criteria of the Mental', *Synthese*, 22 (1971), pp. 323–45.

Kim, Jaegwon, 'Phenomenal Properties, Psychophysical Laws, and the Identity Theory', *Monist*, 56 (April 1972), pp. 177–92.

Kim, Jaegwon, 'Events as Property Exemplifications', in M. Brand and D. Walton (eds.), *Action Theory* (Dordrecht: D. Reidel, 1976), pp. 159–77.

Kim, Jaegwon, 'Supervenience and Nomological Incommensurables', *American Philosophical Quarterly*, 15, 2 (April 1978), pp. 149–56.

Kim, Jaegwon, 'Causality, Identity, and Supervenience in the Mind-Body Problem', in *Midwest Studies in Philosophy*, vol. IV (Minneapolis: University of Minnesota Press, 1979), pp. 31–50.

Kim, Jaegwon, 'Supervenience and Supervenient Causation', in *The Southern Journal of Philosophy*, vol. XXII, supplement (Spindel Conference: The Concept of Supervenience in Contemporary Philosophy) (1984), pp. 45–56.

Kim, Jaegwon, 'Concepts of Supervenience', *Philosophy and Phenomenological Research*, XLV, 2 (December 1984), pp. 153–76.

Kim, Jaegwon, 'Psychophysical Laws', in E. LePore and B. McLaughlin (eds), *Actions and Events* (Oxford: Basil Blackwell, 1985), pp. 369–86.

Kim, Jaegwon, '"Strong" and "Global" Supervenience Revisited', *Philosophy and Phenomenological Research*, XLVIII, 2 (December 1987), pp. 315–26.

Kitcher, Patricia, 'Narrow Taxonomy and Wide Functionalism',

Philosophy of Science, 52 (1985), pp. 78–97.

Kripke, Saul, 'Identity and Necessity', in M. Munitz (ed.), *Identity and Individuation* (New York: New York University Press, 1971), pp. 135–64.

Kripke, Saul, 'Naming and Necessity' in D. Davidson and G. Harman (eds), *Semantics of Natural Language* (Dordrecht: D. Reidel, 1972), pp. 253–355.

Leder, Drew, 'Troubles with Token Identity', *Philosophical Studies*, 47 (1985), pp. 79–94.

Lemmon, E.J., 'Comments on D. Davidson's "The Logical Form of Action Sentences"', in N. Rescher (ed.), *The Logic of Decision and Action* (Pittsburgh, Pa: University of Pittsburgh Press, 1968), pp. 96–103.

LePore, E., and McLaughlin, B. (eds), *Actions and Events* (Oxford: Basil Blackwell, 1985).

Levin, Michael, 'Phenomenal Properties', *Philosophy and Phenomenological Research*, 42 (1981-2), pp. 42–58.

Levison, Arnold, 'An Epistemic Criterion of the Mental', *Canadian Journal of Philosophy*, XIII, 3. (September 1983), pp. 389–407.

Lewis, David, 'An Argument for the Identity Theory', reprinted in *Philosophical Papers*, vol. I (Oxford: Oxford University Press, 1983), pp. 99–107.

Lewis, David, 'Psychophysical and Theoretical Identifications', *Australasian Journal of Philosophy*, 50, 2 (December 1972), pp. 249–58.

Lewis, David, 'How To Define Theoretical Terms', reprinted in *Philosophical Papers*, vol. I, pp. 78–95.

Lewis, David, 'Mad Pain and Martian Pain', reprinted in *Philosophical Papers*, vol. I, pp. 122–30.

Lewis, David, 'New Work for a Theory of Universals', *Australasian Journal of Philosophy*, 61, 4 (December 1983), pp. 343–77.

Lewis, David, 'Events', in *Philosophical Papers*, vol. II (Oxford: Oxford University Press, 1986), pp. 241–69.

Lewis, Harry, 'Is the Mental Supervenient on the Physical?', in B. Vermazen and M. Hintikka (eds), *Essays on Davidson: Actions and Events* (Oxford: Clarendon Press, 1985), pp. 159–72.

Loar, Brian, *Mind and Meaning* (Cambridge: Cambridge University Press, 1981).

Lombard, Lawrence, 'Events', *The Canadian Journal of Philosophy*, IX, 3 (September 1979), pp. 425–60.

Lombard, Lawrence, 'Events and Their Subjects', *Pacific Philosophical Quarterly*, 62, 2 (April 1981), pp. 138–47.

Lombard, Lawrence, *Events: A Metaphysical Study* (London: Routledge & Kegan Paul, 1986).

Loux, M., *Substance and Attribute* (Dordrecht: D. Reidel, 1978).

Macdonald, Cynthia, and Macdonald, Graham, 'Mental Causes and Explanation of Action', *The Philosophical Quarterly*, 36, 143 (April 1986), pp. 145–58.

Macdonald, Graham, 'The Possibility of the Disunity of Science', in G. Macdonald and C. Wright (eds), *Fact, Science and Morality* (Oxford: Basil Blackwell, 1986), pp. 219–46.

McDowell, John, 'Physicalism and Primitive Denotation: Field on Tarski', *Erkenntnis*, 13 (1978), pp. 131–52.

McDowell, John, 'Functionalism and Anomalous Monism', in E. LePore and B. McLaughlin (eds), *Actions and Events* (Oxford: Basil Blackwell, 1985), pp. 387–98.

McGinn, Colin, 'Mental States, Natural Kinds, and Psychophysical Laws', *Proceedings of the Aristotelian Society*, supp. vol. LII (1978), pp. 195–221.

McGinn, Colin, 'Functionalism and Phenomenalism: A Critical Note', *Australasian Journal of Philosophy*, 58, 1 (March 1980), pp. 35–46.

McGinn, Colin, 'Philosophical Materialism', *Synthese*, 44 (1980), pp. 173–206.

McGinn, Colin, 'The Structure of Content', in A. Woodfield (ed.), *Thought And Object* (Oxford: Clarendon Press, 1982), pp. 207–58.

McGinn, Colin, Critical Notice of *The View From Nowhere*, *Mind*, XCVI, 382 (April 1987), pp. 263–72.

McLaughlin, Brian, 'Anomalous Monism and the Irreducibility of the Mental', in E. LePore and B. McLaughlin (eds), *Actions and Events* (Oxford: Basil Blackwell, 1985), pp. 331–68.

Martin, R.M., 'On Events and Event-Descriptions', in J. Margolis (ed.), *Fact and Experience* (Oxford: Basil Blackwell, 1969), pp. 63–73.

Nagel, Thomas, 'What Is It Like to Be a Bat?', reprinted in *Mortal Questions* (Cambridge: Cambridge University Press, 1979), pp. 165–80.

O'Connor, John (ed.), *Modern Materialism: Readings on Mind-Body Identity* (New York: Harcourt, Brace, & World, Inc., 1969).

Owens, Joseph, 'The Failure of Lewis's Functionalism', *The Philosophical Quarterly*, 36, 143 (April 1986), pp. 159–73.

Peacocke, Christopher, *Holistic Explanation* (Oxford: Clarendon Press, 1979).

Peacocke, Christopher, 'Demonstrative Reference and Psychological Explanation', *Synthese*, 49 (1981), pp. 187–217.

Petrie, Bradford, 'Global Supervenience and Reduction', *Philosophy and Phenomenological Research*, 48 (1987), pp. 119–30.

Place, U.T., 'Is Consciousness a Brain Process?', reprinted in John O'Connor (ed.), *Modern Materialism: Readings on Mind-Body Identity*, (New York: Harcourt, Brace & World, inc., 1969), pp. 21–31.

Plantinga, Alvin, *The Nature of Neccessity* (Oxford: Clarendon Library, 1974).

Post, John, 'Comment on Teller', *The Southern Journal of Philosophy*, vol. XXII, supplement (Spindel Conference on Supervenience) (1984) pp. 163–7.

Putnam, Hilary, 'Psychological Predicates', in W.H. Capitan and D.D. Merrill (eds), *Art, Mind and Religion* (Pittsburgh Pa: University of

Pittsburgh Press, 1967), pp. 44–5.

Putnam, Hilary, 'Is Semantics Possible?', reprinted in *Mind, Language, and Reality*, vol. II (Cambridge: Cambridge University Press, 1975), pp. 139–52.

Putnam, Hilary, 'The Meaning of "Meaning"', reprinted in *Mind, Language, and Reality*, vol. II, pp. 215–71.

Quine, W.V., 'Two Dogmas of Empiricism', in *From a Logical Point of View* (Cambridge, Mass.: Harvard University Press, 1964), pp. 20–47.

Quine, W.V., 'Events and Reification', in E. LePore and B. McLaughlin (eds), *Actions and Events*, (Oxford: Basil Blackwell, 1985), pp. 162–71.

Quinton, A., *The Nature of Things* (London: Routledge & Kegan Paul, 1973).

Rescher, N. (ed.), *The Logic of Decision and Action* (Pittsburgh, Pa: Pittsburgh University Press, 1968).

Rescher, N. (ed.), *Essays in Honor of Carl G. Hempel* (Dordrecht: D. Reidel, 1969).

Robinson, Howard, *Matter and Sense* (Cambridge: Cambridge University Press, 1982).

Rorty, Richard, 'Mind-Body Identity, Privacy, and Categories', *The Review of Metaphysics*, 19 (1965), pp. 25–54.

Sher, George, 'On Event-Identity', *Australasian Journal of Philosophy*, 52, 1 (May 1974), pp. 40–7.

Shoemaker, Sydney, 'Functionalism and Qualia', reprinted in *Identity, Cause, and Mind* (Cambridge: Cambridge University Press, 1984), pp. 184–205.

Shoemaker, Sydney, 'Absent Qualia Are Impossible', reprinted in *Identity, Cause, and Mind*, pp. 309–26.

Shoemaker, Sydney, 'The Inverted Spectrum', reprinted in *Identity, Cause, and Mind*, pp. 327–57.

Smart, J.J.C., 'Sensations and Brain Processes', reprinted in John O'Connor (ed.), *Modern Materialism: Readings on Mind-Body Identity* New York: Harcourt, Brace & World, Inc. 1969), pp. 32–47.

Smith, Peter, 'Bad News for Anomalous Monism?', *Analysis* 42 (1982), pp. 220–4.

Smith, Peter, 'Anomalous Monism and Epiphenomenalism: A Reply to Honderich', *Analysis*, 44 (1984), pp. 83–6.

Swinburne, Richard, 'Are Mental Events Identical with Brain Events?', *American Philosophical Quarterly*, 19, 2 (1982), pp. 173–83.

Teller, Paul, 'Comments on Kim's Paper', *The Southern Journal of Philosophy*, vol. XXII, supplement (Spindel Conference on Supervenience), (1984), pp. 57–61.

Tennant, Neil, 'Beth's Theorem and Reductionism', *Pacific Philosophical Quarterly*, 66 (1985), pp. 342–54.

Thompson, Judith Jarvis, 'Individuating Actions', *The Journal of Philosophy*, 68 (1971), pp. 774–81.

Thompson, Judith Jarvis, *Acts and Other Events* (Ithaca, NY: Cornell University Press, 1977).

White, Steven, 'Curse of the Qualia', *Synthese*, 68 (1986), pp. 333–68.

Wiggins, David, *Sameness and Substance* (Oxford: Basil Blackwell, 1980).

Wilson, Neil, 'Facts, Events and Their Identity Conditions', *Philosophical Studies*, 25 (1974), pp. 303–21.

Woodfield, Andrew, Foreword to A. Woodfield (ed.), *Thought and Object* (Oxford: Clarendon Press, 1982), pp. v–xi.

Woodward, James, 'Scientific Explanation', *British Journal of the Philosophy of Science*, 30 (1979), pp. 41–67.

Woodward, James, 'A Theory of Singular Causal Explanation', *Erkenntnis*, 21 (1984), pp. 231–62.

Woodward, James, 'Are Singular Causal Explanations Implicit Covering-Law Explanations?', *Canadian Journal of Philosophy*, 16, 2 (June 1986), pp. 253–80.

Index